KU-663-044

# Holocaust Poetry

Awkward Poetics in the Work of Sylvia Plath,
Geoffrey Hill, Tony Harrison and Ted Hughes

Antony Rowland

Edinburgh University Press

| ABERDEENSHIRE LIBRARY AND INFORMATION SERVICE | |
|---|---|
| 1702291 | |
| CAW | 358455 |
| 821.914 | £16.99 |
| AD | PORP |

© Antony Rowland, 2005

Edinburgh University Press Ltd
22 George Square, Edinburgh

Typeset in Adobe Sabon
by Servis Filmsetting Ltd, Manchester, and
printed and bound in Great Britain by
Antony Rowe Ltd, Chippenham

A CIP record for this book is available from the British Library

ISBN 0 7486 1553 9 (paperback)
ISBN 0 7486 2256 X (hardback)

The right of Antony Rowland
to be identified as author of this work
has been asserted in accordance with
the Copyright, Designs and Patents Act 1988.

Holocaust Poetry

**Aberdeenshire Library and Information Service**
**www.aberdeenshire.gov.uk/libraries**
**Renewals Hotline 01224 661511**

1 4 FEB 2017

2 9 FEB 2019

ABERDEENSHIRE
LIBRARIES

WITHDRAWN
FROM LIBRARY

ROWLAND, Antony

Holocaust poetry

A L I S

1702291

To Polly Rowland, 2004–

# Contents

# Acknowledgements

Thanks are primarily due to Jackie Jones at EUP, whose efficient dealings with this book were essential to its completion, and also to the AHRB: without an award from the Research Leave Scheme this book could not have been completed for several years. The support from Brian Longhurst, Martin Bull and the School of ESPaCH at the University of Salford – in terms of the well-timed sabbatical to match the AHRB award – was also invaluable. Generous financial help was also forthcoming from the European Studies Research Institute at Salford, and the university's Research Development Fund, which allowed me to visit the Ted Hughes archives at Emory University (Atlanta). Emma deserves constant credit for her patience, pies, and scuffles over the laptop.

Tony Harrison (via the cheerfully indefatigable Gordon Dickerson) kindly provided me with a day's access to the workbooks and photograph albums for *Prometheus*. The members of staff at the Ted Hughes archives (particularly Steve Enniss), the British Library and the Poetry Library (Royal Festival Hall) were extremely helpful in chasing down those essential articles, letters and manuscripts. The readers of the manuscript gave their time selflessly, and made me think hard about certain aspects of the drafts: they include Susan Gubar, Sue Vice, Neil Roberts, Jeffrey Wainwright, Peter Lawson and Sandie Byrne. Others chipped in with invaluable suggestions, comments (or ruminations) on some of the ideas herein, including Rainer Emig, Jane Kilby, Rick Crownshaw, Ursula Tidd, Robert Eaglestone, Sue Powell and the audiences at papers delivered at the University of Frankfurt, the University of Aberystwyth and the University of Manchester. (Ian Copestake also sent me a book and article from Germany that aided the completion of the chapter on Sylvia Plath.) Stan Smith must also be thanked for his support throughout the composition of this book.

The editors of *Critical Survey* have kindly allowed me to reproduce (with amendments) some of the material in my article entitled 'Peephole

Metaphysics in the Poetry of Ted Hughes'. Permission has been sought to reproduce quotations from Faber and Faber. Every attempt has been made to contact the publishers and authors for permission to use primary material. The British Library granted permission to use the Jacques Callot illustrations, and the photographer Phil Hunt to use the photographs from *Prometheus*. Extracts from *The Triumph of Love* by Geoffrey Hill (Penguin Books, 1999) © Geoffrey Hill, 1998, reproduced by permission of Penguin Books Ltd.

# Illustrations

# Introduction

Awkward poetics can be regarded as an integral response to the current development of post-Holocaust writing, as the number of survivor poets decreases. This contention is in no way meant to denigrate what Frieda W. Aaron calls the 'marvel' of those who 'wrote poetry in the shadow of gas chambers'.[1] Dora Apel argues that secondary witnesses display self-consciousness when they place the Holocaust in relation to 'the circumstances of its representation in the present': these witnesses include post-Holocaust poets concerned with the epistemological question of how writers not involved in the Holocaust gain access to its historical reality.[2] The discussion of post-Holocaust poetics in this book contributes to related debates in Holocaust studies about postmemory, secondary witnessing, proxy-witnesses, received history and the vicarious past: many post-Holocaust poets have reflected self-consciously on their non-participation in the historical events between the departure of refugees from Germany in the 1930s and the liberation of the camps in 1945. Such self-reflexivity has much in common with the work of postmemory, such as Art Spiegelman's '*story of the telling of the story*' in the two *Maus* books: Marianne Hirsch's concept focuses on transgenerational haunting, the traumatic imprint of history in the lives of children of murdered inmates or Holocaust survivors.[3] However, post-Holocaust poetry can be distinguished from the literature of postmemory in that this 'deep personal connection' is absent from the backgrounds of the poets discussed in this book, but is replaced with their determination to provide ethical responses to the events in Europe between 1933 and 1945.[4] Post-Holocaust poets, as Susan Gubar argues in *Poetry after Auschwitz*, 'discern the ways [the Holocaust] can be recognized and felt in the present' (p. 7).

Such a stance by writers uninvolved in the Holocaust has courted suspicion, as the following extract from George Szirtes's introduction to *Camp Notebook* demonstrates:

Another major Hungarian poet of the century, János Pilinszky, thought that Sylvia Plath would have been the ideal translator of Radnóti, the case being that Plath, a non-Jew, was best placed to interpret the work of a victim of the holocaust. But it's an odd view at best, for what distinguishes Radnóti's last poems is a turning away from the aestheticised or mythologised self to the brute world outside that he records with remarkable steady-eyed clarity.[5]

Post-Holocaust poets have been accused of aesthetic larceny, but have also been appraised as displaying a moral intelligence attuned to European history and culture. The first response, aware of the potential improprieties of fictionalising the Holocaust, has been more commonplace. In 1965, George Steiner asked whether Plath, and 'anyone, themselves uninvolved and long after the event, commit a subtle larceny when they invoke the echoes and trappings of Auschwitz and appropriate an enormity of ready emotion to their own private design?' At the same time, he argued that 'Perhaps it is only those who had no part in the events who *can* focus on them rationally and imaginatively'.[6] Steiner overstates his argument in the latter comment, which diminishes the value of 'rational' testimony and 'imaginative' literature written by survivors. However, he illustrates the paradox that Plath's poetry might be creative and intellectually rigorous, but also suspiciously appropriative; by doing so, Steiner became one of the first critics to sense a discrepancy between Holocaust and post-Holocaust writing. The assumption that poets who were not directly involved in the events in Europe do not have the right to represent the Holocaust was a persistent one until more recent discussions about secondary witnessing, postmemory, and the vicarious past. Szirtes baulks at the suggestion that Plath, a writer born in America, could be the 'ideal translator' of Miklós Radnóti, a Hungarian poet who died during a forced march in 1944. Szirtes puzzles over Pilinszky's 'odd' view, despite Steiner's contention that the post-Holocaust poet might be able to focus on the Holocaust 'imaginatively'. This book argues that the post-Holocaust poetry of Sylvia Plath, Geoffrey Hill, Tony Harrison and Ted Hughes does not comprise (on the whole) exploitative poems that simply 'aestheticise' or 'mythologise' the lyrical self. One of the ways in which artistic commitment attempts to avoid exploitation is through a direct dialogue with Holocaust poetry. This process allows post-Holocaust poets to look beyond the 'individual national frameworks' that have constructed particularised narratives of the Holocaust.[7] Hill and Hughes in particular are influenced by Holocaust poetry: Hill engages with the work of Radnóti, and also that of Robert Desnos, a French poet who died at Terezín in 1945; Hughes's friendship with Pilinszky is registered in the correspondence held at Emory University in Atlanta. In Chapter 1, I outline the possibility that

Plath's reading of Paul Celan influenced the abstract lyricism of her later poems. Harrison is the only poet in this list who may have ignored Holocaust poetry entirely.

'Holocaust poetry' can be a misleading phrase. The title of this book retains it for the same reason that Hilda Schiff entitled her 1995 anthology *Holocaust Poetry*: it can be deployed as an umbrella term to encompass both Holocaust and post-Holocaust writing. 'Holocaust poetry' also avoids the potentially misleading title 'post-Holocaust poetry', which could be read as appertaining to all poems written since the liberation of the camps. Aaron justifiably uses it in this sense when the intention is to distinguish between Holocaust poetry written in the ghettos and camps, less concerned 'with issues of aestheticism', and poems by writers such as Celan and Nelly Sachs, who were granted 'a temporal and spatial perspective' denied to poets who did not survive.[8] This book argues that, under the general term 'Holocaust poetry', distinctions need to be made between Holocaust poems written by those involved in the events unfolding in Europe from 1933 to 1945 (including Celan and Sachs), and post-Holocaust poems, composed by those who were not. Postmemory writers, children of those involved in these events, are distinguished from post-Holocaust poets who have no (or only tenuous) personal connections to them; who have felt compelled to engage with representations of the Holocaust, despite their temporal, geographical, but not imaginative, distance from the camps. As with Aaron and Gubar's studies, this book is not meant to survey all the poetry produced by well-known Holocaust and post-Holocaust poets. For the sake of concision and clarity (and the author's expertise), this study concentrates on post-Holocaust poets in Britain.[9] Following the publication of my previous book, *Tony Harrison and the Holocaust*, there has been some discussion as to whether the British writer can be 'a post-Holocaust poet or (simply put) a poet writing in the aftermath of the Holocaust'.[10] Harriet L. Parmet justifiably separates the two categories: this critical study argues that post-Holocaust poets who write about the events in Europe without any personal connections to them (such as Harrison) can be distinguished from those who choose to ignore the effects of the Holocaust on post-war culture.

## Holocaust and Post-Holocaust literature

Holocaust and post-Holocaust literature have often been distinguished – as in Steiner's comments on Plath – by constructing an opposition between authentic testimony and creative rumination. After reading

Albrecht Goes's *The Burnt Offering*, Primo Levi reaffirmed that 'there are human experiences of such enormity that they can be narrated only by those who were "actually involved" in them.'[11] However, Levi did not mean to separate the genres of testimony and literature entirely: *The Truce*, his account of his return to Italy after the liberation of Auschwitz, does not eschew literary frameworks (most obviously that of *The Odyssey*). When Levi incorporates stories into his narrative such as the old woman who sent Hitler a letter imploring him to desist from his total-itarian ways, Ian Thomson argues that the writer does not so much embellish the truth, as add to it.[12] And even though Levi states in his preface to *If This is a Man* that it seems 'unnecessary to add that none of the facts are invented', the overall authenticity of the book still allows for the alteration of specific details, such as the fact that the character Alberto (based on Dalla Volta) could not speak German, when he was actually fluent in that language.[13]

Berel Lang has responded to the literariness of testimony by devising an ingenious system to categorise Holocaust genres. In the first category, Holocaust writing 'aspires to the condition of history': this encompasses diarists as well as post-Holocaust writers, 'non-fictional fiction' and testimony rendered through the 'filter of memory' (Lang mentions *Fragments*, 'the sparest or least self-indulgent memoir' of Benjamin Wilkomirski).[14] The second category includes work which 'appears with only a sub- or con-text of historical reference', such as Celan's poetry; the third, 'historical writing itself'.[15] Lang's divisions are valuable in that they stress the connections between Holocaust and post-Holocaust texts (in the same way as the umbrella term 'Holocaust poetry'), and the gap between genres that aspire to history, rather than the writing of history itself, at the same time as acknowledging historians' use of rhetoric. As Lang admits, however, even Holocaust denial 'aspires to the condition of history', however falsely. The fake memoir could be added to this cate-gory. Lang asks if readers would respond to Levi's early books differently if we suddenly discovered that they represented invented experiences: the question can be addressed to the aforementioned Wilkomirski, whose 'least self-indulgent memoir' was exposed as a fabrication in 1998.

Does the fake memoir really deserve to be classed in the same category as Levi's testimony? As Daniel R. Schwarz states in *Imagining the Holocaust*, 'Surely we need to differentiate between memoirs and docu-mentary fiction posing as memoirs, and between realistic novels and fables'?[16] Despite similar literary devices that might be deployed by the two types of writing, a post-Holocaust writer with no experience of the camps (or starvation) would be unlikely to attack a wild persimmon bush 'on a walk one day, chewing on the fruit'.[17] This description of Levi soon after his return from Auschwitz focuses on the author-figure, rather than any analysis of the texts in question. Yet this distinction is central to Holocaust studies at the beginning of the twenty-first century. The production of Holocaust and post-Holocaust literature has reached a stage where the icons of atrocity have become so familiar that a post-Holocaust writer born during the war, and who lived safely in Switzerland during the conflict, can ape them to such an extent that the resulting text is lauded as autobiography. Textual details purporting to refer to a childhood in the camps successfully regurgitate synecdoches of Holocaust literature to the extent that Wilkomirski's 'memoir' was awarded the National Jewish Book Award, the Jewish Quarterly Literary Prize and the *Prix de Mémoire de la Shoah*.

*Fragments* illustrates the point that Holocaust and post-Holocaust writing are mutually enhancing, but still distinct, categories. (In the University of Manchester's John Rylands Library in 2004, the book was still catalogued under the 'History' rather than 'Literature' section.) Any reader who tries to adduce authentic experience from textual evidence without knowledge of the author encounters problems.[18] François Mauriac's comments in the foreword to Elie Wiesel's *Night* could be appropriated as an *apologia* for Wilkomirski when he argues that 'It is not always the events we have been directly involved in that affect us the most . . . nothing I had seen . . . had left so deep a mark upon me as those trainloads of Jewish children standing at Austerlitz station. Yet I did not even see them myself.'[19] However, there is still an important difference between *Fragments* and a comparable literary depiction of a child affected by the Holocaust, such as W. G. Sebald's *Austerlitz*. The distinction lies between the first word of *Fragments*, 'I', and the phrase 'said Austerlitz', which is repeated throughout Sebald's novel.[20] *Austerlitz* records imagined conversations between a narrator and a character who traces his origins back to a forgotten, war-time childhood in Prague. Whereas *Fragments* opens with a photograph of 'The author at about age 10', which connects the subtitle ('Memories of a Childhood, 1939–1948') on the next page to the 'I' of the opening sentence, *Austerlitz* contains a photo (p. 326) of the (perhaps) adult Austerlitz, which is clearly distinguished – particularly after the repetition of 'said Austerlitz' – from Sebald's photograph on the inside back cover of the novel. *Austerlitz* is concerned with the character's recovery of his 'deep memory', and the pathos of his fruitless search for his parents' fate; *Fragments*, in contrast, attends to gleaning pity for the author in the present, and at 'about age 10'.[21] Despite the narrative similarities between the books' protagonists – both are orphans, and uncover their childhood histories in middle age – the books are different in the way that they deal with authorship, which forms an integral part of what Susan Rubin Suleiman has termed the 'conventional', the 'set of implicit and explicit understandings that frames the publication and reception of any work'.[22]

Yet there are also uncomfortable, structural similarities between a narrative that falsely purports to be authentic, and the 'rescued memory' of a fictionalised memoir.[23] Sebald and Wilkomirksi both draw on Holocaust literature and historical narratives (H. G. Adler's *Theresienstadt 1941–45: Das Antliz einer Zwangsgemeinschaft* in Sebald's case) in order to construct their fiction. *Austerlitz* also teases the reader into ruminating whether the main character is fictionalised or not: the improbable, chance meetings between the protagonist and narrator across Europe initiate a suspicion – complemented by the expectation of a unexpected denouement – that Austerlitz may turn out to be the fictive narrator. The latter may, or may not, be representative of Sebald; is the final photo meant to link with the cover photograph, purportedly that of Austerlitz as a child, but possibly (without knowledge of Sebald's features, or the fact that he bought many of the pictures from antique shops) that of the author? Such faultlines and overlaps between testimony, literature and memoirs that Sue Vice has analysed in relation to 'faction' are evident in Elena Lappin's comments on *Fragments*: 'If only he would admit that he was a writer . . . It would have been a very clever piece of writing if it wasn't fraudulent'.[24] By 'writer' Lappin means 'a writer of fiction' (someone who pens memoirs is also a writer). '[F]raudulent' refers to the author's fictional account of his childhood, and would not be applicable to an evaluation of *Fragments* as post-Holocaust fiction. As Vice argues, now Wilkomirski has been uncovered as Bruno Doessekker, 'the work of textual analysis can begin on what remains a striking and unusual *novel* about a childhood in the death camps'.[25]

Geoffrey Hill, a post-Holocaust poet concerned (as Sebald is, and Wilkomirski – if he is aware of the deception in *Fragments* – is not) with the ethical depiction of history in literature, is wary of ventriloquising the voice of someone in the camps. 'Domaine Public' illustrates this wariness: the epigraph refers to Desnos, but Hill combines an abstract narrative voice with that of the French poet; Desnos's surrealism merges with the macabre ruminations of the poet of *King Log* ('The days/ of the week/ are seven pits').[26] The case of Sylvia Plath is more complicated, since she has been accused of equating her own suffering with those who died during the Holocaust. Yet in the Szirtes quotation above, Pilinszky is purported to have said that Plath would have been the 'ideal translator' of Radnóti. Pilinszky's argument appears to have been that Plath was clearly interested in those who suffered under Nazi tyranny, and that, as a non-Jew, she could distance herself from the atrocities. (Of course, many non-Jews – such as Charlotte Delbo – also suffered during the Nazi regime.) Szirtes is rightly suspicious of Pilinszky's statement: any split between Holocaust and post-Holocaust poetry based solely on Jewish identity would be misleading; Szirtes notes in the introduction to Radnóti's *Camp Notebook* that 'Hardly ever does he touch on the reason that he was condemned to forced labour and eventual death, in other words on his Jewish origins' (p. 15). Despite the complex interactions between representations of the Holocaust and post-war constructions of Jewish identities, Tony Kushner argues that 'The Holocaust . . . is far too large an event for its impact to be felt only in the Jewish community'.[27] Its 'impact' is registered in the work of the non-Jewish poets discussed in this book.

Pilinszky himself is a troubling case when distinguishing Holocaust and post-Holocaust writing. He could be labelled a Holocaust poet in that he worked in a camp, but Hughes's introduction to his poetry in *The Desert of Love* obscures the fact that he was enrolled, rather than interned, by the retreating Nazis. Schiff's *Holocaust Poetry* is similarly vague in that Pilinszky is described as having 'spent some time in the camps' during the war.[28] The selection of writers in *Holocaust Poetry* illustrates other grey areas between Holocaust and post-Holocaust poets. It includes Holocaust poets such as Levi and Celan, but also writers such as Lotte Kramer – who was born in Mainz and came to England as a child refugee in 1939 – and Bertholt Brecht, who found refuge in Denmark, Finland and, later, America. Poems by the latter two writers are included in the 'Alienation', 'Persecution' and 'Destruction' sections of the anthology: should they be considered post-Holocaust poets, since they were not inmates of the camps, or – to use Gubar's phrase – 'differently authentic' Holocaust poets (p. 55), since their background credits them with a closer connection to the events of mid-century Europe than Plath, Hill, Harrison or Hughes? Equally, should the Anglo-Jewish poets Michael Hamburger, Michael Horovitz, Lotte Kramer, Karen Gershon and Gerda Meyer, all of whom 'emigrated [to Britain] to escape Nazism in the 1930s' be labelled as Holocaust, post-Holocaust or postmemory authors?[29] And how should poets such as Abraham Sutzkever or Abba Kovner be categorised? Neither was an inmate in a camp, but both were involved in underground movements in the Vilna ghetto, and then fought the Nazis as partisans in the surrounding forests. Holocaust and post-Holocaust poetry must be distinguished with criteria based on temporality, personal experience or connections to the camps and ghettos, but also taking into account refugees, and members of resistance movements. Such distinctions are central to this book, since they separate authors who were directly affected by the advent of the Final Solution from post-Holocaust writers such as Plath, Hill, Harrison and Hughes.

However, such criteria unavoidably create grey areas. How can a 'connection' to, or 'involvement' in, the Holocaust be separate from variegated imaginative investment? Perhaps a distinction should also be made in terms of identity politics: Sachs, 'Though geographically distant from the death camps themselves nevertheless participated imaginatively in the destruction of her people and sought to speak for those who could not speak for themselves'.[30] The key phrases here are 'her people' and 'speak for': Schiff interprets Sachs's poetry as taking a stance on behalf of Jewish people. This differentiates Sachs's work from that of a post-Holocaust poet such as William Heyen. Both poets adopt the voices of those who suffered during the Holocaust: in Heyen's 'Passover: the Injections', 'We', children, are murdered by German soldiers; in 'A Dead Child Speaks', the interlocutor is 'led to death' (pp. 60, 67). Nevertheless, Schiff argues that Sachs is participating 'imaginatively' in the child's demise as a Jew, unlike the American poet Heyen, whose writing responds to his German ancestry. Since Szirtes is suspicious of Pilinszky's equating of the Holocaust with only Jewish suffering, a distinction between Holocaust and post-Holocaust poetry based only on identity politics would clearly be simplistic. Yet, even though 'Passover: the Injections' and 'A Dead Child Speaks' are similar texts, a temporal, identitarian and generational gap separates the two poets. Some of Heyen's relatives were (former) Nazis: his post-Holocaust poems are the work of postmemory, since, as Hirsch outlines, 'Postmemory characterizes the experience of those who grow up dominated by narratives that preceded their birth'.[31] This contrasts with Sachs's Holocaust poetry: Sachs was forced to emigrate from Germany to Sweden in 1940; she 'imaginatively' engaged with the events in central Europe as they were unfolding, and through subsequent conversations and correspondence with Celan.[32]

Peter Huchel's poem 'Roads' in Schiff's anthology clearly demonstrates that criteria based solely on imaginative investment and identification, rather than encompassing temporality and experience, are not specific enough to separate Holocaust from post-Holocaust poetry. The title (and the third line, 'Roads. Roads') could lead to a misinterpretation of the poem as a depiction of a death march by a camp inmate, particularly since it is positioned so close to Pilinszky's 'Harbach 1944' (p. 53). A letter from Michael Hamburger quoted by Schiff reveals that it '"is about the exodus of Germans from Eastern Germany at the end of the war"' (p. 212). Abstract, apocalyptic images such as the 'sky in flames' and 'fire/ that sullenly chewed the darkness' mean that this can only be only adduced from authorial intention: the poem could have been written by a former inmate of a camp, an SS commander, an eastern European or a German civilian. It is unsettling that 'Roads' has been inserted into the 'Destruction' section of the anthology: the corpses on the railway line make it clear why this is so, but the Hamburger letter suggests an uneasy equivalence between the Holocaust and the tribulations of the German population, a comparison that was opened up as a possibility during the revisionist *Historikerstreit* debates in Germany in the 1980s.[33] Is it possible for a (non-refugee) German writer who had no experience of the camps, or relatives who perished therein, to be categorised as a Holocaust poet, despite the fact that Huchel 'received a prize for his first collection of poems in 1932 but withdrew his manuscript when the Nazis came to power a year later'? Hamburger's comments suggest he should instead be classed as a post-Holocaust poet, since he '"was much concerned with the Jews and wrote a prose piece about the Jewish cemetery at Sulzbach, not far from his refuge in West Germany"' (p. 212). Yet again, we are unavoidably led back to the author's biography, as when Szirtes makes a distinction between Plath and Radnóti. Roland Barthes's 'The Death of the Author' has sometimes been misunderstood as a poststructuralist attack on the author-figure per se rather than as a warning against 'authorcentric' critics: without knowledge of the author's life, it becomes possible to give a fraudster prizes for 'authentic' memoirs. Barthes would have no doubt deplored Wilkomirski's triumphs, at the same time as conceding that mistakes can be made if the text is relied on to ascertain the authenticity of the narrative. Distinctions between Holocaust and post-Holocaust poets such as Radnóti and Plath cannot but rely on some knowledge of the author-figures. Wilkomirski's is an extreme case: in many instances the two categories can be distinguished through features such as the self-conscious engagement of the post-Holocaust poet with images of atrocity (Hill) or the discussion of ideas first expounded by Holocaust poets (Hughes).

## Awkwardness and Postmemory

Due to the 'grey areas' between Holocaust and post-Holocaust literature outlined above, awkward poetics can be regarded as a response to the current stage of post-Holocaust writing. Writing may not be able '"to reference its own authenticity"', as Maurice Blanchot has stated, but it can at least self-consciously discuss the process of inscription.[34] '[T]he problem of boundaries between Holocaust fact and Holocaust fiction' is not a new one, as Lawrence L. Langer comments in relation to Tadeusz Borowski's *This Way for the Gas, Ladies and Gentlemen*, which was first published in 1946.[35] This quandary has attained a specific urgency in the twenty-first century, however: as Schwarz argues, 'it is the artistic rendering of the Holocaust that will keep it alive in the imagination particularly as memoirists dwindle'.[36] Rather than ransacking others' experience for the sake of aesthetic purchase (of which Plath has been accused), the tensions between contemporary poets' reactions to the Holocaust and their lack of personal connections to the camps can be highlighted as twenty-first century responses to 'rescued memory'. In this way, post-Holocaust art might assuage Lang's concern that '"literature divorced from the precise historical moment inspiring it may go astray, leading others astray in its wake"'.[37] As James E. Young asks in *At Memory's Edge: After-Images of the Holocaust in Contemporary Art and Architecture*, how is a post-Holocaust generation of artists 'supposed to "remember" events they never experienced directly?'. His answer is that these artists engage with their 'hypermediated experiences of memory', the 'vicarious past' and the 'memory of the witness's memory'.[38] The poets discussed in this book display an awareness of this vicariousness: Hill, for example, dramatises his position as a non-victim in early poems such as 'Of Commerce and Society' and 'Two Formal Elegies', and in a more sophisticated way in *The Triumph of Love* – written over forty years later – where lyrical moments vie with an exposition of the art of atrocity.

Such self-reflexivity is embedded in the exposition of awkward poetics in *Tony Harrison and the Holocaust*. The theory of awkwardness arose out of my interpretation of Theodor Adorno's famous statement in 'Cultural Criticism and Society' that 'To write poetry after Auschwitz is barbaric'.[39] Adorno's main point is that poems should not be written in the same way as they were before the Holocaust. His warning is particularly pertinent if – as Leonard Forster argues in *German Poetry 1944–48* – atrocities 'are commonly followed by an outburst of lyric poetry'.[40] To ignore the ways in which the Holocaust has changed pre-war conceptions of aesthetics, Adorno argues, would be obscene. His contentions that art has not been attentive enough to this process – and the fact that the advent of the Holocaust makes its unreflective savouring appear unseemly – are registered in the less epigrammatic statement in *Negative Dialectics* that 'All post-Auschwitz culture, including its urgent critique, is garbage.'[41] Such a 'pungent' view, as Langer terms the latter maxim, can be interpreted as a plea for awkward poetics, in which art might register the worries that Adorno expounds within the texture of the artworks themselves.[42] Post-Holocaust poets, as Gubar argues, 'often find a mandate for their work . . . by laying bare the reasons why the composing of poetry after Auschwitz had to become suspect' (p.

210). Harrison registers these suspicions by inserting irregular metrics into mellifluous pentameters, and discussing how the advent of the Holocaust challenges the concept of classical humanism. His attention to metrical intricacies in his sonnets highlights Adorno's implication that it would be insensitive to continue blindly with traditional forms without registering the impact of the Holocaust on contemporary culture. In Levinasian terms, awkward poetics enable the poet to 'adopt a position of interpretative responsibility towards the victims they are representing', which includes the rigorous examination of inherited structures.[43] In a wider sense, ethical responses in literature are also bound up with the notion of authorship: they link with Suleiman's notion of the 'conventional', expressing the author's conception of his or her relationship to the 'implicit and explicit understandings' that frame the publication and reception of any book (p. 546). Inherited conventions include the contract between the author and reader, an implicit understanding that has been violated in the case of Wilkomirksi's *Fragments*, but which awkward aesthetics call attention to, as in Hill's famous interjection in 'September Song' that, whilst ostensibly writing a post-Holocaust elegy for an unnamed victim, he has made 'an elegy for [himself] it/ is true'.[44] Unlike *Fragments*, 'September Song' admits, and emphasises, its own fictionality.

Hill's self-critique responds to the 'awkwardly *un*poetic nature of [the poem's] subject matter', and inaugurates a '*non*cathartic artistry of disaster'.[45] This 'artistry' resists the notion that true poetry can only draw on mellifluous aesthetics. Glancing at any dictionary of literary terms, the critic might assume that traditional poetics are based on a taxonomy of technical perfection, but perfect metre comprises substandard doggerel. Awkward poetics highlight the fact that, historically, poets have always relied on subtle irregularities to inaugurate creative tensions in their texts. Post-Holocaust aesthetics utilise these self-conscious moments to emphasise the specific difficulties of engaging with an event so resistant to artistic representation. In the introduction to *Tony Harrison and the Holocaust*, I illustrate aspects of this aesthetic struggle in relation to the work of Harrison, Plath and Hill. Metrical breaks in Harrison's poems, and the daring mixture of rhythms in Plath's 'Daddy', register the 'seismic' impact – as Harrison terms it – of twentieth-century atrocities.[46] Plath's poems display a marked suspicion towards the aesthetic: the narrator's concerns about unreflective glamorisations of Austria's beauty in 'Daddy' lay bare the reasons 'why the composing of poetry after Auschwitz had to become suspect'.[47] In Hill's 'September Song', awkward poetics are evident in linguistic compression: the poem's economy of language foregrounds its failure to provide an adequate elegy for the Holocaust victim. Responding to what Gubar has termed 'the ethical ramifications of "consuming trauma"', this anti-elegy calls attention to the gleaning of aesthetic profit out of atrocity: economic language is figured as resisting, but also complicit with, the Nazis' (sometimes) efficient disposal of victims; 'September Song' makes the 'reader fully aware of their own suspicions about the aestheticizing in which [post-Holocaust poets] engage'.[48] A taxonomy of awkward poetics includes these poets' 'suspicions', as well as metrical tension, the anti-elegiac, self-questioning, embarrassed rhetoric, anti-rhetoric, juxtaposition, incongruity, self-declared inadequacies, paradox, minimalism, non-catharsis, heightened tone, hermeneutics, the anti-redemptive, archaisms, anti-objectivism and 'stylistic eccentricities'.[49] These (anti-) poetic qualities are bound up with the impossible necessity of representing the Holocaust; like choliambus and ischiorrhogic verse, they constitute regular irregularities. Some of the stylistics are contradictory: heightened tone is clearly not the same as anti-rhetoric, but the embarrassing sentimentality of the Auschwitz sequence in Harrison's *Prometheus* and the minimalism of Hughes's *Crow* collection are both responses to the pressure of silence surrounding post-Holocaust poetry. Not all post-Holocaust poets, of course, adhere to the taxonomy above in its entirety: in this book, I focus on awkward poetics in the form of intense self-critique in Hill's *The Triumph of Love*, the self-critical discussion of aesthetic prurience and spectacle in Hill and Plath's work, the subversive juxtaposition of alternative perspectives in *Prometheus* and the 'plain and ugly' language of the 'Crow' poems.[50]

Some critics have detected piety in Hill's self-conscious (and often self-flagellating) poetics: Ian Hamilton accuses the author of 'recondite grandiloquence . . . locked into his quasi-vatic' self-importance.[51] The charge can be redirected towards awkward poetics, which could be regarded as a pious attempt to register the difficulties of historical representation, a conundrum that the poet then resolves all too easily through self-castigation masquerading as appropriation. In *Mourning Becomes the Law*, Gillian Rose refers to the phenomenon of Holocaust piety in relation to theories that espouse the impossibility of representing atrocities. Awkward aesthetics could be located in a continuum extrapolated from Rose's theory: although they do not adhere to the misreading of Adorno that 'poetry is [entirely] impossible after Auschwitz', they nevertheless indicate an ethical struggle in their engagement with the Holocaust that may be blithely ignorant of the ease in which popular culture has encompassed representations of atrocity, as in the famous example of the television show *Holocaust*. The latter example provides an unwitting defence for awkward poetics, since the alternative to 'interpretive responsibility' is the unreflective seizure of Holocaust icons. However, as critics have argued in relation to Hill, the self-conscious recognition of authorial responsibility does not necessarily exculpate a pious tone.[52] These detractors are particularly wary of the author's voice in the poetry; their criticism can, again, be appended to the notion of awkward aesthetics, which could be charged with a conservative erudition that privileges the author's version of the work, to the detriment of lesser mortals, such as other readers. One counterargument would be that the author-figure is not as stable as these critics suggest: Hill actually presents 'Hill' in various, and sometimes contradictory, guises; Francis Spufford characterises one of them as a 'nasty old git gobbing on contemporary culture'.[53] These multiple perspectives grate against the post-Movement poetics that Hill clearly distrusts, in which the poem is '"an anecdote, where language has a deft, satisfactory, empirical function, inoffensively conveying the gist of an interesting experience"'.[54] As with the charge of piety, the alternative to poetry open to its own postures, contradictions and responsibilities is an unreflective writing that leaves the 'interpretive responsibility' entirely – rather than partly – up to the reader.

As opposed to most of contemporary British poetry, which responds to Adorno's 'lacerating cry' about 'barbaric' poetry with 'blank-faced' indifference, William Logan acclaims the 'painful regard' of Hill's long poem *The Triumph of Love* (p. 208). Nevertheless, awkward poetics – even though they arose out of a study of Harrison's poetry – could appear to be merely an accurate description of Hill's 'painful regard'. This book makes no apology for presenting Hill's work as exemplary in terms of its 'interpretive responsibility' towards the representation of history: Hill has explored the problems of secondary witnessing and the vicarious past for over fifty years. Such a stance leaves awkward aesthetics open to the charge of offensive erudition: they could be dismissed as the preserve of a few academic poets and critics. Encountering them in poetry could be figured – recalling Edna Longley's hyperbole on *The Triumph of Love* – as 'like swallowing barbed wire'.[55] '[I]t can be irritating,' James Wood argues, 'when Hill's more pious admirers speak as if verse's highest theme should be not the intolerable wrestle with words, but, as it were, a further wrestle with the wrestle'; in other words, poetics akin to the 'gravel of the joyless'.[56] Criticism of Hill's work has tended to construct an opposition between intellectual rumination and sensuous appreciation: Hamilton accepts that 'there are glints of lyric simplicity and power' in *The Triumph of Love*, but they are 'all too eagerly subsumed by a general straining for recondite grandiloquence' (p. 12). Self-questioning is mistaken for pomposity: lyrical epiphanies are hard-earned in Hill's work. Awkward poetics cannot be deployed ignorantly without 'painful regard' for the historicity of the sensual, whatever the aesthetic risks of a 'further wrestle with the wrestle'.

Ethical responses to the dialectic between the lyric and history in post-war British poetry have been inextricable from what Jon Harris terms 'distancing'.[57] Asking whether it is possible 'to identify a specifically British response to the Holocaust', Harris argues that 'The best non-Jewish, British Holocaust poems are either set at a horrified uncompre-hending distance', like Mervyn Peake's 'The Consumptive. Belsen 1945', or 'set in a fictional distance', as with 'September Song' or George Macbeth's 'The Auschwitz Rag' (pp. 212, 228). Harris distinguishes Peake from Hill and Macbeth because – like the American poet Anthony Hecht – Peake had first-hand experience of the camps: Andrew Sinclair notes in *War Like a Wasp: The Lost Decade of the 'Forties* that Peake was sent to Belsen in 1945 to 'prepare a series of drawings for the *Leader* magazine'.[58] Poetry, as well as drawings, ensued: 'The Consumptive. Belsen 1945' is one of the first examples of 'interpretive responsibility' in British, post-Holocaust poetry. The poem comprises a self-conscious response to Peake's status as a poet and painter sent to record the misery of the camp for a British audience: he berates his artistic 'traffic' (trade); the fact that his 'schooled eyes' can see the 'ghost of a great painting' (as well as an elegy) in a dying girl.[59] 'If such can be a painter's ecstasy,' the poet enquires, '(Her limbs like pipes, her head a china skull)/ Then where is mercy?' (p. 269). Peake admits to a lack of compassion in his official capacity as a war artist: aesthetic culpability is extended to historical nar-ratives in another poem ('Victims'), which continue 'witlessly', despite their inability to register the disappearance of the 'hush of love' amongst the 'smoothed sheets of death'.[60]

'The Consumptive. Belsen 1945' and 'Victims' are based on sketches reproduced in *Drawings by Mervyn Peake*: number 31 contains the note 'Girl dying of consumption at Belsen, a month after the Burning[?]'; another (32) is inscribed, simply, with '17 years'.[61] The poems, unlike the Chinese brush drawings, highlight Peake's 'interpretative responsibility'. Peake's poetics could be read as 'quasi-vatic' self-importance, but a more generous response would be to regard the self-exposure of the witness as an honest attempt to register the 'distance' of the post-Holocaust poet from the suffering in the camps, even as he sees it unfolding. The poet's pity is unveiled as suspicious when he watches the girl dying: depicting himself as 'glass' in *War Like a Wasp*'s 'The Consumptive. Belsen 1945', the narrator bemoans the grief that 'so glibly slides' from his pen as her agony 'slides through' him (pp. 269–70). Only her last breath 'grips' him with any emotion; despite this (and the intermittent, strained rhetoric), Peake is confident that the poem will not 'betray' the 'last cough of her small, trembling head'. In contrast to Peake's awkward poetics, Harris argues that, even though Anglo-Jewish poets such as Gershon are 'no more able to conceive . . . horror than any non-Jew', they also cancel 'any suggestion of a fictional or distancing approach' (p. 231). Some poets included in Peter Lawson's anthology of post-war Jewish poetry in Britain (see Note 29) may seem to support Harris's thesis: for example, Richard Burns ruminates in 'The Blue Butterfly' that his 'Jew's hand' was 'Raised from unmarked graves of my obliterated people'; Dannie Abse argues in 'White Balloon' that 'Auschwitz made [him]/ more of a Jew than Moses did' (pp. 53, 26). However, metaphysics of 'raising' and 'making' still register the fictional distance of post-Holocaust poets from the events in Europe: such secondary witnesses can, as the narrator does in 'A Night Out', munch chocolate while taking in a Polish film about Auschwitz (p. 25). The limitations of Harris's sense of 'closeness' – as implied by the poems themselves – are illustrated when he argues erroneously that Plath, 'another Jewish poet', demonstrates her personal connection to the Holocaust with 'impartial description' in 'Mary's Song' (p. 230).

Harris's article does usefully demonstrate that the overall reaction of Jewish, and non-Jewish British poets to the Holocaust in the 1940s and 1950s was not an attempt to forge awkward poetics, but primarily that of silence. His research reveals the 'amazingly small number of poems' about the Holocaust in contemporaneous journals; he recounts that Abse printed a section on young Jewish poets in an edition of *Poetry Quarterly* in 1948, 'which did not contain a single poem on the theme in question' (p. 220). As early as 1944, George Orwell wrote that England lacked a 'concentration-camp literature' because no British writer had experienced 'totalitarianism from the inside'.[62] This was in spite of a few British POWs who were interned in camps at the time, such as Auschwitz and – in the case of Christopher Burney – Buchenwald. Burney, like other prisoners, returned to provide testimony of his experiences: his book entitled *Dungeon Democracy* berates the 'depravity' of the inmates and the 'obsequiousness' of the Jewish inmates towards the SS.[63] As Orwell predicted, a literature responding directly to the *Lager* did not flourish from such (biased) testimony, which, as Mark Rawlinson notes, is at odds with Levi's notion of the 'grey zone', where prisoners are so enmeshed in the systems of the camps, and the struggle to survive, that they might, for example, collaborate in the victimisation of others (pp. 12–13). Rawlinson illustrates that British war novels in the 1940s, including H. E. Bates's *Fair Stood the Wind*, respond to the conflict primarily through adventure stories, and the figures of 'escapers and evaders at large in Western Europe': this tends to occlude the happenings in the death camps in the East, and the daily machinations of Nazism (p. 7).

The danger of 'Allied' responses to the Holocaust is compounded for second-generation writers in Britain, since their knowledge of the events of 1933 to 1945 is based on, for example, newsreel of the camps, fictional films (as in Abse's 'A Night Out'), books like the American Central Office of Information publication – which contained 'the most terrible photographs of Belsen, Auschwitz and Buchenwald' – and the waxworks exhibition in London of 'All the Horrors of the Concentration Camp'.[64] Awkward poetics call attention to the difficulties for post-Holocaust writers in trying to gain access to the historical reality of the Holocaust, rather than chasing the chimera of a purely objective response to the events in Europe. Harrison remembers watching newsreels in Leeds of the liberation of Belsen and Buchenwald by Allied troops in 1945: the question is whether narratives of liberation lead to simplistic readings of the war which celebrate hopes for the future at the expense of the voices of survivors, who, as in Levi's poem 'The Survivor', may be disturbed by images of dead compatriots and inmates, the 'submerged people' who are 'Tinged with death in their uneasy sleep'.[65] The former perspective risks presenting the moment of liberation as a caesura in history, the point at which Allied justice can begin, the atavistic years of Nazi rule can be expunged, and Western civilisation can be returned to normality. As Kushner argues, '[T]he battle to establish the singularity and specificity of the Jewish tragedy in the war would have to [be] waged *against* the perceptions of spring 1945.'[66] In *The Drowned and the Saved*, Levi takes issue with Allied narratives of the camps' liberation. They offer a 'ster[e]otyped picture, proposed innumerable times', as in the final frames of Roberto Benigni's *Life is Beautiful*, when the mother and child realise they have just 'won' the 'game' inside the camp. Levi contrasts such celebrations of the 'end of the storm' with the shame of actual survivors.[67] Rawlinson argues that key historical moments in the Allied version of the war, including the liberation of the camps in Germany, are invested with so much symbolic potential that references to the Holocaust 'in the decades after the war were often skewed by the tendency . . . to view things through the prism of the familiar' (p. 20). Walter Abish criticises the 'familiar' in a German context in his novel *How German Is It*: the schoolteacher Anna asks her pupils to think about the concept; the scene's proximity to those in which the corpses of former inmates of a nearby camp (Durst) are uncovered suggests that the refusal to mourn the events of World War II has become a national disgrace. For this book, the question is whether British post-Holocaust poets are guilty of perpetuating the familiar narratives of liberation, camp escapees, and wooden horses, thereby obscuring 'the singularity and specificity of the Jewish tragedy'.[68]

Whereas *Tony Harrison and the Holocaust* (see Note 10) focused on the work of one poet, this book looks at the ways in which Plath, Hill, Harrison and Hughes might respond to, or resist, awkward poetics. Rather than just 'apply' Adorno's thesis to each author, this study is attentive to the ways in which awkwardness is figured differently in each poet's work. In relation to Plath, I argue that the furore over her appropriation of Holocaust imagery ignores a word which critics have rarely used to describe her infamous monologues: camp. The campy poetics of 'Lady Lazarus' appear an inappropriate context in which to mention Ilse Koch's lampshade, since they highlight the artifice of the text, and have a tendency to over-dramatise. Rather than being an instance of Nazi chic, or what Saul Friedlander has called the 'new discourse', however, I argue that Plath is more self-conscious in her deployment of Holocaust iconography in her dramatic monologues than most critics have suggested. Whereas Plath is only edging towards an ethical response to history, Hill is more attuned than any of the other post-Holocaust poets discussed in this book to the difficulties of writing about the events of 1933 to 1945. In *The Triumph of Love*, Hill's development of a self-conscious (and often self-critical) voice within the long poem allows him to critique his poetic assumptions and shortcomings. These awkward poetics offset the palimpsest imagination at work elsewhere, when Hill reinterprets pre-Holocaust texts (such as The Book of Daniel) in the light of the advent of Auschwitz. Moral intelligence, empathy and erudite philosophical and historical musings are never far from accusations of prurience, exploitation, and cowardice. Such self-critique is, unfortunately, absent from one of Hughes's post-Holocaust poems, 'Lines about Elias', where the camp guards are depicted as suffering as much as the inmates. The correspondence between Hughes and Pilinszky in the archives at Emory University reveals that this negative awkwardness (or, more simply put, offensiveness) arises out of Hughes's reading of Pilinszky's concept of the literature of extremity, which evolves out of the moment of extinction. Hughes is on much surer ground, I argue, when he engages with twentieth-century history in his earlier, less 'representational' texts, and poems about violence, such as 'Pike' and the Crow sequence. Harrison also risks giving offence in his film/poem *Prometheus*, where the film crew speeds through scenes of atrocity in Europe with the alacrity of tourists. The ways in which digital editing allows Harrison to link visual metaphors is arresting, but also potentially confusing and controversial. Prometheus, in the form of a huge golden statue, is an astonishing device to register the immobility of Aeschylus's hero, but its defiant salute outside Auschwitz could be read as according with Nazi, as much as classical, and Stalinist, iconography. Similarly, the image of a crucifix after the visit to Auschwitz cannot help but encourage a reading of the Holocaust in which the Jews are punished for killing Christ. Such frames without a voiceover invite multiple interpretations, but eschew the awkward poetics that abound in Harrison's lyrics, but are absent from the monologues of Hermes, the insensitive (main) narrator. However, my discussion of *Prometheus* does not set up an opposition between self-reflexive lyrical poetry and cinema, since unsettling self-questioning forms an integral part of other post-Holocaust films, such as Alain Resnais's *Night and Fog*. Nor does it privilege the lyric over the monologue: both forms can contain awkward poetics, whether through the imaginary voice of a persona, or the fictional representation of the author's perspective.

Such expositions of awkward poetics (or the lack of them) are an attempt to provide a critical vocabulary to discuss post-Holocaust poetry.[69] They are attuned to what Michael Rothberg has termed 'an emerging interdisciplinary consensus about the importance of taking account of the psychic and social aftermath of genocide, as well as the problem of the transmission of knowledge, in considerations of the Holocaust's significance'.[70] Critical discourses surrounding the 'aftermath' of the Holocaust in terms of post-Holocaust poetry in Britain and America in particular are rare at present (Gubar's book and Parmet's *The Terror of Our Days* form two of the few exceptions).[71] Rothberg chooses not to distinguish postmemory from the 'post-Holocaust' when he refers to 'the latecomer' or 'the "postmemory generation"', which 'inherits the detritus of the twentieth-century', whereas Hirsch stresses that 'postmemory is distinguished from memory by generational distance and from history by deep personal connection'.[72] This is not to suggest that the literature of postmemory does not deal with similar issues to post-Holocaust poetry. Yet critical responses to a poem such as Karen Gershon's 'I Was Not There' – which mourns the fact that the poet was not there 'to comfort them' when 'Both [her] parents died in camps' – should take into account the 'deep personal connection', whereas an account of such a situation written by a post-Holocaust poet would not. Gershon and Plath's poetry skirts around the label 'confessional', but Plath has been accused of parading a personal anguish incommensurate to the suffering of postmemory writers such as Gershon.[73] Whatever the moral imperatives involved in Plath's fictionalising, her poetry certainly forms an instance of what Kaja Silverman has termed 'heteropathic recollection', in the light of her 'imaginative investment' in the camps, but this cannot cover up the fact that her personal connections to the Holocaust are tenuous, based only on her status as a second-generation German.[74]

Awkward poetics are not the preserve of post-Holocaust writers, despite the differences between postmemory texts and post-Holocaust literature. As I demonstrated in *Tony Harrison and the Holocaust*, the stilted grammar, tentative adjectival phrases and heightened tone of a passage from *The Truce* (pp. 15–16) illustrates that Levi is deploying an aesthetics of awkwardness to seek out apt words for the survivors' experiences after the liberation of Auschwitz. Lexical difficulties give way to awkwardness in the form of conceptual juxtapositions in Czeslaw Milosz's 'Campo dei Fiori'. During a visit to Italy, the poet – who was involved in the Polish Underground during the war – savours the colours of 'rose-pink fish', 'dark grapes' and 'peach-down' in the square.[75] Stanza two immediately subverts these tourist pleasures: 'On this same square/ they burned Giordano Bruno' (an Italian philosopher murdered in 1600 for his heretical views on Catholicism). Plath similarly juxtaposes the beauty of the landscape against the atrocities committed there with the narrator's denunciation in 'Daddy' of the 'snows of the Tyrol, the clear beer of Vienna' which are not 'very pure or true'.[76] One difference between the awkward poetics of Holocaust and post-Holocaust writers lies in the latter's self-conscious engagement with the ramifications of their non-participation in the events of mid-twentieth-century Europe. Hence Hill worries in *The Triumph of Love* about the possibilities of aesthetic prurience when he watches a newsreel of the ghettos, and his cowardice compared to the valour of war poets such as Butterworth. Cinematic interpretations of the war for a British audience are emphasised in the work of Hill and Harrison in particular: in *Prometheus*, the cheering of contemporaneous audiences at the bombing of Dresden is undercut as the newsreel is replayed for the Old Man; he applauds at first, but then begins to cry as he realises his implication in the perspective of the perpetrator.

Self-conscious aesthetics of awkwardness in post-Holocaust poetry have more in common with the concept of countermemory than postmemory: James Young praises German countermonuments as '"brazen, painfully self-conscious memorial spaces conceived to challenge the very premises of their being"'.[77] This description, which introduces his commentary on the monument against Fascism in Harburg, could be appropriated to describe awkward poetics. Just as the Gerzs's disappearing monument suggests that the artists are 'Ethically certain of their duty to remember, but aesthetically skeptical of the assumptions underpinning traditional memorial forms', Hill and Harrison subvert the trajectory of consolation in traditional elegies, at the same time as committing themselves to writing within, and about, these structures. The Gerzs's scepticism is also mirrored in Hill's critique of what Rose has termed the 'fascism of representation': in *The Triumph of Love*, Quadriga, the statue on Constitution Arch, is appraised as a fascistic glorification of supreme authority and pompous military aggrandisement.[78] The Harburg monument responds to the current generation's memory of memory, just as the poetics of awkwardness stress the need for a self-conscious ethics of remembering that emphasise post-Holocaust writers' self-doubt in representing the events of mid-twentieth-century Europe. By doing so the poets cannot help but rely on the notion of the authentic.

Andrew Leak and George Paizis claim that 'It is difficult to imagine anything more alien to a postmodern sensibility than an insistence on the ethical imperative of authenticity.'[79] Awkward poetics do bear comparison, though, with the self-referential, postmodernist techniques of post-memory texts, such as the two *Maus* books, and James Friedman's photographs of the camps. Apel defines her version of postmodernism in her approach to the art of secondary witnessing (such as Friedman's pictures) as 'a self-consciousness that always places the Holocaust in relation to the circumstances of its representation in the present, eschewing the stance of objective observer who recognises timeless truths'.[80] Plath, although writing long before the term 'postmodernism' became popular in critical discourse, is edging towards a self-conscious appropriation of Holocaust imagery with her emphasis on the artifice of the dramatic monologue. Hill's self-critique in *The Triumph of Love* more obviously rejects objectivity, and rigorously examines 'the circumstances of its representation'. However, despite the similarities between Hill's deliberations and Apel's definition of postmodernism, the traditional uses of form in Hill and Harrison's poetry and (to a lesser extent) in Plath and Hughes's work, hardly qualifies these writers as postmodernist poets. Whereas Friedman's postmodernist photographs of the camp focus on objects such as toys in a car park, a delivery van and a table in a café, Harrison, for example, constructs a modernist version of Auschwitz in *Prometheus* (according to Apel's terminology) when he includes recognisable frames of the entrance to Birkenau, railway tracks and barbed wire.[81]

Sue Vice's challenge to monologic conceptions of the authorial voice in *Holocaust Fiction* can be framed within this debate about postmodernism and Holocaust art. Vice defends Helen Darville's *The Hand that Signed the Paper* as a polyphonic text that should be evaluated – along with Wilkomirski's *Fragments* – outside debates about the authors' false identities. Darville's novel is exculpated of aesthetic larceny; in contrast, the critic Robert Manne laments the lack of a '"clearly identified and morally unambiguous authorial voice"' in the book.[82] Vice argues that the various voices in the book demand the reader's imaginative engagement: polyphony does not lead to relativism (a charge often made against postmodernist art), since some of the voices are clearly more authoritative, or less prejudiced, than others. These contentions provide the most serious challenge to the notion of awkward poetics. Are the poet's self-conscious ruminations nothing more than a conservative, monologic wish for a 'clearly identified and morally unambiguous voice'? Or do they merely form part of the more authoritative voices in the text? Given that Vice illustrates that some voices are of less value than others, awkwardness can be defended within the Bakhtinian framework as an important exposition of an author's position, but one which should not be regarded as authoritarian; awkward poetics may, after all, be situated amongst a variety of authorial perspectives. Vice's arguments about polyphonic Holocaust fiction are complex and persuasive, and leave this critic troubled only by the apparent freedom of the reader to interpret the open-ended text. As he or she sifts among the dialogic 'tissue of signs', they carry the 'interpretive responsibility' towards the material; unless, as in the case of the Gerzs's countermonument, neo-Nazis' responses to a text (in this case, their inscriptions on the countermonument) are to be given equal space to those of more enlightened respondents.[83] Awkward poetics provide the reader with a self-reflexive position with which to engage, but one that anticipates, following Vice's argument, critical thinking, and possible rejection.

## Notes

1. Frieda W. Aaron, *Bearing the Unbearable: Yiddish and Polish Poetry in the Ghettos and Concentration Camps* (New York: State University of New York Press, 1990), p. 211. In *Poetry after Auschwitz: Remembering What One Never Knew* (Bloomington: Indiana University Press, 2003), Susan Gubar argues that the decreasing number of survivors provides one reason for the Holocaust's 'dying', and that 'if only the reports of those who personally witnessed the destruction of the Jewish people can be judged meaningful . . . then the Holocaust is doomed to expire' (p. 4).
2. Dora Apel, *Memory Effects: The Holocaust and the Art of Secondary Witnessing* (New Brunswick, New Jersey and London: Rutgers University Press, 2002), p. 7.
3. *Between Hope and Despair: Pedagogy and the Remembrance of Historical Trauma*, ed. Roger Simon, Sharon Rosenberg and Claudia Eppert (New York: Rowman and Littlefield, 2000), p. 7.
4. Marianne Hirsch, 'Mourning and Postmemory', in *The Holocaust: Theoretical Readings*, ed. Neil Levi and Michael Rothberg (Edinburgh: Edinburgh University Press, 2003), pp. 416–22, p. 416.
5. George Szirtes, 'Introduction', in Miklós Radnóti, *Camp Notebook*, trans. Francis Jones (Todmorden: Arc, 2000), pp. 13–16, p. 14.

6. George Steiner, 'Dying is an Art' (rev. of *Ariel*), in *Language and Silence* (London: Faber, 1967), pp. 324–34, p. 330. Harold Bloom has also stated that 'Elie Wiesel, Paul Celan, Nelly Sachs can touch the horror with authority', but that 'British and American writers need to avoid it, as we have no warrant for imagination in that most terrible of areas' (quoted in Gubar, p. 9).

7. Tony Kushner, *The Holocaust and the Liberal Imagination: A Social and Cultural History* (Oxford: Blackwell, 1994), p. 24.

8. Aaron, p. 8.

9. There has not been enough space in this book to discuss numerous Holocaust, and post-Holocaust, poets, including Dannie Abse, Karen Alkalay-Gut, Yehuda Amichai, W. H. Auden, Ingeborg Bachmann, Anita Barrows, Józef Bau, Stephen Berg, John Berryman, Elizabeth Bishop, Johannes Bobrowski, Alan Bold, Edward Bond, Dietrich Bonhoeffer, Lily Brett, Rachmil Bryks, Jean Cayrol, Robert Desnos, Olga Drucker, Hans Magnus Enzenberger, Christopher Fahy, Ruth Fainlight, Howard Fast, Elaine Feinstein, Irving Feldman, Ruth Feldman, James Fenton, Jerzy Ficowski, Carolyn Forché, Sari Friedman, Pavel Friedmann, Mike Frenkel, M. Gebirtig, Amir Gilboa, Jacob Glatstein, Hirsh Glik, Hayim Gouri, Jorie Graham, Uri Zvi Greenberg, Marilyn Hacker, Michael Hamburger, Anthony Hecht, Judith Hemscheyemer, Magda Herzberger, Philip Hobsbaum, Michael Horovitz, Lynda Hull, Barbara Helfgott Hyett, Ada Jackson, A. C. Jacobs, Randall Jarrell, Mieczysław Jastruń, Shmerke Kaczerginski, Dori Katz, Yitzhak Katzenelson, A. M. Klein, Gertrud Kolmar, Bernard Kops, Jan Korr, Yala Korwin, Abba Kovner, Maxine Kumin, Isreal Meir Lask, H. Leivick, Denise Levertov, Olga Levertov, Lyn Litshin, Emanuel Litvinoff, Michael Longley, George Macbeth, Derek Mahon, Itzik Manger, Gerda Mayer, W. S. Merwin, Bert Meyers, Robert Mezey, Czeslaw Milosz, Kadya Molodowsky, Amos Neufeld, Pastor Niemöller, Sharon Olds, Charles Olson, Jiří Orten, Jacqueline Osherow, Alicia Ostriker, Dan Pagis, Marge Piercy, Sonia Pilcer, Vasko Popa, Peter Porter, Evelyn Posamentier, Anne Ranasinghe, Naomi Replansky, Charles Reznikoff, Adrienne Rich, Menachem Rosensaft, Jerome Rothenberg, Carol Rumens, Anne Sexton, Hilda Schiff, Gregg Shapiro, Harvey Shapiro, Simkhe-Bunem Shayevitsh, Robert Sheppard, Danny Siegel, Jon Silkin, Charles Simic, Louis Simpson, Myra Sklarew, Antoni Slonimski, Boris Slutsky, Harry Smart, W. D. Snodgrass, Kirtland Snyder, Jason Sommer, Stephen Spender, Isiah Spiegel, Gerald Stern, Marguerite M. Strair, Abraham Sutzkever, Anna Swirszczynska, George Szirtes, Władyslaw Szlengel, Hermen Taube, Hilary Tham, R. S. Thomas, David Vogel, Burton D. Wasserman, Florence Weinberger, C. K. Williams, Karl Wolfskehl, Itamar Yaoz-Kest, Yevgeny Yevtushenko, Natan Zach, Aaron Zeitlin and Adam Zych.

10. Harriet L. Parmet (rev. of *Tony Harrison and the Holocaust*, *Holocaust and Genocide Studies*), 17: 3 (winter 2003), pp. 515–17. Michael Murphy asks the same question as Parmet in his review in *Critical Survey*, 14:3 (2002), pp. 89–91, p. 91. See also Steve Padley, 'Poetry and Atrocity' in *English*, 52: 204 (autumn 2003), pp. 278–82.

11. Ian Thomson, *Primo Levi* (London: Vintage, 2003 [2002]), p. 300. Goes

was an anti-Nazi pastor: *Das Brandopfer* is 'the literal German translation of Shoah, or Holocaust'.

12. Thomson, p. 301.
13. Thomson, p. 277; Primo Levi, *If This is a Man/The Truce* (London: Abacus, 1987 [1958]), p. 16. George Perec's *W, or the Memory of Childhood* is interesting in this context, since it is based on the author's experiences in children's homes during the war, but highlights the fraught processes of remembering by confusing dates, and announcing wrong biographical and historical facts.
14. Berel Lang, 'Holocaust Genres and the Turn to History', in *The Holocaust and the Text: Speaking the Unspeakable*, ed. Andrew Leak and George Paizis (London: Macmillan, 2000), pp. 17–31, pp. 19, 21.
15. Lang, pp. 21, 28.
16. Daniel R. Schwarz, *Imagining the Holocaust* (London: Palgrave, 1999), p. 4.
17. Thomson, p. 221.
18. Of course, even with knowledge of the author's experience it is sometimes difficult to adduce authentic experience from textual details.
19. François Mauriac, 'Foreword', in Elie Wiesel, *Night*, trans. Stella Rodway (London: Penguin, 1981 [1958]), pp. 7–11, p. 7.
20. W. G. Sebald, *Austerlitz*, trans. Anthea Bell (London: Penguin, 2002 [2001]).
21. The concept 'deep memory' is taken from James E. Young's *The Texture of Memory*.
22. Susan Rubin Suleiman, 'Problems of Memory and Factuality in Recent Holocaust Memoirs: Wilkomirski/Wiesel', *Poetics Today*, 21: 3 (fall 2000), pp. 543–59, p. 546.
23. The term 'rescued memory' comes from Efraim Sicher's discussion of *Maus* and Aryeh Lev Stollman's novel *The Far Euphrates* in 'The Future of the Past: Countermemory and Postmemory in Contemporary American Post-Holocaust Narratives' (*History and Memory: Studies in Representations of the Past*, 2 (2000), pp. 56–91, p. 74). Sicher writes that 'fictional accounts cannot always be easily distinguished from documentary or autobiographical memoirs' (p. 81).
24. Elena Lappin is quoted in 'Fragments of a Fraud', *The Guardian*, 15 October 1999 (www.guardian.ac.uk/Archives); Sue Vice, *Holocaust Fiction* (London: Routledge, 2000). In her recent work on Holocaust diaries by children and teenagers, Vice has illustrated that the deployment of the present tense creates a sense of authenticity, simultaneity, and the opportunity to write about writing at the moment of inscription, as in Ana Novac's *The Beautiful Days of my Youth* (New York: Henry Holt & Co., 1997) when she states that 'Now I'm writing. I'm writing that I'm writing' (p. 20). The temporality of 'writing that I'm writing' in a diary whilst the events of the war are unfolding distinguishes the genre from memoirs written since 1945. This aura of simultaneity means that post-Holocaust authors are less likely to pen pastiches of Holocaust diaries (with, for example, subheadings comprising particular dates), whereas fictionalised memoirs, such as *Austerlitz*, are much more common. (Vice discussed Novac's diary, amongst others, during a paper entitled 'Children's eye views of the Holocaust' at the One-Day

Workshop on 'Representing the Holocaust' at The University of Manchester (24 October 2003)).

25. Vice, p. 164. In 'Binjamin Wilkomirski's *Fragments* and Holocaust Envy: "Why Wasn't I There Too"?', Vice reiterates that 'It is possible to read Wilkomirski's *Fragments* as a novel' (*Representing the Holocaust: In Honour of Bryan Burns* (London and Portland: Vallentine Mitchell, 2003), pp. 249–68, p. 250). In contrast, Suleiman has argued that *Fragments* is 'neither an authentic memoir nor a novel but a false or deluded memoir' (p. 543). Suleiman bases this observation on the 'criterion of the truth claim': since Wilkomirski stubbornly insisted in 1999 that his book was a memoir, it must be evaluated as 'not a novel but a false – or better, a deluded – memoir' (p. 552). She notes that discredited memoirs are usually forgotten, rather than being lauded as fiction (pp. 552–3). However, the latter categorises writing according to reader response and the reactions of publishing houses; the 'criterion of the truth claim' bases generic distinctions on the author's intentions. Suleiman's complex and cogent argument has recourse to the 'conventional', the 'set of implicit and explicit understandings that frame the publication and reception of any work' (p. 546). Intentionality is not the same as biography, however: I agree with Vice that *Fragments* can be classed as a novel due, in the light of Bruno Doesseker's biographical details, to its deployment of Holocaust synecdoches. Vice's detailed analysis of its complex narrative in *Representing the Holocaust* suggests that this might not form an example of the forgotten, discredited memoir.

26. Geoffrey Hill, *King Log* (London: André Deutsch Ltd, 1981), p. 37.

27. Kushner, p. 26.

28. *Holocaust Poetry*, ed. Hilda Schiff (London: Harper Collins, 1995), p. 214.

29. *Jewish Poetry in Britain Since 1945: An Anthology*, ed. Peter Lawson (Nottingham: Five Leaves Publishers, 2001), p. 5.

30. Schiff, pp. 216–17.

31. Hirsch, p. 416.

32. See John Felstiner, *Paul Celan: Poet, Survivor, Jew* (New Haven: Yale University Press, 1995) for a discussion of the correspondence. In '"Some Gold Across the Water": Paul Celan and Nelly Sachs' (*Holocaust and Genocide Studies*, 14: 2 (fall 2000), pp. 197–214), Joan Peterson makes a case for a discussion of the two writers as Holocaust poets.

33. See Charles Maier's comment that 'Nazi crimes' may be 'comparable to other . . . atrocities' (quoted in Dominick LaCapra, 'Representing the Holocaust: Reflections on the Historians' Debate', in *Probing the Limits of Representation*, ed. Saul Friedlander (Cambridge, MA and London: Harvard University Press, 1991), pp. 108–27, p. 109. 'Stalinist terror' – rather than the Germans' suffering at the hands of the retreating Soviet army – formed the main point of comparison with 'Nazi crimes' during the *Historikerstreit*.

34. Quoted in Geoffrey Hartman, *Scars of the Spirit: the Struggle against Inauthenticity* (New York and Basingstoke: Palgrave, 2002), p. 22.

35. Lawrence L. Langer, 'Recent Studies on Memory and Representation', *Holocaust and Genocide Studies*, 16: 1 (spring 2002), pp. 77–93, p. 80.

36. Schwarz, p. 23.

37. Quoted in Langer, p. 85.

38. James E. Young, *At Memory's Edge: After-Images of the Holocaust in Contemporary Art and Architecture* (New Haven and London: Yale University Press, 2000), p. 1.
39. Theodor Adorno, 'Cultural Criticism and Society', in *Prisms*, trans. S. and S. Weber (London: Neville Spearman, 1967), pp. 17–35, p. 34.
40. Leonard Forster, *German Poetry 1944–48* (Cambridge: Bowes and Bowes, 1949), p. 9.
41. Theodor Adorno, *Negative Dialectics*, trans. E. B. Ashton (New York: Seabury Press, 1973 [1967]), p. 367.
42. Lawrence L. Langer, p. 77. Awkward poetics may still, according to Adorno in *Negative Dialectics*, be 'garbage'.
43. D. G. Myers, 'Responsible for Every Single Pain: Holocaust Literature and the Ethics of Interpretation', *Comparative Literature*, 51: 4 (fall 1999), pp. 266–88, p. 282.
44. Schiff, p. 96. These awkward poetics could, of course, be the product of false posturing rather than honest self-evaluation, which is why I use the term 'author's conception'. The reader's possible rejection of the author's self-evaluation is discussed later in relation to Sue Vice's *Holocaust Fiction*.
45. Gubar, p. 14.
46. Harrison refers to the 'seismic events of the twentieth century which we're still quaking from' in an episode of *The South Bank Show* (1999).
47. Gubar, p. 210.
48. Gubar, pp. 22, 64.
49. Gubar, p. 24.
50. Hughes mentions the 'plain and ugly' language of the Crow poems in a letter to Gerald Hughes (27 October 1969) held at Emory University (Box 1).
51. Ian Hamilton, 'Between Me and We' (rev. of *The Triumph of Love*), *Sunday Telegraph*, 21 February 1999, p. 12.
52. In 'The Triumph of Geoffrey Hill' (*Parnassus*, 24: 2 [May 2000], pp. 201–20), William Logan argues that Hill's reaction to the difficulties of historical representation, 'to worry and wring his hands, isn't quite good enough . . . Hill's "introspection" [is] more conspicuous than [the] memory of the dead (more conspicuous, or more self-satisfied – there's something dishonestly gratifying in his self-inflicted stigmata, his designer hair-shirt)' (p. 209).
53. Francis Spufford, 'Geoffrey Hill Goes into Injury Time' (rev. of *The Triumph of Love*), *Evening Standard*, 1 February 1999, p. 50.
54. Quoted in David Sexton, 'The Strongest Voice' (rev. of *The Orchards of Syon*), *Evening Standard*, 9 September 2002, p. 45.
55. Edna Longley, 'All You Need is Love' (rev. of *The Triumph of Love*), *Metre*, 6 (summer 1999), pp. 70–4, pp. 73–4.
56. James Wood, 'Too Many Alibis' (rev. of *Canaan* and *The Triumph of Love*), *London Review of Books*, 1 July 1999, pp. 24–6, p. 24.
57. Jon Harris, 'An Elegy for Myself: British Poetry and the Holocaust', *English*, 41:171 (1992), pp. 213–33, p. 221.
58. Andrew Sinclair, *War Like a Wasp: The Lost Decade of the 'Forties* (London: Hamish Hamilton, 1989), p. 184.
59. *The War Decade: An Anthology of the 1940s*, ed. Andrew Sinclair (London: Hamish Hamilton, 1989), pp. 269–70, p. 269.

60. Mervyn Peake, *A Reverie of Bone and Other Poems* (London: Bertram Rota, 1967), p. 7

61. *Drawings by Mervyn Peake* (London: The Grey Walls Press, 1949), pp. 29–33.

62. Quoted in Mark Rawlinson, 'This Other War: British Culture and the Holocaust', *Cambridge Quarterly*, 25: 1 (1996), pp. 1–25, p. 6.

63. Quoted in Rawlinson, p. 12.

64. Sinclair, pp. 185, 191.

65. Primo Levi, 'The Survivor', trans. Ruth Feldman and Brian Swann, in Schiff, p. 118 (see Note 28).

66. Kushner, p. 225 (see Note 7).

67. Primo Levi, *The Drowned and the Saved*, trans. R. Rosenthal (London: Abacus, 1986), p. 52.

68. I am referring here to Eric Williams's popular POW narrative *The Wooden Horse*, which was turned into a film in 1950.

69. Gubar refers to 'stylistic eccentricities' that 'display the place of the *unpoetic* and the *non*cathartic in Holocaust poems – their authors' distance from eyewitnessing' (p. 24). These 'eccentricities' are akin to 'unpoetic' awkward aesthetics. Gubar notes that her use of the word 'awkward' is indebted to Julia Kristeva: I discuss Kristeva's 'aesthetics of awkwardness' in relation to grieving, and Marguerite Duras's work, in *Tony Harrison and the Holocaust* (Liverpool: Liverpool University Press, 2001), p. 158.

70. Michael Rothberg, *Traumatic Realism: The Demands of Holocaust Representation* (Minneapolis and London: University of Minnesota Press, 2000), p. 12.

71. Other studies of post-Holocaust poetry include: Gloria Young, 'The Poetry of the Holocaust', in *Holocaust Literature: A Handbook of Critical, Historical, and Literary Writings*, ed. Saul S. Friedman (Westport and London: Greenwood Press, 1993), pp. 547–74; Sidra DeKoven Ezrahi, '"The Grave in the Air": Unbound Metaphors in Post-Holocaust Poetry', in *Probing the Limits of Representation: Nazism and the "Final Solution"*, pp. 259–76; R. K. Meiner, 'Mourning for Ourselves and for Poetry: The Lyric after Auschwitz', *The Centennial Review*, 35: 3 (fall 1991), pp. 545–90; Efraim Sicher, *Beyond Marginality: Anglo-Jewish Literature after the Holocaust* (Albany: State University of New York Press, 1985), pp. 139–67; Dori Laub, 'Holocaust Themes: Their Expression in Poetry and in the Psychological Conflicts of Patients in Psychotherapy', in *The Nazi Concentration Camps: Structure and Aims; the Image of the Prisoners; the Jews in the Camps* (Jerusalem: Yad Vashem, 1984), pp. 573–87; Brian Murdoch, 'Transformations of the Holocaust: Auschwitz in Modern Lyric Poetry', *Comparative Literature Studies*, 11: 2 (June 1974), pp. 123–50, 142. Peter Lawson's *Singers of the Diaspora: Anglo-Jewish Poetry from Isaac Rosenberg to Elaine Feinstein* is due to be published by Vallentine Mitchell in 2005.

72. Rothberg, p. 13; Marianne Hirsch, 'Mourning and Postmemory', in Levi and Rothberg, pp. 416–22, p. 416 (see Note 4).

73. Schiff, p. 133. The label 'postmemory' covers varied responses to this 'deep personal connection': Gershon, for example, was unable to consult her father's memory of the Holocaust, unlike Art Spiegelman.

74. Quoted in Levi and Rothberg, p. 416.
75. Schiff, p. 167.
76. Plath, *Collected Poems*, p. 223.
77. James E. Young, 'The Countermonument: Memory Against Itself in Germany', in Levi and Rothberg, pp. 431–8, p. 431.
78. Gillian Rose, *Mourning Becomes the Law: Philosophy and Representation* (Cambridge: Cambridge University Press, 1996), p. 41.
79. Andrew Leak and George Paizis, 'Introduction', in *The Holocaust and the Text: Speaking the Unspeakable* (London: Macmillan, 2000), pp. 1–16, p. 12.
80. Apel, p. 7 (see Note 2).
81. Apel argues that contemporary artists have 'largely rejected the iconic forms of barbed wire, corpses, guard towers, train tracks, and smokestacks as clichéd images whose power has been vitiated through overuse' (p. 20).
82. Sue Vice, 'The Demidenko Affair and Contemporary Holocaust Fiction', in *The Holocaust and the Text: Speaking the Unspeakable*, pp. 125–41, p. 132.
83. Roland Barthes, 'The Death of the Author', in *Literature in the Modern World*, ed. Dennis Walder (Oxford: Oxford University Press, 1990), pp. 228–31, p. 231.

# Chapter 1

# Camp Poetics and Holocaust Icons in the Poetry of Sylvia Plath

'Satire's perennial complaint is that people are so in thrall to the trivial, the sensual, the spectacular, that they have lost all identity as moral beings.'

'out of the pain of history it creates clowns.'[1]

Many of the remarkable poems that Sylvia Plath wrote in October 1962 have never been appraised with an adjective they deserve: camp.[2] Parading their artifice, 'The Detective', 'The Courage of Shutting-Up', 'A Secret', 'The Applicant', 'Lesbos' and 'The Tour' in particular display, as a whole, the campy stylistics of exaggeration, theatricality, insistent repetition and iteration, outrageous surrealism, overstatement, mock-amazement, melodramatic keening, vamping, bitchiness, sarcasm, interjections, incongruity, black comedy and queer poetics. Famously, this productive month for Plath also heralded two monologues that deploy Holocaust imagery: 'Lady Lazarus' and 'Daddy'.[3] These two poems have been criticised for appropriating historical suffering for the sake of titillation and personal aggrandisement.[4] Criticism of the poems has been bound up with Plath's status as a post-Holocaust poet: in 1965, George Steiner was one of the first critics to debate Plath's use of Holocaust imagery, wondering whether writers who were not camp inmates 'commit a subtle larceny when they invoke the echoes and trappings of Auschwitz and appropriate an enormity of ready emotion to their own private design?'[5] For such critics, the awkwardness of 'Lady Lazarus' arises from a tension between the appropriation of Holocaust icons and Plath's 'private' mental anguish. Many of these critics also react to the form of the poetry, sensing an ethical gulf between the camp poetics of the monologue, and the suffering of those murdered in the *Lager*. In this chapter, I argue that Plath's 'private design' is not simply to highlight, and exaggerate, her own suffering within a melodramatic poem that takes sideswipes at history to the exasperation of many critics.

Instead, I illustrate that the camp poetics of 'Lady Lazarus' are inextricably bound up with its critique of Holocaust spectacle: Plath's satire is moving in the direction of the more self-reflexive, awkward poetics to be found in the work of Geoffrey Hill and Tony Harrison. 'Lady Lazarus' satirises people who are 'in thrall to the trivial, the sensual, the spectacular', and highlights the difficulty for contemporaneous audiences in separating recent history from sensational reportage: media obsessions with the more macabre details of the Holocaust are evoked in 'Lady Lazarus', such as the Buchenwald lampshade made out of human skin, and soap reputedly manufactured out of human fat. However, the critic must concede that in Plath's poems it is sometimes unclear where the unreflective reproduction of such Holocaust icons ends, and the satire begins. The quotations above illustrate the central paradox of her satirical monologue: it criticises an unreflective reception of spectacle, at the same time as the camp poetics suggest that Plath might be turning tragic, historical figures into clowns.

In 1982, the publication of Saul Friedlander's *Reflections of Nazism: An Essay on Kitsch and Death* illustrated the critical concern within Holocaust studies about the interplay between historical representation and spectacle. For Friedlander, a 'new discourse' was created at the moment when Hitler became part of the entertainment industry; an ensuing, and insidious, fascination with Nazi chic is regarded as a product of the late 1960s.[6] The exposition of Holocaust icons as spectacle in 'Lady Lazarus' forms an uncanny portent for Friedlander's argument, but unlike his chosen texts that replicate the new discourse, camp poetics allow for a more self-conscious critique of representation in 'Lady Lazarus'. In *At Memory's Edge*, James E. Young discusses Friedlander's theory in relation to David Levinthal's Nazi figurines.[7] Both Plath and Levinthal leave the question unanswered as to whether investigations of the new discourse are ultimately attempts to understand spectacle, or whether they betray 'mute yearnings' towards Nazi iconography. Young argues the former with respect to the artist, at the same time as pointing out that Levinthal cannot transcend the discourse through mere critique. The same critical generosity should be extended to Plath: like Levinthal, Plath confronts readers with their own role in the representation of suffering. Over ten years before the figurines in Levinthal's *Hitler Moves East*, Plath was calling into question 'the seeming innocence of our preoccupations' with icons of atrocity. When Levinthal sets out '"to remember" the Holocaust, all he can actually remember are the numberless images passed down to him in books, films, and photographs': Young's appraisal of the artist can be applied to Plath's post-Holocaust monologues, which register her vicarious reception of the Holocaust through sensationalist media images (p. 44).

Young and Tim Kendall both argue that Plath is not a Holocaust poet in the sense that she writes as a survivor of the camps, or in the way that she openly cites specific historical incidents.[8] However, she does cite the detail of the sensationalist lampshade in 'Lady Lazarus', which evokes Ilse Koch's alleged predilection for the tattooed skin of inmates in Buchenwald. Young claims that Plath's 'Holocaust tropes do reveal indirectly her own grasp of events' (p. 118). '[H]er own grasp' stresses that Plath's allusions to the Holocaust are mediated. They are also specific, often, to a particular camp: in his Foreword to the American edition of *Ariel* in 1966, Robert Lowell mistakes Belsen for Buchenwald when asserting the supposed origin of the lampshade; William Heyen's 'Riddle' contains the (historically inaccurate) line 'from Auschwitz a skin lampshade'.[9] Along with this particular, macabre article of Nazi paraphernalia, Koch herself has become a symptom of Nazi chic: various newspaper articles, books, plays and documentary films display an obsessive fascination with her symptomatic of the new discourse. In 1974, Koch was even graced with a 'video nasty': the film *Ilse – She-Wolf of the SS* paraded a relentless gamut of executions, castrations, torture and softcore sex. A. Alvarez has commented that Koch's actions were generally known in Britain in 1962.[10] Yet the danger of the intertwining of historical narratives about Koch and the new discourse indicates that many of these supposed 'actions' may have been historically inaccurate; paradoxically, as Young argues in *At Memory's Edge*, 'whether we like it or not, once icons of the Holocaust enter the popular imagination, they also turn mythic, hard and impenetrable' (p. 50). The Holocaust icons are not self-evident signs of atrocity in 'Lady Lazarus', but citations of citations: Plath utilises her knowledge of Koch gained via the media and conversations with friends such as Gerry Becker; these sources were themselves the results of fascination with Koch's delinquency.[11] Plath's choice of icons proves shrewd, since Koch, the lampshade and the soap form prime examples of how Holocaust icons are partly the products of media spectacle.

In the article 'Camp Comedy', Slavoj Žižek contends that, by the late 1990s, the era of Holocaust tragedy was over, replaced by comedies such as Roberto Benigni's *Life is Beautiful*, which at least openly admit their failure of representation in relation to atrocity.[12] Mark Rawlinson also signals the possibility of black humour surpassing the pathos of tragedy when – in relation to the episode in Martin Amis's *Time's Arrow* in which piles of corpses are brought back to life – he asks, '[C]an comedy . . . be bleaker than a detached solemnity?'[13] The black comedy of 'Lady

Lazarus' results in an opposite movement in Plath's work, as opposed to Žižek and Rawlinson's discussions of Holocaust representation in general. Ted Hughes illustrates in *Winter Pollen* that Plath's final poems display a marked change in tone from the pieces written in October 1962.[14] This movement could be described as a switch from camp poetics to abstract lyricism. 'Mary's Song', a post-Holocaust poem written in November 1962, fulfils this description: reserve dominates the narrator's engagement with historical suffering. There is a correlation between Plath's rejection in 'Mary's Song' of the camp poetics in 'Lady Lazarus', and Paul Celan's dismissal of his early monologue 'Todesfuge' as too direct, and his subsequent forging of a more indirect, lyrical response to the Holocaust. The stylistic similarities between 'Lady Lazarus', 'Mary's Song' and Celan's poetry will be analysed towards the end of this chapter.[15] Before this, I illustrate the camp aspects of 'Lady Lazarus' using David Bergman's four defining categories, outlining their relationship to awkward poetics, and Holocaust icons.

## Camp poetics

Many of the October 1962 poems are camp, but they are not products of the Camp movement: this highlights the difference between critical attempts to define a gay (usually male) sensibility, and a literary style. In Fabio Cleto's *Camp: Queer Aesthetics and the Performing Subject*, Bergman discusses camp as both an aesthetic choice in general, and eroticism associated specifically with gay culture:

> First, everyone agrees that camp is a style (whether of objects or of the way objects are perceived is debated) that favors 'exaggeration', 'artifice', and 'extremity'. Second, camp exists in tension with popular culture, commercial culture, or consumerist culture. Third, the person who can recognize camp, who sees things as campy, or who can camp is a person outside the cultural mainstream. Fourth, camp is affiliated with homosexual culture, or at least with a self-conscious eroticism that throws into question the naturalisation of desire.[16]

Exaggeration, 'extreme' metaphor and an emphasis on artifice have been instrumental to camp since the term's coinage in the nineteenth century, when it denoted 'actions and gestures of exaggerated emphasis' (p. 9). These are key components of 'Lady Lazarus'. It opens with a campy tone of exasperated weariness seemingly at odds with the poem's overall list of Holocaust icons: 'I have done it again' immediately presents the narrator as childish, someone who has just revelled in committing yet another naughty misdeed.[17] After the daring – or, as Steiner muses, perhaps inappropriate – comparison of the skin tone with the lampshade, Lady Lazarus employs either outrageous surrealism in her equating of the foot with a paperweight, or provides a description of a heavily bandaged, or club, foot:

> A sort of walking miracle, my skin
> Bright as a Nazi lampshade,
> My right foot
>
> A paperweight (p. 244)

The movement from simile ('as a Nazi lampshade') to metaphor ('A paperweight') across the stanzas indicates that the narrator's propensity for potentially awkward, incongruous tropes is gaining in confidence. Esther Newton argues that 'Camp usually depends on the perception or creation of *incongruous juxtapositions*': this connects with the lampshade, paperweight and other 'extreme' surrealist images encountered in the poems Plath wrote in October 1962.[18] For example, in 'Fever 103°', a camellia has multiple orgasms, a head forms a Japanese lantern, and an orchid proves akin to a leopard (pp. 231–2). In 'The Detective', the Dali-like mouth of the murder victim, 'like brown fruit', is left outside 'To wrinkle and dry' (p. 209). The narrator in 'Stings' indicates that which she is not, at the same time as evoking a surreal image with its mere suggestion ('I am no source of honey') (p. 213). In 'A Secret', the bizarre mixed metaphors juxtapose opposites to the point of either incredulity or turgidity: a secret is a brandy snap, which is like an extra finger, and also like a dove which roosts and accuses ('"You, you"'). (Or maybe the present participles suggest that only the finger is akin to a bird.) The secret – or the finger, or the bird (or all, or some of them) – is located behind eyes that cannot see anything but monkeys (p. 219). By stretching metaphor until it breaks down, Plath highlights both the artifice of the October poems, and the potentially camp nature of poetry itself, which has the capacity to transform a mundane incident – such as the moving of the virgin bees in 'The Bee Meeting' – into a metaphysical dilemma.

After the seemingly awkward juxtaposition of camp poetics and the Nazi lampshade in the second stanza of 'Lady Lazarus', campy rhetoric is established with a parody of apostrophe and invocation in the fourth stanza. The narrator offers a macabre invitation to the, as yet unnamed, foe ('O my enemy') to peel off her napkin, accompanied by the teasing interrogative 'Do I terrify?' According to *A Concordance to the Collected Poems of Sylvia Plath*, 'O' – a word that commonly denotes the use of apostrophe – occurs sixty-nine times in her *oeuvre*, eight more times than the popular 'moon', and eighteen more than 'death'.[19] Frequently employed by poets such as Virgil, Dante and Wordsworth, apostrophe denotes a figure of speech which consists in addressing a (usually absent) person or thing: it 'gives life and immediacy to language, but is also subject to abuse and open to parody'.[20] By 1962, apostrophe had become such a commonplace of rhetorical poetics that contemporaneous poets could employ it to write hackneyed poetry, or 'abuse' it with the more sophisticated forms of parody and pastiche. Plath's work, with its sixty-nine instances of 'O', falls into the latter category. Her use of apostrophe links with the self-conscious poetics elsewhere in 'Lady Lazarus': Plath does not appear to be parodying a poet or movement in particular; she simply parodies a poetic device in order to emphasise its artificial, and potentially campy, nature. Philip Larkin similarly subverts apostrophe in 'Sad Steps' ('O wolves of memory! Immensements!'), but whereas he also laments the passing of his youthful, romantic self, Plath's usage demonstrates both a fondness for, and impatience with, the high rhetoric of appeals to nymphs, dryads, goddesses and other such classical spectres.[21]

In 'Lady Lazarus', the campy interjection 'O my enemy' instigates a post-Holocaust rewriting of apostrophe, replacing the addressees of classical invocations with a Nazi: the unnamed adversary ('Herr Enemy') is revealed to be 'Herr Doktor' in stanza twenty-two.[22] Teasingly, Plath's narrator does not reveal in the first four stanzas what Herr Doktor might be terrified by: the reader may assume, from the title, that a resurrection in the style of Lazarus is being witnessed, or recounted. However, the two instances of 'it' in stanza one are initially unspecified:

I have done it again.
One year in every ten
I manage it – (p. 244)

The second 'it' may refer to the opening clause of the next stanza ('A sort of walking miracle'), but it may equally refer to 'my skin' as a miraculous biped. Plath's use of the ambiguous pronoun at the beginning of the poem complements the concurrent parody of a striptease: the nose, eye pits and teeth are unveiled in stanza five at the same time as the narrator teases the reader to identify the exact denotation of 'it'. Lady Lazarus's vocation as an entertainer becomes clearer in the teasing appeal to 'my enemy'. 'Called' on stage as an actress, Lady Lazarus appears trapped by her surroundings, dependent on the repellent, Nazi 'enemy'. This scenario is emphasised by the pun on 'call': as well as referring to a religious 'calling', 'call' puns on a 'caul', a tight-fitting head-dress, which is represented by the napkin clinging to the narrator's face. Plath borrows this detail from the depiction of Lazarus in The Book of St John (v. 44):

'And he that was dead came forth, bound hand and foot with grave-clothes: and his face was bound about with a napkin. Jesus saith unto them, Loose him, and let him go.' Plath deliberately switches the gender of the biblical character; Lady Lazarus's offer of the napkin calls attention to the unveiling process of the poem's narrative, its portrayal of a performing vamp, and its status as a dramatic monologue. Critical responses to Plath since the beginning of the 1990s have shifted from arguing that the poems written in October 1962 aggrandise Plath's self (whatever that might be) and 'private design'. Many of the poems are now accepted to be dramatic monologues primarily concerned with the proclivities of different speakers; once this is grasped, the self-conscious artifice of Plath's post-Holocaust poems becomes more evident. Plath illustrated the multi-vocal, and self-reflexive, nature of these texts when she read 'Daddy' in November 1962 to a friend, Clarissa Roche, in a 'spooky, comical voice' and fell about laughing. This campy rendition is more appropriate to 'Lady Lazarus' than the lyrical monotone of the British Council reading, since the poem constantly flaunts an audacious sarcasm and knowing chutzpah.[23]

Gestures of exaggeration in the form of apostrophe, incongruous metaphor, and the emphasis on performing allow the critic to label this monologue 'camp' according to Bergman's first definition of the concept. The second definition appertains to 'Lady Lazarus' as much as the first: tension between the narrator and 'popular culture, commercial culture, or consumerist culture' is located in the performance of the striptease, and the emphasis on artifice. Repetition and iteration in the October poems stresses, as Kendall notes, that poetic language itself is 'rhetorical and incantatory, conscious of its status as performance' (p. 149); as the narrator regains her eyes to complement the 'full set of teeth', a parallel is established between the 'theatrical/ Comeback' in the text and the theatre of the monologue itself (*Collected Poems*, pp. 245–6). Dramatic monologues conventionally require a dual audience: an implied addressee, and the reader. Many of the October poems are directly addressed to an interlocutor, such as 'Daddy', and 'The Applicant'; in 'Fever 103°', the 'you' denotes the reader as well as (possibly) adulterous lover/s, the 'Not you, nor him', depicted earlier as rather greasy (p. 231). Roberts notes that 'approximately half the poems in the "two" *Ariels* have explicit addressees' (p. 22). The venom directed at the 'peanut-crunching crowd' in 'Lady Lazarus' encompasses the poetry reader as much as the silent voyeurs. She dismisses the vulgar audience that 'Shoves in to see' her 'big strip tease' (p. 245), at the same time as the reader of the supposedly 'high' art of poetry is berated for enjoying her pain as aesthetic fodder: her rejection of the absorbed voyeurs forms an instance of

Plath's questioning of the 'seeming innocence of our preoccupations' with images of suffering. The diatribe against the 'peanut-crunching' crowd also subverts the high/low split within simplistic definitions of camp. In Christopher Isherwood's *The World in the Evening*, the character Charles Kennedy makes a distinction between high camp (ballet, Baroque art, and, presumably, opera), and the low camp of 'a swishy little boy with peroxided hair, dressed in a picture hat and a feather boa, pretending to be Marlene Dietrich'.[24] In Plath's work, camp poetics upset this opposition by juxtaposing lowbrow burlesque with the highbrow genre of poetry itself.

Plath's fusion of sensational incident and the monologue form did not find favour with many poetry editors. Her comparative lack of publications (compared to Hughes), and her increasing involvement with the stylistics of camp in October 1962, links with Bergman's third concern, that the person who can 'recognize camp' is outside the cultural mainstream; this marginality is compounded by Plath's attempts to publish as a woman poet in a field dominated, in the early 1960s, by male poets and editors. Isolated and humiliated on stage, Lady Lazarus reflects the figure of the rejected poet, desperate for acclaim. Divergence between the two figures occurs when the mythical persona announces a 'Comeback': 'Lady Lazarus' may represent a stage name for a previously successful actress, a Marilyn Monroe-figure determined to return to form, even in a flea-pit or music hall whilst performing the burlesque, primarily for the peanut-eating crowd who may have previously adored her. Her reverse strip-tease, as she regains her features, parodies the process of a make-over, or plastic surgery: the monologue can be interpreted as a specific instance of female camp, a text which insists that the production of femininity proves inseparable from an aesthetics of violence. 'I am the same, identical woman' can be read as ironic in this context, since femininity itself is uncovered as a process of naturalisation. This links with the simpering bewilderment of the narrator in 'The Bee Meeting' ('does nobody love me?'): infantilism here is deployed as a parody of conventional femininity (p. 211). Lady Lazarus's comeback extracts an 'Amused shout' from the munching crowd: the pun on the phrase 'That knocks me out' indicates that this is at the expense of a physical violation beyond their ken. Live on stage, she is paradoxically 'dead': her performance is likened to that of a debased saint, charging for a touch of 'filament' (a piece of hair); these icons are snapped up like souvenirs after the death of a famous actress, enjoying a 'charge' out of the reification of the corpse. However, 'dying' allows Lady Lazarus a modicum of agency: the routine is pure theatre; the artifice of this act, and the poem as a whole, is underlined by the repetition, 'masculine' rhymes and aggressive oratory.

This self-reflexive focus on an outsider figure seems to set up an awkward tension between railing, camp poetics and the evocation of the Holocaust icons of the lampshade, soap, crematoria ash, wedding ring and gold filling in the poem as a whole. Does this potential awkwardness court insensitivity, as Seamus Heaney has argued, by underscoring artifice when death was clearly not an 'art' to those who perished during the Holocaust?[25] Plath does not appropriate the Holocaust imagery, as Heaney contends, for 'a vehemently self-justifying purpose' in 'Lady Lazarus'. However, unlike the awkward aesthetics in Geoffrey Hill or Tony Harrison's poetry, camp poetics cannot help – as Susan Sontag argues in 'Notes on Camp' – but convert the 'serious into the frivolous', even if, as Isherwood's character contends, '"High Camp always has an underlying seriousness"'.[26] Plath's monologue is self-conscious, but not self-reflexive enough to be clearly understood as an attempt at awkward poetics in my (more positive) sense of the term. In this way, it bears comparison with Harrison's *Prometheus*, since both writers address Holocaust imagery through the words of their narrators; in doing so, the ethical position of the author remains indeterminate. The lack of awkward poetics leaves Plath open to attacks of insensitivity, at the same time as it encourages – following Vice's argument about post-Holocaust fiction – multiple readings. When Harold Bloom accuses Plath of sneakily making use of a coercive rhetoric, it must be retorted that the Holocaust tropes do comply with the logic of the camp narrator's iconography of suffering, even if the author remains ultimately responsible for their deployment. Susan Gubar defends Plath by arguing that the poet adopts the rhetorical figure of prosopopoeia in an attempt to speak for the victims of the death camps, and asserting that this technique 'surfaces in some of the most powerful poems about the Shoah'.[27] Lady Lazarus is not simply an example of the *'rehabilitation of the dead'*, however, since the mythical persona only *compares* her suffering to that of a Holocaust victim in the first half of the poem. Nevertheless, as Gubar contends, Plath's work can be seen as an aesthetic reaction to postmemory, since Plath had a 'sense of personal connection to events not experienced firsthand [but] articulated by many of her contemporaries' (p. 194). In her 1962 essay 'Context', Plath herself argues that her work does not engage with atrocity directly; instead, the poems are 'deflections': 'They are not about the terrors of mass extinction, but about the bleakness of the moon over a yew tree.'[28]

'Lady Lazarus' successfully 'deflects' the Holocaust, as Gubar argues, into a post-Holocaust poem about the spectacle of suffering, but the second half risks losing the reader's sympathy for the narrator's plight due to the campy way in which she rails against her tormentors. Shouting, the beastly crowd (not specifically, but probably, composed of men) is described as 'brute', a camp phrase in itself, since it evokes the image of an actress in a 1950s Hollywood romance screaming at the handsome, cigar-toting male.[29] This adjective connects with the (definitely male) character in 'Daddy', who, clearly a 'brute', also owns a 'brute/ Brute heart' (p. 223). 'Lady Lazarus' is certainly anti-patriarchal in its insistence that men insist that women perform femininity.[30] With the twist of the 'extreme' metaphor, the consumers of the peanuts and strip-tease metamorphose into Nazi-figures, 'Herr Doktor' and 'Herr Enemy', then 'Herr God' and 'Herr Lucifer'. The gender-specific 'Herr' links with the ironic reversal of the conventional stage address in stanza ten: the phrase 'Gentlemen, ladies' indicates that the politics of politeness reveal that women (or, more exactly, 'ladies', like 'Lady' Lazarus) are deferred to only linguistically, which occludes the extent of their actual power.[31] Patriarchy here is regarded as an all-encompassing system, with Nazis at its apex, in which powerful men denigrate women (and weaker males), as in Virginia Woolf's critique of masculinity in *The Three Guineas*. By camping her distaste towards these (abstract) historical, and then mythical, male characters, Plath cements her memorable image of an actress now outside the 'cultural mainstream' of brutish Hollywood.

Textual expositions of female camp, as in the example above, do not necessarily slip into the auspices of Bergman's fourth definition of the elusive concept: an affiliation with homosexual culture. After all, 'real' and imagined heterosexual women from Mae West to Lady Lazarus recognise that the performance of femininity can be parodied by simply camping it up. Nevertheless, as Bergman suggests, this act inherently suggests that something queer is afoot, since it vies with the naturalisation of gender identity. In contrast, Mark Booth and Fabio Cleto, amongst others, argue that camp should be reclaimed as a specifically gay, not queer, quality: Sontag has often been accused of appropriating the concept for straight, 'kitschy middle-class pretensions'; it may thus become an exponent of 'degayified taste'.[32] Plath's poems may be symptoms of 'degayified taste', but this interpretation would be based on the assumption that the straight author mainly produces straightforwardly heterosexual narrators. Plath's camp poems were published only on the cusp of the Camp movement in the mid- to late 1960s; nevertheless, in the *OED*, the first citation of 'closet' (as in 'to come out of the closet') appertains to one of these October poems, 'The Applicant'.[33] This reading of the poem may seem perverse, since it appears to be a monologue with a male narrator addressing a male addressee, who needs convincing that he requires a new suit and a synthetic wife. 'Come, here, sweetie, out of the closet' seems to apply to the silent, 'female' robot, queering the moment in Keats's 'The Eve of St Agnes' when Porphyro sneaks out of the closet to entertain his lover with a pile of fruit (p. 221). Plath replaces Keats's active male character with a subservient female: 'coming out of the closet' might denote, as in Jane Austen's novels, the moment when the heroines express their availability for marriage by attending their first ball; in her journals, Plath utilises this version of the phrase when she dreams of having a wealthy 'coming-out party . . . with fur coats, social contacts, and a blasé pout' (p. 34). Or, according to the *OED* reading, 'sweetie' might refer to the primary addressee, the male consumer, who might be 'coming out of the closet' in the sense of purchasing a male or female 'doll': in a queer version of the classical myth of Baucis and Philemon, the robot will 'dissolve of sorrow' when the man dies. Perhaps 'sweetie' retains its American denotation of a young woman: after all, at the beginning of the poem, the applicant is asked if (she?) wears 'Rubber breasts'. The *OED* citation indicates that the purchaser's gender identity – which initially appears to be self-evidently male – is actually less stable than has been remarked: the reader might assume 'he' is male from the line 'Will you marry it?', but equally 'you' could be a 'she' who is ready to buy a 'he' (or a 'she').

The possibility of a queer reading of 'The Applicant' has not been emphasised by Plath critics. Such gender confusion in the poem cannot help but align the camp poetics of the poem with queer aesthetics. Jacqueline Rose famously troubled the Plath estate with her queer reading of 'The Rabbit Catcher' in *The Haunting of Sylvia Plath* (see Note 4): less controversially in this monologue, it can be seen that the slipperiness of the pronouns complicates the gender identity of the unnamed applicant. The *OED*-based interpretation of 'The Applicant' opens out the possibility of a queer reading of 'Lady Lazarus'. I have assumed so far in this chapter that the narrator is female. 'She' appears to be a female impersonator of the biblical character, and 'she' calls 'herself' a woman twice ('And I a smiling woman'; 'I am the same, identical woman') (p. 245). Equally, the 'she' might be a he in drag, especially since, as previously noted, the title forms a stage name for the narrator. If the 'she' is a 'he', then this compounds my interpretation of the poem as a vehicle for stressing the ways in which femininity can be performed (by both males and females, she-hes, and so on). In this sense, the two references to 'woman' would either be ironic, or, perhaps, indicate that, through the performance of femininity, the male drag queen becomes a woman. In the next section, I argue that these camp aesthetics indicate that aspects of Nazism can be read as camp performances; the problem with this, following Sontag, is that the subversion of 'the serious' risks kitsching the Holocaust, and turning it, obscenely, into a frivolity.

### The spectacle of Holocaust icons

Plath's self-conscious deployment of camp poetics in 'Lady Lazarus' highlights the poem's critique of the Holocaust as spectacle. Whereas Harrison's *Prometheus* replicates the modernist icons of Auschwitz – with the film/poem's frames of barbed wire, barracks, guard towers and railway tracks – Plath's monologue demonstrates the way in which supposedly self-evident, historical images can actually be bound up with sensationalism. Awkward poetics situate the author in relation to their reception of the vicarious past: the narrator's camp extravaganza in 'Lady Lazarus' means that Plath cannot display this level of self-reflexivity, but her compliance with the character's scathing attack on voyeurism can be vouchsafed. Campy renditions of history could also be read less positively as mere comic flippancy. In 'The Holocaust as Entertainment', Alvin Rosenfeld attacks comic representations of the Holocaust, evaluating Leslie Epstein's *King of the Jews: A Novel of the Holocaust* as a '350-page slapstick comedy of the Holocaust . . . fun swiped from someone else's grave', which results in 'rhetorical indulgence in the pleasures of self-aggrandizement . . . out of the pain of history it creates clowns'.[34] When Lady Lazarus dismisses her three 'deaths' and resurrections as 'trash', the word – as in the American 'trash-can' or 'white trash' – calls attention to the possibility that the initial reference to the 'Nazi lampshade' may have taken place in a monologue where the narrator begins to admit, even if ironically, that her monologue might be nonsensical talk, or a flawed literary production. Alvarez worried about the possibly flippant appropriation of historical baggage when he accused Plath of hitching 'an easy lift by dragging in' the victims of Hiroshima and Nagasaki: she subsequently cut 'I may be skin and bone, I may be Japanese' from the poem, although the lines crop up again in the later BBC reading of 'Lady Lazarus'.[35] Critics might also argue that Plath deploys Koch's lampshade to 'drag in' the murdered inmates of Buchenwald for a 'vehemently self-justifying purpose'.

Rather than ransacking others' experience for the sake of a dubious 'private design', however, 'Lady Lazarus' forms an early example of a post-Holocaust poem that engages with secondary witnesses' reception of the Holocaust as, partly, a series of media images. Towards the end of the monologue, the narrator presents herself directly as a victim of Nazism: she metamorphoses into 'A cake of soap,/ A wedding ring,/ A gold filling' (p. 246). 'A cake of soap' is particularly significant in terms of the reception of the Holocaust as spectacle. As Young argues in *At Memory's Edge*, such icons of the Holocaust have entered the popular imagination, turning 'mythic, hard and impenetrable'. Rather than leading to a better understanding of history, they can obfuscate the facts, as Young argues in relation to traditional monuments. Icons may in fact – like these monuments – encourage forgetting rather than an appreciation of the vicarious past. 'A cake of soap' may appear to be a self-evident reference to the Holocaust, but a historicist reading of 'Lady Lazarus' actually reveals the way in which secondary witnesses may receive history in the form of misleading icons. Just as the character-signs in Plath's poetry (the 'Applicant', Lady Lazarus, the narrator of 'Daddy') are not as self-evident as they might at first appear, the soap is not a transparent signifier of atrocity.[36] One of the secondary witness's duties is precisely to investigate the reception of Holocaust icons such as the 'cake of soap', as Levinthal does when he interrogates the fact that his memory of the Holocaust comprises not authentic experience, but 'numberless images passed down to him in books, films, and photographs'. Awkward poetics in Hill's *The Triumph of Love* register this lack of authenticity within the text itself, but Plath is certainly moving towards this level of self-reflexivity with her insertion of Holocaust icons into a campy narrative that critiques the relationship between spectacle and suffering.

The soap and lampshade in 'Lady Lazarus' form examples of objects transformed into sensationalist images in news reports and journal articles about Koch, and media accounts of the Nuremberg trials. Young reports in *Writing and Rewriting the Holocaust* (see Note 8) that in the early 1960s, Holocaust 'Images selected by the media for their spectacular and often horrifying qualities became the most common figures of all' (p. 120).[37] The reception of such icons has led to historical inaccuracies: Brian Murdoch refers to the soap as part of Plath's 'references to the grisly pastimes of Ilse Koch', despite the fact that Koch has never been officially accused of ordering, producing or owning such soap.[38] Media images from the early 1960s are not the only examples of the concretion of icons: during the Nuremberg trials (1945–6), the Holocaust was already being depicted as spectacle within the confines of the legal system. Just after the exhibition of the shrunken head of Buchenwald and a display of flayed skin, the Soviet prosecutor presented a bar of soap allegedly made from human fat. On one level, exhibit USSR-393 had the effect, like the head and skin, of depicting Nazism as a temporary and atavistic aberration from Western civilisation. Lawrence Douglas has demonstrated that rumours about the soap circulated widely during the war, particularly amongst the Poles, so much so that 'segments of the Polish population actually boycotted the purchase of soap'.[39] Rumour turned into 'fact' during the trials: Douglas recounts that a British corporal and a laboratory assistant in Danzig claimed to have witnessed the production process (p. 53). The 'fact' of the (apocryphal) soap then 'hardened' into a Holocaust icon. Alain Resnais's film *Night and Fog* contains contemporaneous photographs of flayed and beheaded corpses with the subtitle, 'With the bodies, they tried to make bars of soap.' In *This Way for the Gas, Ladies and Gentlemen*, Tadeusz Borowski refers to an unspecified 'elsewhere' outside Auschwitz-Birkenau, where 'they make soap out of people, and lampshades out of human skin, and jewellery out of the bones'.[40] Post-Holocaust literature also replicates the 'fact' of the soap: in Kurt Vonnegut's *Slaughterhouse-Five*, British POWs present the new American servicemen with candles and soap; 'The British had no way of knowing it, but the candles and the soap were made from the fat of rendered Jews and Gypsies and fairies and communists, and other enemies of the State.'[41] Randall Jarrell's poem 'A Camp in the Prussian Forest' also refers to camp inmates who were 'rendered into soap'.[42]

In the early 1990s, the United States Holocaust Memorial Museum 'tested several bars of soap purportedly made from humans, but no human fat was detected'. Douglas argues that 'no positive evidence has ever been adduced proving that the Nazis used human fat to make soap' (he does not comment on the photographs filmed in *Night and Fog*).[43] Rather than forming a mimetic sign, and an uncomplicated synecdoche for the Holocaust, the soap has become a misleading icon for Nazi atrocities. To state this is not to fall into the camp of Holocaust deniers and argue that the soap, and other items of atrocity, categorically never existed; it is only to question the self-evident nature of the icon.[44] Douglas mentions that Nazis such as Himmler knew of rumours about the production of soap, and did nothing to discourage them, given that they added to the vision of Nazism as a fearsome spectacle (p. 53). Young argues in *At Memory's Edge* that Levinthal's art partly subverts the subsuming of politics into aesthetics: the artist finds 'in films like Leni Riefenstahl's *Triumph of the Will* . . . this sense of pageantry and spectacle whence the Nazis derived so much of their public power and appeal' (p. 50). In 1962, long before the investigations of the United States Holocaust Memorial Museum, Plath may well have believed that the soap was a 'true' referent of the Holocaust, but its insertion into a post-Holocaust monologue which self-consciously camps, and critiques, its material necessarily puts a spotlight on the deployment of such sensationalist icons. As I argued in the last section, when Lady Lazarus rails at both 'Herr Doktor' and 'the peanut-crunching crowd', she includes the reader in her venomous attack. '[E]nemy' in stanza four could refer to the spectators as much as the Nazi figure: the peanut eaters are akin to the Nuremberg 'crowd', scandalised by the exhibits, but also revelling in the spectacle. Plath's satire links with Levinthal's manipulation of erotic

Japanese dolls in *Mein Kampf*, which emphasises the viewer's role in the spectatorship of suffering. As with Plath's focus on the reader's collusion in voyeurism, Levinthal's photographs suggest that we 'may be no less complicit in the continuing degradation of the victim than the original Nazi photographer' (pp. 57–8).

The process of 'hardening' spectacle into iconic objects was perhaps inevitable at Nuremberg, given the nature of the exhibits. Douglas argues that the skin and head functioned 'at best, as pieces of "stark reality" meant to penetrate the "air of remoteness that . . . hung over the Nuremberg trial"; at worst, as grotesque artifacts offered more to satisfy voyeuristic impulses than to clarify questions of legal guilt' (p. 41). Lady Lazarus refers to herself, and her reduction into ashes and soap, as, inevitably, the Nazis' 'opus': similarly, the trials could not help but replicate the Nazis' manipulation of spectacle to reinforce ideological might by bringing the soap and shrunken heads into the courtroom. In 'Lady Lazarus', a secondary meaning of 'opus' indicates the vulgar unseemliness of the Nazis' obsession with spectacle: Plath would have been aware that in America, 'opus' can also mean (according to the *OED*) 'slighter' productions, as in '"B" films and other ghastly opuses'.[45] By replicating the '"hiccups of barbarism"' at Nuremberg, 'Lady Lazarus' risks being derided as an opus in this secondary sense, as a '*twisted discursive building*', to apply one of Cleto's definitions of camp; the site of an 'improvised and stylised performance' of history as aesthetic (p. 9).[46] Plath's choice of Holocaust icons may, however, have been entirely deliberate: the monologue's scathing critique of masculinity subverts Nazi obsessions with images of power, as with the example of the lampshade. Sontag purports that 'Camp sees everything in quotation marks. It's not a lamp, but a "lamp"; not a woman, but a "woman".'[47] This statement proves incisive in relation to Koch, since it emphasises that the 'Nazi lampshade' itself is an instance of audacious spectacle, or grotesque kitsch; a functional object turned into an ornate and obscene parody of itself. Cleto argues that 'The totalitarian deployment of the spectacle, in its highly coded rituals, hypnotic fascination with hierarchy, uniforms and parades, contributes to the *display . . . of power* at the very core of the camp "frivolity"'.[48] In other words, as in 'Lady Lazarus', campy exhibitionism cannot be extricated from exaggerated displays of ideological might. The queer, 'discursive building' of Plath's monologue may critique Nazism's manipulation of sensationalism – and Western societies that reject Nazis as atavistic, but still revel in depictions of their misdeeds – but it cannot transcend the reception of history as spectacle. Her choice of icons, like Levinthal's photographs, leaves the following questions unanswered: 'To what extent do these images ironize and thereby repudiate such representations? Or how heavily do these images feed on the same prurient energy they purportedly expose?'[49] 'Lady Lazarus' is dependent upon the citation of icons without the deployment of the self-questioning, awkward poetics to be found in Hill or Harrison's work. Camp poetics do allow for a self-conscious investigation of spectacle, but, unlike the reflexivity of awkward poetics in *The Triumph of Love*, they highlight and reflect the post-Holocaust writer's reception of 'spectacular' history, rather than rigorously challenging it.

Nevertheless, since 'Lady Lazarus' highlights the camp nature of Nazi spectacle, and the way in which history can be received as sensationalist images, the poem predates Friedlander's concerns with the new discourse by nearly twenty years. As Gubar argues, Plath's post-Holocaust poems succeed in chronologically preceding, but also deriding, 'the highly profitable entertainment industry the Holocaust has so recently become' (p. 207). In *Reflections of Nazism: An Essay on Kitsch and Death*, Friedlander explains that the new discourse iterates the obsessive hold (for some) that Nazism originally paraded. Both the narrator of 'Lady Lazarus' and Plath could be regarded as perpetuating this obsession rather than deriding it, but this would grate against the poem's depiction of suffering, and the speaker's rejection of masculine power in the form of 'Herr Doktor'. More worrying is the possibility of the narrator and author's complicity with Nazi ideology as a 'gratuitous reverie' in the sense that, not profound fears, but 'mute yearnings' are expressed in the lady's flirtatious behaviour towards 'Herr Enemy' at the beginning of the poem (p. 19). Such 'reveries' are revealed more openly in the line 'Every woman adores a fascist' in 'Daddy' (p. 223). Friedlander argues that if such statements in literature are meant as attempts to understand the original allure of Nazism, then fine, but 'in the midst of meditation rises a suspicion of complacency. Some kind of limit has been overstepped and uneasiness appears: It [*sic*] is a sign of the new discourse' (p. 21). Maybe, Friedlander concludes, the issue is one of '*indiscriminate word and image overload on topics that call for so much restraint, hesitation, groping*' (p. 96). Friedlander goes on to contend that the 'kitsch of death' forms the 'bedrock of Nazi aestheticism': this is illustrated in *Eichmann in Jerusalem* when a female 'leader' of the Nazis speaks to Bavarian peasants in the summer of 1944 and extols the Führer, who '"*in his great goodness [has] prepared for the whole German people a mild death through gassing in case the war should have an unhappy end*"'.[50] Is Plath's post-Holocaust poetry an endorsement of the kitsch of death, and does she overstep the 'limit' with her use of particularly sensationalist Holocaust icons? 'Daddy' resists such a reading by vilifying the kitschy, picture-postcard landscape of Austria as not very 'pure' or 'true', since it occludes the recent horrors of Nazism (p. 223). Similarly, 'Lady Lazarus' does not neutralise Nazi atrocities by turning them into 'some sentimental idyll', but scathingly depicts them as the products of unchecked, masculine power.[51] However, Plath's choice of icons, 'by playing on all the facets of horror', cannot help but shift 'the attention to the aesthetic element'.[52] The examples of spectacle from Nuremberg indicate, unlike Friedlander's text, that no representation of such disturbing icons can be entirely free from this possibility. At the same time as Plath's post-Holocaust poems highlight the secondary witness's reception of spectacle, by replicating sensationalist icons they cannot transcend the new discourse.

By choosing to refer to 'A cake of soap' in 'Lady Lazarus', Plath anticipates Friedlander's exposition of the new discourse, but also risks 'indiscriminate word and image overload' (p. 21). This danger is equally present in the citation of the 'Nazi lampshade'. Long before *Ilse – She-Wolf of the SS* in 1974 (and the sequel, *Ilse – Keeper of the Harem*), the sign of 'Ilse Koch' was being transformed into an icon of the Holocaust, due mainly to the increasing notoriety of the lampshade. This process began immediately after the liberation of Buchenwald in 1945, and increased considerably in 1948, when the US military governor Lucius D. Clay pardoned Koch, just over a year after her conviction by an American military court. The article 'The Bitch Again' from the 'War Crimes' section of *Time* in October 1948 is representative.[53] Like Lady Lazarus, Koch is depicted as flaunting a dangerous infantilism: the photograph accompanying the article depicts her head as slightly tilted, with an index finger touching her cheek, as if she were a child bemused by the court surroundings. 'Tattoos preferred', the caption under the photo, forms the first example in the article of the potential of Nazi spectacle to displace historical truth. In her essay 'Transfixed by an Image: Ilse Koch, the "Kommandeuse of Buchenwald"', Alexandra Przyrembel argues that no definitive proof yet exists that Koch ordered the tattooed skin of inmates, or that she chose the prisoners to be murdered, despite the fact that in the *Time* article, witnesses said that she 'collected human skin, *preferably tattooed*, for lampshades and bookbindings'.[54] '[P]referably tattooed' suggests that she had a predilection for collecting human skin even if it did not sport a tattoo. That a Buchenwald laboratory was set up independently of Koch to experiment with, amongst other things, tattooed skin, is not mentioned in *Time*. Przyrembel recalls the testimony of Werner B., who worked in the pathology lab at Buchenwald, and had been '"entrusted" with both the preservation of skins and the production of the legendary lamp-shade' (p. 384).

A lampshade constructed out of skin certainly existed, but its fate remains indeterminate: Holocaust deniers have contradictorily denied its existence, but also claimed that it was planted in the Koch household. According to Werner B., an SS Doctor, Müller, took the lamp out of Buchenwald when it was finished, but it then reappeared in the pathology laboratory shortly afterwards; the pieces of skin were placed in a portfolio, and the base was left lying around. By the 1947 trial at Dachau, the American military authorities reported that the lampshade had gone missing (pp. 384, 390).[55] Przyrembel concludes that it remains undeniable that Koch instigated acts of cruelty, given the weight of evidence from witnesses in the camp, but it is unclear whether she requested, and then owned, the particular detail of the lampshade. At the same time, Przyrembel insists that as a figure outside the main power system of the camp (as only the wife of the Kommandant), Ilse Koch's influence on the day-to-day running of Buchenwald has been overstated. Revealingly, the Washington lawyer William Dowdell Denson complained in the *Time* article about the reduced sentence in 1948 due, not to her influence in the camp, but to the spectacle of Koch as 'one of the most sadistic defendants' (the paragraph before labels her 'the most vivid of the defendants'), and primarily because 'she was a woman'. Przyrembel argues that this is because, as a woman, she offered an exotic image of atavistic greed and sexual iniquity for the male inmates, 'a symbol of unbridled violence', who fixed on her as a hate-figure; understandably, since she is purported to have emphasised her allure to humiliate them in the camp (p. 370). However, the transformation of Ilse Koch into an icon of the Holocaust has had the effect of occluding the role of the SS in Buchenwald, and the collusion of Germans living nearby the camp.

In the 1960s, the organisation of former Buchenwald inmates referred to Koch's '"unusual perversity"' and her household of '"shrunken heads, skulls and table lamps with shades made of human skin and other parts of human bones"'; Plath adds her own, imagined detail of the paperweight to this list in 'Lady Lazarus'. This sensational 'phantasmagoria' surrounding Koch meant that her name was transformed into the embodiment of Buchenwald (p. 372). At the beginning of the *Time* article, she is described as the '"Bitch of Buchenwald"'. A year earlier, *Nachtexpress* illustrated the potential slippage between fact and icon by denouncing her as *the* archetypal Nazi, the 'most despicable . . . Nazi beast' (p. 375). Koch's sexuality is both revelled in, and stigmatised, by the onlookers; in this case, the 'peanut-crunching crowd' of journalists. In *Time*, she becomes 'the red-haired, sexually psychopathic "Bitch of Buchenwald", the Nazi concentration camp where more than 50,000 died'. The correlation between the two clauses in this sentence, strengthened by the genitive, hints that she might be directly responsible for these deaths, at the expense of the SS officers, of whom no mention is made throughout the entire article. By the time of a Channel 5 production of a documentary film in 2002, as part of the series *The Most Evil Men and Women in History*, it had become historical 'fact' that Ilse Koch commandeered the laboratory and requested tattooed skin, personally selected prisoners for execution, subsequently sentenced them to death, then forced other inmates to decorate the skin of the dead; and that she used the shrunken heads as decorations in her dining room, where she entertained guests and played with her children.[56] Koch's transformation into a sensational icon for the British and American media – unlike female SS personnel from death camps further east, such as 'Blutige ("Bloody") Brigide' from Majdanek – did not only lead to historical inaccuracies on television. In *Hitler's Elite: Biographical Sketches of the Nazis who Shaped the Third Reich*, Louis L. Snyder argues that Koch, an SS-Aufseherin, indulged in her 'special hobby' of 'collecting lamp shades, book covers, and gloves made from the skin of dead prisoners', while her husband 'went about the business of gassing thousands'.[57] There were no gas chambers at Buchenwald, unlike Majdanek – which contained seven gas chambers – where Karl Koch was Kommandant between September 1941 and July 1942; neither was Ilse Koch an official SS 'overseer' in the camp.[58] More reliable historical sources than Snyder's sensationalist tome, such as the *Dictionary of the Holocaust* and the *Encyclopedia of the Holocaust*, still agree – contra Przyrembel – that Koch chose inmates to be killed for their tattoos, but then disagree as to the destination of the skin samples. In the former, Ilse Koch collects them 'for her husband': Karl Koch constructed 'lampshades from the tattooed skin of inmates', and 'had a hobby of collecting skulls and tattooed skin'; whereas in the *Encyclopedia of the Holocaust*, Ilse Koch selects prisoners 'for her own collection and for use in making lampshades'.[59]

As with my discussion earlier of the icon of the soap, the intention here is not to fall into the camp of Holocaust deniers by highlighting conflicting accounts of the Kochs' behaviour, but only to question the self-evident nature, and appropriation, of the Holocaust icon of the lampshade. In 'Lady Lazarus', camp poetics illustrate the process in which post-Holocaust writers can receive knowledge of the Holocaust via sensational, and misleading, media icons such as Ilse Koch. Unlike the detail of the soap, the evocation of Koch at the beginning of the poem then has discomforting repercussions for a post-Holocaust reading of the narrator's character in the light of the new discourse. My historicist reading of the lampshade is not meant to exculpate Koch's cruelty in Buchenwald, or to draw simplistic parallels between media attacks on what Snyder calls 'a new low for womankind' (p. 263), and the victimhood of Lady Lazarus. Nevertheless, once Plath indirectly evokes Koch at the beginning of 'Lady Lazarus' to explore an iconography of suffering, it is difficult to displace her presence from the rest of the monologue. In *A Journey into the Red Eye: The Poetry of Sylvia Plath*, Janice Markey offers an interpretation of the line 'I rise with my red hair': 'The dumb redhead, so often satirised in contemporary American cinema (the films of Judy Halliday being a typical example) takes her revenge.'[60] Since the poem initially invokes the spectacle of the '*red-haired*, sexually psychotic' Koch, the more disturbing possibility arises that media representations of this icon inform the character of Lady Lazarus.[61] By deploying the sign of the red-haired Koch, Plath clearly did not wish to celebrate the historical figure herself. Her narrator is not simply representative of Koch, but a displaced, mythic persona of no specific origin: she is, after all, a victim of 'Herr Doktor' towards the end of the monologue. The price of invocation, however, is that the shadow of Koch cannot be banished from the text: this has repercussions for readings of the last line, 'I eat men like air', as the narrator re-emerges to cannibalise men in an abstract rejection of patriarchy, but also reveals an appetite for aestheticised violence symptomatic of the new discourse. As early as 1972, Anne Cluysenaar recognised the discomforting ramifications of the atavistic ending of 'Lady Lazarus', when she argued that 'Lady Lazarus' delights in domination, as well as railing against subservience: the closure 'is an assertion of power, over death but also (less attractive but psychologically authentic) over other human beings'.[62] For 'human beings', read 'men': 'I eat men like air' suggests a parity of violence, in which women can be just as destructive towards the opposite sex, after aeons of suppression, if required. This 'psychologically authentic' action has proved attractive to some feminist critiques of Plath, but the radical nature of this call to arms is surely undercut by the evocation of Ilse Koch.[63]

## The rejection of camp: Paul Celan and 'Mary's Song'

'I rise with my red hair/ And I eat men like air' may also contain an echo of Celan's 'Todesfuge'. If this is so, then it is ironic that Plath mixes camp poetics and an item of the phantasmagoria surrounding Ilse Koch with a reference to a Holocaust poet who epitomises lyrical restraint. Murdoch was one of the first critics to suggest a connection between Plath and Celan in his essay 'Transformations of the Holocaust: Auschwitz in Modern Lyric Poetry'.[64] '[T]here is perhaps a conscious echo,' he contends, 'of Celan's "Todesfuge" here in the combination ash/hair/air' (p. 141). Plath was certainly interested in follicles: she uses 'hair' thirty-four times in her *oeuvre*, and nine times in the October poems; in 'Stings', 'Medusa', 'The Jailer', 'Lesbos' (twice), 'The Tour', 'Ariel' and 'Lady Lazarus' (also twice). Murdoch's evocation of Celan is astute, since the hypnotic tone of 'Todesfuge' – and the ending of 'Lady Lazarus' – is partly achieved through the rhyming motif of 'hair' and 'air'.[65] Janice Markey similarly connects Plath's work with that of Celan, as 'The intensity of Celan's poetry and his declamatory style are strikingly similar to Plath's.'[66] Steven Gould Axelrod also refers to the lyrical 'I''s 'Shadow existence' in Plath's later poems, which reminds him of 'Celan's ash-haired Shulamith being granted a "grave in the air" by the Nazis'; the fire imagery in 'Lady Lazarus' also recalls, for him, Celan's work.[67] There is no proof in the journals or letters that I am aware of that indicates that Plath was familiar with Celan's poems; Alvarez commented to me that they never discussed his work in conversation. Nevertheless, she may have come across the Hamburger and Middleton anthology of German poetry, published early in 1962, which was one of the first English translations of Celan's work (after its appearance in *The Jewish Quarterly* in 1955).[68] Similarities certainly exist between 'Todesfuge' and 'Lady Lazarus' apart from the use of full rhyme and half rhyme: both are monologues spoken, apparently, by victims of the Nazis (although Lady Lazarus's status is unclear at the beginning of the poem); Plath's burlesque links with the *danse macabre* in 'Todesfuge'; the famous surreal opening of 'Black milk of daybreak' connects with the surrealist imagery in 'Lady Lazarus'; both speakers rail against their captors with bitter irony ('Do not think I underestimate your great concern'/ 'in the breezes there one lies unconfined'); the repeated motifs in both texts suggest a fairy tale or nursery rhyme structure.

The tone of the two pieces is remarkably different, however: a friend of Celan remembers him reading 'Todesfuge' with a 'cold heat', as opposed to the melodramatic, campy rhetoric of 'Lady Lazarus'.[69] There is also no dialectic of power in Celan's poem: whereas the last word in 'Lady Lazarus' ('air') denotes the possibility of escape from 'Herr Doktor' (as in the 'through' which ends 'Daddy'), *'in den Lüften'* represents death in 'Todesfuge'; John Felstiner translates the relevant line as 'we shovel a grave in the air there you won't lie too cramped' (p. 31). The 'heat' that Celan's friend detected in these lines indicates that the poem can be read at great pace: the initially surreal image can be explicated through the possibility of split clauses (as in 'we shovel a grave/ in the air you won't lie too cramped'). '[R]ed hair' also replaces 'your golden hair Margarete/ your ashen hair Shulamith' at the closure of 'Lady Lazarus'. However, both Plath and Celan may have had the myth of the Lorelei in mind when depicting the hair of their female characters. As Felstiner shows, Celan would have been familiar with the siren in a Heinrich Heine poem, who 'combs her golden hair'; Plath refers to this lyric in her journals, when she remembers 'the plaintive German song Mother used to play and sing to us beginning *"Ich weiss nicht was soll es bedeuten"'*.[70] *'Die Heimkehr'* ('The Homecoming') is the poem in question: Heine refers to *'Die schönste Jungfrau . . . Sie kämmt ihr goldenes Haar'*; the result of Plath's recollection was the poem 'Lorelei'.[71] This also calls attention to a (partly) shared cultural heritage between Plath and Celan. Plath defended her right to engage with the Holocaust in the BBC interview due to her Germanic background: Peter Orr contends that Americans are not familiar, in 1962, with Dachau, Auschwitz and *Mein Kampf*; Plath replies that 'my background is . . . German and Austrian . . . and so my concern with concentration camps . . . is uniquely intense.'[72] As a survivor of a labour camp whose parents both died during the war, Celan's 'concern' with the camps throughout his work reveals Plath's statement to be woefully over-assertive, but by 'uniquely intense' she does limit her remit to other British and American poets at the time. Whereas the ending of 'Todesfuge' – with its contrast between the Nordic blondness of Margarete and the ashen hair of Shulamith – demonstrates that 'German and Jewish ideals will not coexist' in the poem, Plath's 'concern' in 'Lady Lazarus' partly results in a rejection of her (male) Germanic heritage as she eats 'Herr Doktor' and 'Herr Enemy' 'like air'.[73]

Acutely aware of its status as a dramatic monologue, with its 'quickenings, emphases, retards, pauses, caustic articulation', Celan later rejected the 'tango' aesthetics of 'Todesfuge'.[74] For Friedlander, the fusion of music and death formed an integral part of Nazi kitsch: perhaps Celan became unconvinced that his poem exerted enough resistance to what Friedlander would later term the new discourse. Michael Hamburger, in his edition of Celan's poems, illustrates the fact that Celan refused permission to have 'Todesfuge' reprinted in anthologies in his later years, because 'he had refined his art in the meantime to a point where the early poem seemed too direct, too explicit' (p. 24). Plath's decision to switch from campy poetics to a more abstract lyricism links with Celan's change of heart about 'Todesfuge'. After the completion of 'Lady Lazarus' on 29 October 1962, the next post-Holocaust poem that Plath wrote – on 19 November – proved very different in tone. 'Mary's Song' diverges from the trajectory in 'Lady Lazarus' from camp poetics towards the possibility of awkward poetics that might challenge the poet's relationship to Holocaust representation more openly and rigorously. Instead, its minimalism connects with the lyrical restraint and autonomous poetics of Celan's later poetry. 'Mary's Song', like 'Lady

Lazarus', is still a monologue, but a restrained tone indicates the suffering of the narrator, as opposed to the camp railing of the earlier piece.

Kendall argues that 'Mary's Song' is a masterpiece of poetic economy: throughout his critical study, he extols the lexical ambiguities of poems such as 'The Other' as opposed to the 'dross' of 'raw material' in blatantly confessional (and campy) pieces; he refers in this instance to 'Words heard, by accident, over the phone' (p. 96) (see Note 8). Ambiguity is immediately apparent in the first stanza of 'Mary's Song':

The Sunday lamb cracks in its fat.
The fat
Sacrifices its opacity . . . (p. 257)

'Opacity' denotes impenetrability to sight, or obscurity of meaning. Fat turns from a white to a clear substance; simultaneously, the lines might refer to the Lamb of God, whose symbolic meaning is somehow becoming clear. Ellipsis is unusual in Plath's work – dashes form a favourite punctuation mark in the October poems – but here it deliberately confuses the syntax: does the following line ('A window, holy gold') appertain to 'opacity', in which case the oven (?) window becomes transparent, as well as the 'holy gold'? Or is 'holy gold' an image for the window, through which the fat 'Sacrifices its opacity'? Is the 'gold' the lamb itself, and (or) Christ? Or does the ellipsis indicate that 'A window, holy gold' forms an entirely separate image (or images)? This compression of language rejects the 'theatrical rhetoric of repetition' in 'Lady Lazarus', as Roberts terms it (p. 24) (see Note 2), for a proliferation of meaning. The process of symbolic progression continues in the fifth of only seven stanzas: 'Gray birds' obsess Mary's heart, but are they literal or symbolic? Do they also obsess the 'Mouth-ash, ash of eye', or are these separate images? Do the ashes of those murdered in the camps settle on Mary's face, and (or) do the lines express her continuing empathy with these people? These ambiguities bear comparison with Celan's minimalist search for meaning in lines such as 'I eat the book/ with all its/ insignia' from 'Todtnauberg' (p. 303). (It would be tempting to make a connection between these lines and 'I eat men like air' from 'Lady Lazarus', were it not for the fact that 'Todtnauberg' was first published in 1968, almost five years after Plath's death.) The book in question is a visitors' book, which Celan signed when leaving the Black Forest retreat of the philosopher Martin Heidegger. Does the act of consumption denote anticipated freedom from the 'insignia' (Nazism?), or the opposite meaning of replication? Does it affirm Heidegger's possible acceptance of his complicity with Nazism, as someone who 'was Rector at Freiburg in 1933–34, who in 1935 declared Nazism's "inner truth and greatness," who in 1936 still signed his letters *Heil Hitler!*, had his classes give the salute, and sported a swastika pin, and who paid party dues until 1945'?[75] Or does it reflect Celan's abject misery at his failure to make the philosopher confess his previous allegiances?

Lexical compression and ambiguity are commonly (and sometimes unconsciously) regarded by poetry critics to be the cornerstones of exceptional talent. In relation to 'Mary's Song', there are problems with this assumption, which have repercussions for the evaluation of camp poetics in 'Lady Lazarus'. In 'Mary's Song', the interjections, apostrophe, interrogatives and exaggeration have disappeared, but does their replacement with ambiguous abstractions necessarily impute higher aesthetic value? A proliferation of meaning can incur unintentional confusion; and, at the far end of the spectrum, turgidity. Young argues in *Writing and Rewriting the Holocaust* that 'the confused exchange between [Plath's] associations' in 'Mary's Song' deliberately demonstrates how the Holocaust victim becomes common currency in the West as a trope for suffering, but this critic remains unconvinced (p. 122). Kendall illustrates that 'Mary's Song' relies on Plath's knowledge of the etymology of the word 'holocaust', which she marked in her Webster's dictionary (p. 127). The origin of 'holocaust' as a sign for Christian sacrifice results in Plath merging the fates of earlier 'tallow heretics' and 'Jews' during World War II. The comparison could cause offence: in what sense were those who died in the camps sacrificial victims (as Hughes similarly contends in the lamentable 'Lines about Elias')? Is it not insensitive to align the secular and Orthodox Jews murdered in the camps with Christian martyrs? In contrast, Jon Silkin's poem on the destruction of the Warsaw ghetto, 'Footsteps on the Downcast Path', carefully distinguishes between the 'Girls/ in a row, on fire' and the deaths of Christian martyrs.[76] Plath's blurring of 'those sacrificed by fire' begins with the 'tallow heretics' in stanza three: the first citation of 'heretic' in the *OED* is from 1330; 'tallow' denotes melted fat to make candles, which might date these heretics more specifically as victims of the Spanish Inquisition, when prisoners were famously burnt at the stake. Tallow is also a substance used in the production of the soap: the image connects those murdered in the camps (still specifically 'Jews' for Plath) with Christian heretics by recalling the icon of the 'cake of soap' from 'Lady Lazarus'. The dictionary definition of 'heretics' as those who hold unorthodox religious beliefs carries a cruel irony for Plath in relation to (Orthodox?) Jews living in Nazi Germany. However, perhaps the sympathy for these people lies purely in the narrator's mind, since Kendall lists the 'troubling' remarks made by Plath about 'Jewy' physiognomy and the 'inhuman Jewy working-class bastards' better known as the Hughes family (p. 111).

Anti-Semitic remarks also crop up in Plath's journals, which draw on stereotypical visions of Jews as greasy, obese and rich: there are 'fat, gold-toothed, greasy-haired Jews sunning themselves' on Preston Beach, 'oiling their plump, rutted flesh', and 'Slimy dark curly Jewish Americans' in Paris (pp. 96, 261). There remains a curious offhanded-ness which may be 'too direct, too explicit' about the phrase 'Ousting the Jews', which jars with the overall tone of Mary's careful empathy. 'Ousting' occludes historical specificity as the Sibyl-like narrator travels through time: it is 'The same fire', according to the persona, which kills the Christians during the Inquisition, and Jews during the Holocaust. 'Ousting' sounds like a euphemism for extermination: in Hill's poem 'September Song', the use of such vocabulary implies a critique ('As esti-mated . . . Things marched, sufficient'), but whether this is so in 'Mary's Song' remains unclear.[77] Historical culpability also remains absent from the opening of the poem: the subject of the sentence, 'The fire', replaces 'Herr Doktor' from 'Lady Lazarus' as the villain of the piece. The theo-logical muddle then continues with 'palls', which primarily indicates the smoke of the camp fires and crematoria, but also contains a Roman Catholic connotation: a 'pall' also means a woollen shoulder band worn by some archbishops, and the Pope in particular. As Young concludes, this poem depicts 'a particularly Christian remembrance of events auto-matically figured by her idea of a "holocaust" as a sacrifice of Jews' (p. 123).[78] Whereas 'September Song' deploys awkward poetics to under-score the partly self-interested nature of the narrator and poet ('I have made/ an elegy for myself it/ is true'), 'Mary's Song' constitutes a confu-sion of images that does not question the ethics of representation, and its Christian framework.[79]

Sylvia Plath's post-Holocaust poetry proves more incisive when it self-consciously indicates the reception of the Holocaust via sensational icons than when it utilises her Webster's dictionary. Whereas 'Mary's Song' is an attempt at autonomous, and committed, poetics reminiscent of Celan, 'Lady Lazarus' registers its own failure of representation in relation to the Holocaust. It displays, as Gubar puts it in relation to Irena Klepfisz's poem 'death camp', 'an awareness of the inescapable inauthenticity at the core of [its] undertaking', since it cannot truly represent the silenced voice of a victim of the Holocaust, even in a 'displaced' manner (p. 197). No other post-Holocaust poet, Gubar argues, 'has been more scathingly critical of the figure of prosopopoeia than Sylvia Plath' (p. 203). Žižek's essay on Holocaust comedy is relevant in this context, with its insistence that tragic modes do not necessarily prove more successful in depictions of the Holocaust than bleak comedy. The camp exuberance of 'Lady Lazarus' has made critics of Plath's post-Holocaust poems as different as

George Steiner, Irving Howe and Seamus Heaney wary from the outset; the poet David Shapiro took this to an extreme in his criticism of her work as a whole when he decried her poems as too 'melodramatic and exaggerated'.[80] In contrast, the restrained, 'tragic' lyricism of 'Mary's Song' carries the danger of duping the critic into believing that this is automatically serious, transcendent art of high aesthetic value. Whereas the camp poetics of 'Lady Lazarus' highlight the transformation of Holocaust imagery into sensational icons, 'Mary's Song' comprises a ponderous monologue on the holocaust as etymology.

## Notes

1. Jeffrey Wainwright, '"Beauty is Difficult": Geoffrey Hill and Literary Modernism', p. 5 (this forms part of a monograph on Hill due to be published by Manchester University Press in 2005); Alvin H. Rosenfeld, 'The Holocaust as Entertainment', *Mainstream*, xxv: 8 (October 1979), pp. 55–8, p. 58.
2. Neil Roberts is one of the few critics to have commented on Plath's camp poetics. In *Narrative and Voice in Postwar Poetry* (Harlow: Longman, 1999), Roberts notes that 'The line "Every woman adores a Fascist" [from 'Daddy'] . . . has a camp, Dietrich-like quality' (p. 23). There is an unfortunate, but unavoidable, pun on the word 'camp' in the context of the Holocaust. The deployment of '*Lager*' throughout this chapter could have drawn attention away from the unintentional pun, but would not have eradicated it. '*Camp*' has been retained because it describes the queer poetics I outline in this chapter more accurately than alternative adjectives.
3. I have discussed 'Daddy' previously in *Tony Harrison and the Holocaust* (Liverpool: Liverpool University Press 2001, pp. 20–3), so the focus will be on 'Lady Lazarus' and 'Mary's Song' in this chapter.
4. Calvin Bedient asserts that Plath 'climbs to self-importance over the bodies of the dead' ('Sylvia Plath, Romantic . . .', *Sylvia Plath: New Views on the Poetry*, ed. Gary Lane (Baltimore: Johns Hopkins University Press, 1979), pp. 3–18, p. 5). Marjorie Perloff argues that 'her identification with the Jews who suffered at Auschwitz has a hollow ring' ('Sylvia Plath's "Sivvy Poems": A Portrait of the Poet as Daughter', in Lane, p. 173). Irving Howe criticises this identification as 'utterly disproportionate' in 'The Plath Celebration: A Partial Dissent' (*Sylvia Plath: The Woman and the Work*, ed. E. Butscher (New York: Dodd, Mead and Co., 1977), pp. 223–35, pp. 231–3). Jacqueline Rose covers the main participants in this debate in *The Haunting of Sylvia Plath* (London: Virago, 1991, pp. 205–38), so I shall not reproduce this summary in its entirety here.
5. George Steiner, 'Dying is an Art', *Language and Silence* (London: Faber, 1967 [1965]), pp. 324–34, p. 330.
6. Saul Friedlander, *Reflections of Nazism: An Essay on Kitsch and Death*, trans. Thomas Weyr (Bloomington and Indianapolis: Indiana University Press, 1993 [1982]).

7. James E. Young, *At Memory's Edge: After-Images of the Holocaust in Contemporary Art and Architecture* (New Haven and London: Yale University Press, 2000), p. 61.

8. James E. Young, 'The Holocaust Confessions of Sylvia Plath', in *Writing and Rewriting the Holocaust* (Bloomington and Indianapolis: Indiana University Press, 1988), pp. 117–33, p. 117; Tim Kendall, *Sylvia Plath: A Critical Study* (London: Faber, 2001). Kendall is correct in his assertion that 'Getting There' is not self-evidently a post-Holocaust poem, since the imagery remains abstract, as opposed to the Nazi lampshade and gold fillings in 'Lady Lazarus', and the extermination of the Jews in Poland in 'Mary's Song'. Similarly, 'The Thin People' is sometimes discussed as a Holocaust text, yet the iconography is not explicit.

9. Robert Lowell, 'Foreword', in *Ariel* (New York: Harper & Row, 1966), pp.vii-ix; William Heyen, *Ericka: Poems of the Holocaust* (New York: Vanguard Press, 1984), p. 36.

10. Private correspondence with Alvarez. Lawrence Douglas mentions a famous *Life* photograph of Koch, carrying the caption 'Lady of the Lampshades', in 'The Shrunken Head of Buchenwald: Icons of Atrocity at Nuremberg' (*Representation*, 63 (summer 1998), pp. 39–64, p. 59). Plath may have seen this photograph (if it exists) in the American journal. Plath's journals prove that she was certainly familiar with the periodical; during a visit to Smith College with Ted Hughes in August 1958, she records being sickened by the Holocaust imagery in one edition (*The Journals of Sylvia Plath 1950–1962*, ed. Karen Kukil (London: Faber, 2000), p. 414). Despite consulting editions of *Life* (1945–68) in the University of Cambridge library, I have been unable to locate the photograph of Koch. It has not been included in the following books: *Life Magazine: Best of Life* (London: Time-life Books, 1973); *Life 50, 1936–1986: The First Fifty Years* (Boston: Little, Brown, c. 1986). I have attempted to contact Douglas via email, and letter, to verify the existence of the photograph, but, as yet, I have not received a response.

11. In *The Death and Life of Sylvia Plath*, Ronald Hayman mentions that Gerry Becker, one of Plath's London friends, had read a lot about the Holocaust, and had visited some of the former camps. Sylvia, Hayman claims, 'who was interested but ill-informed, learnt a lot from him' (London: Minerva, 1992 [1991]), p. 3. Plath met the Beckers in September 1962; her conversations with Gerry Becker may have influenced the writing of 'Daddy' and 'Lady Lazarus' in particular. It is also (probably) impossible, however, to pin down the exact source/s for the citations in 'Lady Lazarus'.

12. Slavoj Žižek, 'Camp Comedy', *Sight and Sound*, 10: 4 (2000), pp. 26–9.

13. Mark Rawlinson, 'The Other War: British Culture and the Holocaust', *Cambridge Quarterly*, 25:1 (1996), pp. 1–25, p. 24.

14. Ted Hughes, *Winter Pollen* (London: Faber, 1994), p. 192. Tim Kendall also makes this point in *Sylvia Plath: A Critical Study*, see particularly pp. 187–208.

15. Plath may have come across Celan's work in M. Hamburger and C. Middleton's anthology *Modern German Poetry 1910–60* (London: Macgibbon & Kee, 1962), which contains 'Todesfuge' (p. 318).

16. *Camp: Queer Aesthetics and the Performing Subject: A Reader*, ed. Fabio Cleto (Edinburgh: Edinburgh University Press, 1999), p. 4.

17. Sylvia Plath, *Collected Poems* (London: Faber, 1981), p. 244.

18. Quoted in Cleto, p. 103.

19. Richard M. Matovich, *A Concordance to the Collected Poems of Sylvia Plath* (New York and London: Garland, 1986).

20. *Princeton Encyclopaedia of Poetry and Poetics*, ed. Alex Preminger (Princeton: Princeton University Press, 1974), p. 42.

21. Philip Larkin, *Collected Poems* (London: Faber, 1988), p. 169. Such inter-jectory moments occur throughout Plath's poems written in October 1962. 'The Secret' opens with sarcasm: 'A secret! A secret!/ How superior' (p. 219). 'The Swarm' contains seventeen exclamation marks, including 'Shh!' (twice) and 'Pom! Pom!' (thrice), and Napoleon's comparison of beekeep-ing to his expansionist dreams ('O Europe! O ton of honey!') (pp. 216–17). 'The Tour' has fourteen bitchy interjections, meant to demean the maiden aunt. In 'The Courage of Shutting-Up', overstatement blends with mock-amazement at an everyday action ('The courage of the shut mouth, in spite of artillery!') (p. 209). This interjection complements the simpering, child-like tone ('Must it be cut out?'), as well as the melodramatic keening ('But how about the eyes, the eyes, the eyes?') (p. 210). Not all the October poems can be read as entirely camp: a calm, yet disturbing, tone dominates 'The Jailor', which switches between flat declarations ('I imagine him') and campy repetition ('Surely . . . Surely'; 'Do . . . Do . . . Do, do, do') (p. 226). 'Lady Lazarus' proves to be the culmination of the extrovert pieces: it was drafted over a week, at the same time as 'Cut', 'By Candlelight', 'The Tour', 'Ariel', 'Poppies in October', 'Nick and the Candlestick' and 'Purdah'. Throughout these poems, the rodomontade is symptomatic of a freewheel-ing imagination that refuses to sieve language into the abstract purity of lyrical restraint. It also points to Plath's new confidence in her camp poetics: in October 1962 she produced twenty-five poems, at the rate of nearly one a day.

22. Herr Doktor could, of course, be just an ordinary German doctor; given the evocation of the 'Nazi lampshade', and the impetus of the Holocaust imagery in the October 1962 poems, however, this seems unlikely.

23. This incident is recounted in Anne Stevenson, *Bitter Fame: A Life of Sylvia Plath* (London: Penguin, 1990 [1989]), p. 277. Many critics of camp insist that its detection lies in the eye of the beholder: perhaps, following Bergman, the 'object' in 'Lady Lazarus' is not inherently camp, but only in the eye of the biased critic. Perhaps the 'lyrical voice', maybe Plath's 'own voice' (whatever that might be), might allow for a different interpretation of the poem from that offered in this chapter. After all, in the British Council reading from 1962, Plath's voice proves to be not camp, but remains monot-onous throughout the programme. Yet there is no 'true' reading of a text in any definitive voice, as Plath's reading to Roche demonstrates.

24. Quoted in Cleto, p. 51.

25. 'The Indefatigable Hoof-taps', in *The Government of the Tongue* (London: Faber, 1989), pp. 148–70.

26. Quoted in Cleto, pp. 54, 51.

27. Susan Gubar, 'Prosopopoeia and Holocaust Poetry in English: Sylvia Plath and Her Contemporaries', *The Yale Journal of Criticism*, 14: 1 (2001), pp. 191–215, p. 191. Gubar's cogent exposition of prosopopoeia suggests that

the form conceives 'of subjectivity enduring beyond the concentration camp, and thereby to suggest that the anguish of the Shoah does not, and will not, dissipate' (p. 192). Gubar incisively analyses Plath's poems alongside other post-Holocaust poets, such as Irena Klepfisz, Anthony Hecht, Randall Jarrell, Charles Simic, Jerome Rothenberg, Adrienne Rich and Michael Hamburger. Much of this material is included in *Poetry after Auschwitz: Remembering What One Never Knew* (Bloomington: Indiana University Press, 2003), but it is not identical to the Plath article: hence I retain references to Gubar's essay in this chapter.

28. Sylvia Plath, 'Context', *Johnny Panic and the Bible of Dreams* (London: Faber, 1977), pp. 98–9, p. 98. Plath's interest in tattoos (linking with Koch's supposed predilection for the tattooed skin of inmates) is indicated in the short story 'The Fifteen-Dollar Eagle' (pp. 65–79).

29. Lady Lazarus does, of course, address her speech to 'Gentlemen, ladies' (*Collected Poems*, p. 245). If this is read literally, then the addressees are both male and female. The campy tone of the piece suggests, however – like Tadeusz Borowski's *This Way for the Gas, Ladies and Gentlemen* (see Note 40) – that the address is ironic, and highlights a stage convention. The phrase would, after all, be inappropriate for a female strip-tease, where the audience is likely to be primarily straight men. As in all dramatic monologues, there is also a disturbing possibility that the narrator is addressing no one but herself. There is no 'real' audience, of course, present in any monologue aside from the reader, so in the case of 'Lady Lazarus', the audience cannot be said to be definitively male, female, or otherwise.

30. 'By Candlelight' forms a counterpoint to 'Lady Lazarus' in that the naturalisation of masculinity is uncovered as a potentially camp phenomenon. Four interjections occur in the last stanza, which depicts a kitsch lamp, complete with a brass man holding up the sky with five balls at his feet. The epitome of hegemonic masculinity under duress, Atlas is transformed into an image of queer masculinity: grappling with the phallic pillar and his own strength, his exertions contrast with the tender relationship between the mother and child; he has 'No child, no wife' (p. 237). Fruitless displays of virility, which will ultimately fail as the male strength declines, are disparaged as queer: the testicular 'Five balls! Five bright balls!' become merely onanistic objects to 'juggle with . . . when the sky falls'.

31. 'Lady' has a curious etymology: according to the *OED* (2nd edn), it originates from words for 'loaf' and 'bread'. Plath utilises the word partly for its aristocratic connotations, 'A woman who rules over subjects', and also for the irony of a secondary meaning, 'A woman who is the object of chivalrous devotion'. It can also mean 'a woman whose chastity is easily available', as the *OED* delicately puts it. Since Plath wrote 'Ariel' at the same time as drafting 'Lady Lazarus', it is possible that she had the figure of Lady Godiva in mind, who famously rode a horse through Coventry in her birthday suit to convince her husband not to levy taxes on artwork. 'Lady' occurs twenty-two times in Plath's work: as an alternative to 'wife' ('The Disquieting Muses'), an aristocratic figure ('The Lady and the Earthenware Head'), to signal the kinship of women ('All the Dead Dears'), to link with roses ('Memoirs of a Spinach- Picker', 'Private Ground'), the addressee of a courtly lover ('Leaving Early'), the sign of an older woman ('Face Lift'), a

reference to holy Mary ('Finisterre'), a queen bee ('Wintering') and a fairy-tale figure in the juvenilia ('On Looking into the Eyes of a Demon Lover').

32. Cleto, p. 10. Mark Booth accuses Sontag of inconsistencies and inaccuracies, and presents a list of what is camp, and what are camp fads and fancies: although he does not state it, the two columns are mainly split between gay and straight icons (pp. 67–8).

33. Entry 2d for the noun 'closet' refers to the phrase 'to come out of the closet', as in 'to admit (something) openly, to cease to conceal, esp. one's homosexuality'. The second example illustrates the 'esp.': '"For those who have come out, tried it and like it, read no more. For those 'in the closet', you need to read on, get right on!"' In contrast, the third quotation refers to fans of horse-racing, who can now 'at last come out of the closet'. It is unclear whether the citation from 'The Applicant' is meant to indicate coming out of the closet in the sense of 'to admit (something) openly', or to 'cease to conceal . . . one's homosexuality'. Raymond Federman puns on hiding in the metaphorical closet of homosexuality, and attempting to evade detection by the Nazis by hiding in an actual closet, in the extraordinary narrative *La Voix dans le Cabinet de Débarras (The Voice in the Closet)* (Buffalo and New York: Starcherone Books, 2001 [1979]).

34. Rosenfeld, pp. 55, 56, 58 (see Note 1).

35. A. Alvarez, *The Savage God* (London: Weidenfeld & Nicolson, 1971), p. 15. There may be an echo of the 'may's in 'Daddy' in these deleted lines.

36. For my discussion of the gender identity of the narrator in 'Daddy', see *Tony Harrison and the Holocaust* (pp. 20–3).

37. The first paragraph of *The Bell Jar* (London: Faber, 1964) subverts the link between media spectacle and death (and peanut eaters) when Esther complains about 'goggle-eyed headlines' concerning the electrocution of the Rosenbergs 'on every street corner . . . and at the fusty, peanut-smelling mouth of every subway' (p. 1). In '"The Boot in the Face": The Problem of the Holocaust in the Poetry of Sylvia Plath', Al Strangeways quotes a school friend of Plath's who remembers a teacher who '"had photographic blow-ups made of the inmates of Bergen-Belsen and Buchenwald, Dachau and Auschwitz. These tragic, skeletal inmates looking out from their packed bunk beds in their ragged striped pyjamas stared down upon our crisply shampooed heads, giving us the shudders"' (*Contemporary Literature*, 37:3 (1996), pp. 370–90, p. 371). The 'packed bunk beds' may refer to an iconic photograph of 'Buchenwald, after the liberation: survivors in their barracks', including Elie Wiesel (*Pictorial History of the Holocaust*, ed. Yitzhak Arad (New York: Macmillan, 1990), p. 370). These pictures still risk the charge of Holocaust spectacle by being used in the context of the bourgeois classroom of bored teenagers. Strangeways also makes an interesting case that Plath's knowledge about the Holocaust was partly gained from reading about the subject at college. The relevant texts include Erich Fromm's *The Fear of Freedom* (New York: Rhinehart, 1941), and, possibly, the later films *Judgment at Nuremburg* (1961), *Exodus* (1960) and *The Diary of Anne Frank* (1959). Given the reference to soap in 'Lady Lazarus', it is possible that Plath saw Alain Resnais's film *Night and Fog* (1958). In the short story 'Superman and Paula Brown's New Snowsuit' from *Johnny Panic and the Bible of Dreams* (pp. 166–72), victimhood is expressed with reference to

(reputed) newsreel pictures of Japanese POWs: the young narrator watches Japanese soldiers 'shooting the prisoners dead, and stamping on them'; she then 'knelt over a toilet bowl and vomited up the cake and ice cream' (p. 169).

38. Brian Murdoch, 'Transformations of the Holocaust: Auschwitz in Modern Lyric Poetry', *Comparative Literature Studies*, 11: 2 (June 1974), pp. 123–50, 142.

39. Douglas, p. 53 (see Note 10). Douglas argues that there is a crucial difference between the soap, and the shrunken head and skin. Civilised jurisprudence was set up against the atavism of Nazism: the latter objects compounded the distinction, constituting the 'materialization of a *legal argument*' (p. 57). In contrast, in the bar of soap 'we find a powerful trope of civilization itself': pondering the head 'we can continue to believe in the intrinsic normativity of civilized practice. Handling . . . the bar of soap, we cannot' (p. 55).

40. Tadeusz Borowski, *This Way for the Gas, Ladies and Gentlemen*, trans. Barbara Vedder (London: Penguin, 1976 [1959]), p. 131.

41. Kurt Vonnegut, *Slaughterhouse-Five* (London: Palladin, 1989), p. 10.

42. *Holocaust Poetry*, ed. Hilda Schiff (London: HarperCollins, 1995), pp. 97–8, p. 97. In *Poetry After Auschwitz*, Gubar discusses Gerald Stern's poem on this topic, entitled, simply, 'Soap' (pp. 222–4). She comments that 'contemporary historians disagree about whether or not the Nazis actually made soap out of the fat of Jewish bodies' (p. 222). Gubar mentions this controversy in relation to 'Lady Lazarus' (pp. 201, 276). In the notes to chapter three, she also refers to Jacqueline Osherow's poem 'To Eva', which imagines a resurrection where the dead will 'come alive as soap', and asks 'What will happen if the soap's been used?' (pp. 269–70).

43. Douglas, p. 54. The spectacle of the soap at Nuremberg differs, therefore, as an apocryphal referent of atrocity, from the referents of the shrunken head, and other, future Holocaust icons: 'Even if one cannot say for sure whether the Nazis in fact used Jews to make soap, no similar uncertainty is associated with the claims that dental gold was deposited in the *Reichsbank*, or that human ash was used as fertilizer, or that human hair was used in manufacturing felt footwear of *Reichsbahn* employees' (Douglas, p. 55). In *Anatomy of the Auschwitz Death Camp* (ed. Yisrael Gutman and Michael Berenbaum), Andrzej Strzelecki refers to 'special soap workshops', but former prisoners 'Miczyslaw Gadomski and Mieczyslaw Kazimierz Wendowski' indicate that 'assorted goods, such as bars of soap, toothpaste, and even white shoe polish, taken from the Auschwitz victims' were turned into soap, rather than human fat (Bloomington: Indiana University Press, c. 1994, p. 256). Strzelecki and Michael Berenbaum both concur (contra the commentary in Resnais's film) that 'There is no evidence (despite "widespread reports") that human fat was used to manufacture soap, or that human skin was treated to make lampshades, book-bindings, purses, or similar objects in Auschwitz' (pp. 262, 80).

44. Douglas notes that the Nuremberg soap 'fell into disfavor' as a quintessential representation of Nazi atrocity due to its questionable authenticity, and has now 'been appropriated by Holocaust "revisionists" as evidence that the entire Holocaust was a hoax' (p. 56).

45. Neil Roberts has pointed out to me that 'opus' has a particular resonance in terms of its alchemical connotations: Herr Doktor is, amongst other things, an alchemist; this is possibly a riposte to Hughes's interest in this activity.

46. Zygmunt Bauman coined the term 'hiccups of barbarism' (quoted in Douglas, p. 45).

47. Quoted in Cleto, p. 56.

48. Cleto, p. 205. This can be evidenced clearly in Isherwood's *Goodbye to Berlin* with the character of Sally Bowles, who camps 'woman' as a sham, as much as the sartorial tastes of Nazis. Plath was aware of this figure, who may have formed a prototype for Lady Lazarus: she refers to her twice in the journals, at one point berating herself for the 'ease of [the] Sally Bowles act' rather than being 'friendly & more subdued' (p. 569) (see Note 10). In contrast to Plath and Isherwood's correlation between camp, spectacle, and displays of power, in 2004 B. Ruby Rich baulked at the inclusion of Leni Riefenstahl's celebration of the 1936 Olympics in the 18th London Lesbian and Gay film festival ('Column', *The Guardian Friday Review*, 12 March 2004, p. 8). '[S]ome objects are unrecuperable', Rich argues, even if 'camp entertainment' can turn tragedy into farce.

49. Young, *At Memory's Edge*, p. 60.

50. Quoted in Hannah Arendt, *Eichmann in Jerusalem: A Report on the Banality of Evil* (London: Penguin, 1964 [1963]), p. 110.

51. Friedlander, p. 26 (see Note 6). I use 'masculine' rather than 'male' to illustrate, as in the case of Ilse Koch, that Nazi atrocities were perpetrated not only by men.

52. Friedlander, p. 95.

53. 'The Bitch Again', *Time* (4 October 1948), p. 17.

54. Alexandra Przyrembel, 'Transfixed by an Image: Ilse Koch, the "Kommandeuse of Buchenwald"', trans. Pamela Selwyn, *German History*, 19: 3 (2001), pp. 369–99. My italics. Przyrembel recounts that in the Augsburg trial of Koch (1950), 'the charge of instigating the fetishization of human skins was dropped'. Koch was then found guilty (on several counts) of 'incitement to murder, attempted murder and bodily injury' (p. 397). In her review of *Tony Harrison and the Holocaust*, Harriet L. Parmet quotes Deborah Lipstadt: '"The Nazis performed innumerable acts of horror . . . In certain camps, e.g. Buchenwald, there were acts even more macabre. There the young wife of the commandant used the skin of Jews to make lampshades and other bric-a-brac for her home"' (*Holocaust and Genocide Studies*, 17: 3 [winter 2003], pp. 515–17, p. 517). Przyrembel's article questions both the charges that Koch constructed the macabre 'bric-a-brac', or ordered it herself.

55. Documentary footage does exist of the reputed lampshade: when General Patten insisted that 1,200 inhabitants of Weimar view the atrocities committed at Buchenwald, a table was brought out exhibiting the shade, amongst other items. For the undoubtedly erroneous case that the lampshade was planted, see Arthur Butz, quoted in Jamie McCarthy, 'Frau Ilse Koch, General Lucius Clay, and human-skin atrocities' (http://www. nizkor.com/features/denial-of-science/clay-koch-01.html). According to this article, in 1976 Clay bizarrely claimed in interview that the Buchenwald

ornaments were actually made of goatskin. McCarthy argues that this sop to Holocaust deniers results from Clay's flawed memory of court proceedings nearly fifty years earlier. There are mistakes in McCarthy's piece, such as the claim that the family album 'was never found': presented to the review process in 1948, the albums allegedly had also been bound in human skin; they are now held in the National Archives in Washington (Przyrembel, p. 388). The main difference between McCarthy's article and Przyrembel's is that the former accepts witness statements prima facie, whereas the latter argues that these are 'memory texts' affected by the media spectacle of Koch (there was a gap of two years between the liberation of Buchenwald and the first trial).

56. *The Most Evil Men and Women in History: Ilse Koch*, Channel 5 (15 April 2002). Barbara Helfcott Hyett's *In Evidence: Poems of the Liberation of Nazi Concentration Camps* refers to an American soldier's testimony about his experiences in Buchenwald: he claims that a prisoner gave him a sailboat from Ilse Koch's household, which was made with '"sails of human flesh"' (quoted in Gubar, *Poetry After Auschwitz*, p. 156).

57. Louis L. Snyder, *Hitler's Elite: Biographical Sketches of Nazis who Shaped the Third Reich* (Newton Abbott and London: David and Charles, 1990 [1989]), pp. 263, 266.

58. In *The Buchenwald Report*, the editor and translator David A. Hackett notes that 'Gassings never took place in Buchenwald itself' despite the fact that '[p]robably near the end of 1943, an order from the Central Building Office of the Waffen SS in Weimar arrived to build a gassing facility at Buchenwald' (Boulder and Oxford: Westview Press, 1995, p. 77). An attempt to carry out the building plans collapsed in the second half of 1944.

59. Shmuel Spector, 'Koch, Karl Otto', in *Encyclopedia of the Holocaust*, vol. 2, ed. Israel Gutman (London and New York: Macmillan, 1990), p. 809; Eric Joseph Epstein and Philip Rosen, *Dictionary of the Holocaust* (London and Westport: Greenwood Press, 1997), p. 160.

60. Janice Markey, *A Journey into the Red Eye: The Poetry of Sylvia Plath – A Critique* (London: The Women's Press, 1993), p. 12. As Sue Vice has pointed out to me, Markey's interpretation is limited in that the sign of the red hair could refer to other Hollywood icons, such as Rita Hayworth and Katharine Hepburn.

61. Przyrembel, p. 396. My italics.

62. Anne Cluysenaar, 'Post-Culture: Pre-Culture?', in *British Poetry since 1960: A Critical Survey*, ed. Michael Schmidt and Grevel Lindop (Manchester: Carcanet, 1972), pp. 215–32, p. 219.

63. See, for example, Carole Ferrier's analysis of the closure of 'Lady Lazarus' as an escape from patriarchy in 'The Beekeeper's Apprentice', in *Sylvia Plath: New Views on the Poetry*, ed. Gary Lane (Baltimore: Johns Hopkins University Press, 1976), pp. 208–11.

64. Murdoch notes the slippage between facts and icons when he argues that, for post-Holocaust poetry, 'the [Holocaust] imagery exists for itself alone. The metaphor has become purely aesthetic' (p. 124). He arrives at this conclusion by developing a teleology of Holocaust poetry, that begins with inmates writing verse in the camps, continues with poems about the Holocaust 'as it was', and then includes texts (such as Celan's 'Todesfuge')

written 'one stage further from the camps themselves'; Sylvia Plath's 'historical' pieces, intellectual *Gedankenlyrik*, form 'the final stage' of pure metaphor. As synecdoches of the Holocaust are repeated, Murdoch's argument goes, they lose their initial references, and become merely instances of aesthetic spectacle. He is correct in his distinctions between the ways that Plath and survivors of the camps utilise these icons, but I would argue that they can never become 'purely aesthetic'. If this were so, it would make no difference, in the case of Koch, the lampshade, and soap, whether Plath refers to icons from Belsen, Buchenwald, or Auschwitz-Birkenau. The argument also constructs an opposition between the aesthetics of post-Holocaust poetry, and the documentary realism of writing by survivors.

65. Paul Celan, *Selected Poems*, ed. M. Hamburger (London: Penguin, 1996 [1988]), p. 65. Murdoch does not note that these rhymes are more apparent in the English translation: '*Luft*' and '*Haar*' combine to form only a half rhyme in German.
66. Markey, p. 94. She then, rather incredibly, insists that Celan's verse 'lacked Plath's breadth of vision'.
67. Steven Gould Axelrod, *Sylvia Plath: The Wound and the Cure of Words* (Baltimore and London: The John Hopkins University Press, 1992 [1990]), pp. 215, 159.
68. The book was stored in the British Library on 11 May 1962. As well as 'Todesfuge', the anthology contains Celan's poems 'Die Krüge' ('The Jugs'), 'Shibboleth' and 'In Memoriam Paul Eluard'.
69. John Felstiner, *Paul Celan: Poet, Survivor, Jew* (New Haven and London: Yale University Press, 1995), p. 32.
70. Quoted in Stevenson, p. 137 (see Note 23).
71. Heinrich Heine, *Selected Verse* (London: Penguin, 1986 [1968]), p. 40.
72. Peter Orr, *The Poet Speaks* (London: Routledge & Kegan Paul, 1966), p. 169. Gubar discusses Plath's Germanic background in *Poetry after Auschwitz* (p. 187).
73. Felstiner, p. 40.
74. Felstiner, p. 32.
75. Felstiner, p. 245. For a summary of the debates about Heidegger's complicity, see Jeff Collins, *Heidegger and the Nazis* (Cambridge: Icon books, 2000).
76. Jon Silkin, *The Ship's Pasture* (London: Routledge, 1986), p. 60.
77. Schiff, p. 96.
78. Harriet L. Parmet concurs with this view in *The Terror of Our Days: Four American Poets Respond to the Holocaust* (Cranbury: Rosemont, 2001), p. 64. Parmet argues in Chapter '2: The Confessional Poetry' that Plath equates 'her pain' with the Jewish victims in 'Mary's Song' (p. 64).
79. Schiff, p. 96.
80. David Shapiro, 'Sylvia Plath: Drama and Melodrama' in Lane, pp. 45–53 (see Note 63).

# 'Beauty . . . remains "a brief gasp between one cliché and another"': Awkward Poetics in Geoffrey Hill's *The Triumph of Love*

The 'painful regard' of Geoffrey Hill's poems highlights a tension between the aesthetic – the 'brief gasp' between one cliché and another – and an ethical response to history.[1] Representations of the Holocaust have preoccupied Hill throughout his *oeuvre*: his post-Holocaust poems include 'Two Formal Elegies', 'Of Commerce and Society', 'Ovid in the Third Reich', 'I had Hope When Violence was Ceas't', 'September Song', 'Domaine Public', 'History as Poetry', 'Two Chorale-Preludes' and *The Triumph of Love*. As a whole, these texts register an uneasy, but necessary, collaboration between the concentrated lyrical moment, and an appreciation of the potential 'barbarism' of unreflective writing in a post-Holocaust context. Whereas Sylvia Plath's immersion in Paul Celan's work can only be surmised, and Tony Harrison engages more frequently with classical, rather than Holocaust, literature, Hill and Ted Hughes have reacted to the pressure of silence surrounding post-war poems by reading much more widely in Holocaust poetry. Hughes's involvement with the journal *Modern Poetry in Translation* from the mid-1960s onwards resulted in his appreciation of Holocaust poets such as János Pilinszky and Vasko Popa; Hill's absorption in European literature has led him to the work of writers such as Miklós Radnóti – a Hungarian poet who perished during a forced march in 1944 – and Robert Desnos, a French surrealist who died of typhoid at Terezín in 1945. Hughes, unlike Hill, was drawn into translating Holocaust poetry. Whereas Hughes worked on versions of Pilinszky's verse for many years, 'Two Chorale-Preludes' from *Tenebrae* is only *'on melodies by Paul Celan'*.[2] In other words, while retaining the trimetrical and tetrametrical forms of the German poems, the melancholic ruminations expand around lines such as *'Es ist ein Land Verloren'* ('There is a country Lost') from 'Eis, Eden' and *'Wir gehen dir, Heimat, ins Garn'* ('to our homeland, snared, we return') from 'Kermovan'.[3] The influence of Celan's terse and allusive poetics on Hill's work as a whole is arguable (as with his deployment of hypercatalectic metre, prevalent in 'Eis, Eden'), but elusive overall, whereas the minimalism of Pilinszky and Popa begins to affect the style of Hughes's verse markedly in the late 1960s. Tom Paulin accuses Hill of aloofness, and ignoring, with his 'mannered pentameters', the 'austere, transparent anti-style' of Holocaust poets such as Tadeusz Różewicz and Zbigniew Herbert.[4] In contrast, this chapter expounds the reference to one particular Holocaust poet in Hill's *The Triumph of Love*, and his forging of awkward poetics that combine traditional notions of the aesthetic with a self-awareness attuned to the difficulties of writing committed poetry in the post-Holocaust era.

The first line Paulin quotes (actually an alexandrine) comes from Hill's 'Of Commerce and Society': the apparently matter of fact 'Many have died. Auschwitz' is compared unfavourably to the symbolism of Różewicz's 'Massacre of the Boys', with its 'tree of black smoke/ a vertical/ dead tree/ with no star in its crown'. Paulin's choices are apt, since both poems respond to the post-war development of Auschwitz into a museum. As he notes, 'Massacre of the Boys' is dated '*The Museum, Auschwitz, 1948*' (as is its companion piece, 'Pigtail', in Różewicz's *Conversations with the Prince and Other Poems*). Różewicz was a former member of the Polish Resistance: the poems' austerity barely conceals an anger that imagines 'a small foot here and there' in the gas chambers, or the collection of women's hair in the museum 'shot through with light'.[5] In contrast, Hill responds, in a more detached way, to the memorialisation process itself: the 'Half-erased' 'furnace chambers and lime pits' mean that, for him, the camp appears 'half-dead', and the events in Auschwitz akin to 'a fable/ Unbelievable in fatted marble'.[6] Paulin is correct to pick up on the discomforting effect of these lines: the Holocaust as a 'fable' appears uncomfortably close to neo-Nazi rhetoric, even if the awkward poetics are openly registering Hill's physical, temporal and emotional distance from the events of mid-century Europe. As recourse to this, Paulin is either intimating that post-Holocaust poets should ape the style of Holocaust writers such as Różewicz (as Hughes does with Pilinszky and Popa), or that they should desist entirely from writing about Auschwitz; if they do not, then they risk producing a 'grisly historical voyeurism which . . . sounds both insular and complacent' (pp. 280–1). 'Of Commerce and Society' can be defended as a self-conscious critique of 'historical voyeurism'. The alexandrine that ends with 'Auschwitz' indicates that the Holocaust cannot be easily subsumed into traditional forms, but rather than this leading to a complete overhaul in technique, Hill compares the poet to a culpable voyeur who engages with atrocity as pathetic fallacy: the thunderous 'tremor/ Of remote adjustment' passes 'on the far side' from those not involved in atrocious events.

Like the critics who chide Hill for succumbing to nostalgia when he is actually delineating the temptations of nostalgia, Paulin accuses him of voyeurism in a poem which uncovers the unseemliness of the voyeuristic poet: the horrific bathos of 'Many have died' is deliberately incommensurate to the word that follows it ('Auschwitz').[7] Hill engages here with the dangers facing the post-Holocaust poet. Since he was not directly involved in the events in Europe between 1933 and 1945, Hill explores the temptations of voyeurism, artistic complacency and piety throughout *The Triumph of Love*. Hill's supposedly 'pious' critics who condone such wrestling 'with the wrestle [of words]' annoy the critic James Wood, but the alternative comprises poets unaware of the 'interpretive responsibility' bound up with representations of the Holocaust.[8]

## Miklós Radnóti and Hill's 'strange children'

Towards the end of *The Triumph of Love*, the voice of an exasperated reader interjects to enquire if '*Geffe*' could offer 'One or two illustrations' to help them 'take a fix on [his] position'.[9] Hill declines to simplify matters by giving only 'One or two' exemplars, but he does provide a list of ten artists in CXXIX to CXXXI as an illustration of particular influences. 'Radnóti/ at Bór' refers to a place in Serbia near the labour camp where the Hungarian poet was interned in 1944, before his subsequent death in November of that year during a forced march. Radnóti's inclusion in the list underlines the distinctions and overlaps between Holocaust and post-Holocaust poetry in relation to Hill's work. Hill adheres to Jon Harris's notion of 'distancing' in post-Holocaust British poetry when the poet imagines only an anonymous victim in a 'dull yard' in *The Triumph of Love* (p. 50).[10] In contrast, 'Postcards (3)', one of Radnóti's last poems, describes in detail the writer's companions on the forced march, who are 'pissing blood' and standing in 'rough and stinking clumps'.[11] After the evocation of Radnóti in CXXX, Hill might have appropriated such images for his post-Holocaust poem, particularly since Paulin demands that he take more note of Holocaust poets such as Różewicz and Herbert. However, *The Triumph of Love* remains distanced from such exact description, preferring indirect reference to appropriations from Radnóti's work. This propriety contrasts with graphic images elsewhere in Hill's work, such as the 'blow from axe or seraph,/ Spattering block-straw with mortal residue' from 'Funeral Music' in the earlier collection *King Log*.[12]

Whereas 'Funeral Music' does, in places, adopt the imagined identities of victims killed at the battle of Towton in 1461, a taboo persists that detracts from authors adopting the voices of those murdered in the camps, and on forced marches. Theodor Adorno's critique of Bertholt Brecht in 'Commitment' includes the proviso that all roles 'may be played, except that of the worker', to which he could have added those killed during the Holocaust.[13] Hence the critical furore over Plath's (supposed) equating of her pain with those persecuted in the camps. The example of Binjamin Wilkomirski's *Fragments* illustrates that the taboo is just if it avoids the unreflective ransacking of others' experience for private gain. '[O]ur' in 'Postcard (3)' indicates the gulf between Radnóti and Hill in that the latter would never include '*Geffe*' in an imagined 'squadron', which 'stands in rough and stinking clumps'. The mixture of Robert Desnos's, and the post-Holocaust poet's, voices in the early poem 'Domaine Public' comes close to such a dubious identification. Nevertheless, the hybrid narrator does not blithely appropriate Desnos's voice. Hill registers the impossibility of engaging with Desnos's Holocaust poetry, for the simple reason that the work that the French writer penned in Compiègne, Auschwitz, Buchenwald, Flossenburg, Floha and Terezín was lost after his death in the last camp. Mary Ann Caws notes in *The Surrealist Voice of Robert Desnos* that 'The contents of a tin box in which Desnos kept what he was writing during his imprisonment were thrown away.'[14] 'Domaine Public', named after a posthumous collection of Desnos's writing published in 1953, imagines what the work in this 'tin box' might have looked like by fusing surrealist images symptomatic of Desnos's pre-journalistic writing with the baroque lamentations of the poet of *King Log*.[15] The latter are not entirely dissimilar to the macabre, and camp, ruminations of the narrator in Plath's 'Lady Lazarus'. Confused intonation in 'Domaine Public' attempts to fill an irrevocable gap in Holocaust poetry; the '*in memoriam*' epigraph registers the possibility of a fictional dialogue between Holocaust and post-Holocaust poets. In contrast, the potential confusion of Holocaust and post-Holocaust identities is more apparent in 'I had Hope When Violence was Ceas't' from the same collection (p. 18), which includes an inclusive 'We' that flinch and grin in an unnamed camp as 'The guards cough 'raus! 'raus!' It remains unclear whether the pronoun denotes the prisoners (in which case, the poem comprises a monologue), post-Holocaust writers, both categories, or those referred to in the title – a quotation from *Paradise Lost* – whose hope is dashed by the advent of the Holocaust.[16] In contrast, *The Triumph of Love* registers a more self-conscious indebtedness to a specific Holocaust poet.

The reference to Radnóti in CXXX connects with the long poem's conclusion that poetry comprises '*a sad and angry consolation*' (p. 82). 'Forced March', written at Bor in September 1944, depicts both poetry and memory as '*sad . . . consolation*': the poet begins with the admonition that only a fool who has fallen 'gets up and trudges on', but after elegiac recollections such as the 'plum jam stood cooling' in the 'old veranda's shade', the narrator implores his companions not to leave him.[17] Most of the poems from *Camp Notebook* unnerve due to the equanimity with which Radnóti accepts his fate (as George Szirtes notes in the Introduction), but 'Eighth Eclogue' does bear comparison with the angry invective of *The Triumph of Love*. Perhaps the distancing effect of the classical structure allows the Hungarian poet to feel free to engage in an attack on Nazism: he rails against those who dash children against the walls, and torch houses and churches. The ancient prophet, 'great in wrath', assures the poet-figure that 'Poison/ keepeth us alive. A prophet's rage is kin to a poet's' (pp. 61, 63). Such rhetoric demonstrates that Holocaust and post-Holocaust poems cannot be separated in terms of a conception of poetry as '*angry consolation*'. Hill's bitterness at post-war 'Ingratitude' can be equated with Primo Levi's curse on forgetful future generations in the poem 'Shemà', or Dan Pagis's sarcastic rejoinder in 'Europe, Late' to those who could not comprehend how the Holocaust could be allowed to happen in such a 'cultured' continent:

> Violins float in the sky,
> and a straw hat. I beg your pardon . . .
> No it could never happen here,
> don't worry so – you'll see – it could.[18]

In contrast to the anger vented by Levi and Pagis – survivors, respectively, of Auschwitz and a concentration camp in the Ukraine – tender apostrophe in Radnóti's 'Letter to My Wife' finds an echo in 'My dear and awkward love' in *The Triumph of Love* (p. 30). Amorous awkwardness for both Hill and Radnóti resides in the difficulty (and the nigh-impossibility in Radnóti's situation) of sustaining love in extreme situations. The distance between Bor and Fanni Gyarmati can only be diminished in Radnóti's imagination; the anonymous 'love' in Hill's poem is 'awkward' partly because the couple live in poverty, and only may 'not need/ to burn the furniture' (p. 30).

Any connections between Hill and Radnóti are then undercut by Hill's awkward poetics in *The Triumph of Love*. These poetics partly comprise a self-critique which emphasises that the post-Holocaust poet can only write self-consciously as a secondary witness of historical events in Europe. 'Croker', Keats's arch-critic, accuses Hill of cowardice and non-participation in World War I, at 'the Salient', Pozières and Arras, where Edward Thomas and 'Butterworth' died in his place (p. 74). (Croker also notes that Hill was absent from the 'coal-face/ in Combs pit'.[19]) The less obvious World War I references are to Ypres (Ypres Salient is an area in Belgium), and the battles at Pozières, in which George Butterworth, a composer, critic and collector of folk songs, who composed Housman's *A Shropshire Lad* to music in 1912, died in August 1916. Hill retorts that his 'cowardice/ is not contested', as opposed to Butterworth, who had a reputation for bravery, and won a Military Cross for successfully defending a trench at Pozières (p. 75). Hill has 'admitted, many times' his absence from armed conflict (p. 74). A young child during World War II, Hill can only depict it from that perspective as a (nevertheless disturbing) comic-book event: 'huge silent whumphs/ of flame-shadow' haunt his memory of the bombing of Coventry (p. 3).[20] Throughout *The Triumph of Love*, Hill is careful not to elide his identity with those of writers killed during the Holocaust, or armed conflict. Hence the echo of *Ulysses* ('Faithful departed. As you are now so once were we') in LVIII, where the poet expresses a 'shamed/ gratitude' to James Joyce, and the dead in general ('they were as he/ now is') (p. 30).[21] Peter McDonald, unlike Croker, lauds this critical self-evaluation as the work of a poem willing to 'change tack' and 'tear holes in its own fabric'.[22] In contrast, Edna Longley insists that 'The quality of Hill's poetic attention flickers when he lacks a personally compelling point of entry into the Raj or the Holocaust.'[23] Such a statement risks negating the possibility of post-Holocaust poems for most British authors, since poetry is reduced to an addendum of the writer's experience. As James E. Young notes in *At Memory's Edge*, how is a post-Holocaust generation of artists 'supposed to "remember" events they never experienced directly'? Hill's tribute to Radnóti is attuned to Young's answer: post-Holocaust artists can only engage with their 'hypermediated experiences of memory', and the 'memory of the witness's memory'.[24] In this case, the 'witness's memory' comprises the remarkable series of poems that the Hungarian poet wrote just before his death.

As a non-combatant – who, as a child in *Mercian Hymns*, could only listen to the 'battle-anthems and the gregarious news' on the radio (XXII) – Hill, unlike Radnóti, primarily engages with the Holocaust through historical and literary narratives. Awkwardness resides here in the self-conscious depiction of the poet's own shortcomings, and impartiality, in his engagement with history. Rodney Pybus's belief that Hill eschews the possibility of artistic perfection in his later poetry can be supported by quoting the following lines from section LXXV in *The Triumph of Love*: 'I am too much moved by hate . . . add greed, self-pity, sick/ scrupulosity, frequent fetal regression, *and*/ a twisted libido' (p. 39. My italics).[25] ('But, to continue–', the end of the section, hints that this may be a self-consciously theatrical outburst rather than a genuine confessional

moment.) Self-hatred finds its apotheosis in one of the fiercest denuncia-
tions by his anonymous critics who 'tear holes' in the fabric of the poem:
'Scab-picking old scab: why should we be salted/ with the scurf of his
sores?' (p. 17). Hill may be a 'scab' in the sense of his non-participation
in armed conflict (rather than a strike); an archaic meaning of the word
also denotes a mean or base fellow. '[S]curf' invites the creative misreading 'scurvy' (which can also mean 'low' or 'mean'), but 'scurf' refers primarily to flakes of skin. If 'the scurf of his sores' is read as Hill's poetry,
then this offers a macabre rejoinder to the texts described as 'aeonic
dense snowflurries' elsewhere in *The Triumph of Love* (p. 9). Lyrical
'snowflurries' actually denote texts that threaten to bury historical narratives. The fact that the production of awkward poetics is figured as the
conjuring of flakes and sores indicates that Hill cannot separate out the
retrieval of history from his own hate, greed, self-pity and punctilious-
ness. In this sense, any attempt at autonomous art would be gainsaid by
the poet's own self-dramatisation. Fulminating on the possibility of an
ethical response to history, the self-flagellation throughout *The Triumph
of Love* betrays a worry that those who perished during twentieth-
century atrocities might be being 'inflicted' with a poem that is really just
about the poet's own worries. After all, for this post-Holocaust poet, the
'essential historical fact' is not – as Igor Webb argues – the Holocaust.
For Hill, the events in Europe were an unprecedented attempt at genocide, but, paradoxically, also (in his own words) part of 'the several holo-
causts' of his age.[26] Whereas Levi was drawn to Jean Améry's statement
that the tortured man remains tortured for the rest of his life (the
Austrian philosopher, a former inmate of Auschwitz, was tortured by the
Gestapo in Belgium), the post-Holocaust author may be obsessed by
the Holocaust one week – as the poet is in 'Of Commerce and Society' –
but the obsession may then be lifted.[27] *The Triumph of Love* critiques the
earlier poem – and possibly David Gervais's essay on Hill and
Wordsworth in *Agenda* – by arguing that the concept of 'obsession' itself
is simplistic: 'There you go', the narrator chides, 'narrow it down to
*obsession*!' (p. 21).[28] In response to 'two or three of the harshest critics
of *The Triumph of Love*' (almost certainly including Adam Kirsch after
his review in the *Times Literary Supplement*), Hill defends his supposed
claim for himself as a prophet-figure of history by arguing that 'no such
claim is made by the author. The author is perfectly aware of the grotesque difference between his own resentments and the plight of millions'
(pp. 284, 285).[29]

One of these 'resentments' is contained in section LXXVII of *The
Triumph of Love*, where the writer implicitly distinguishes between post-
Holocaust poets and those less attentive to 'hypermediated experiences

of memory'. The narrator can only name 'two or three' of the 'millions' affected by World War II: the poet Sidney Keyes, a cousin in a Lancaster, and 'the trapped below-decks watch of Peter's clangorous old destroyer-escort' (p. 40). Valorous combatants are opposed to 'these strange children/ pitiless in their ignorance and contempt'. Boyd Tonkin interprets the 'strange children' as manifestations of 'dumbed-down modernity', but the critic is entitled to search for a more exact source for Hill's venom.[30] Hill, the strange war-child from *Mercian Hymns*, 'Dreamy, smug-faced,/ sick on outings' (V), may be absented from the abstract roll call for the 'pitiless'. Perhaps Hill is attacking a generation of children, many of whom are now adults, who were sick of hearing what their fathers (and others) did in the war 'for them'. The crime in the previous section (LXXVI) would then be that of 'ingratitude', which still 'gets' to the poet (is witnessed by him, but also irritates him). This generation – referred to in CXXXVI as 'children/ of the Thirties' who 'were not there' (at the warfront?) – would then have to include Hill: perhaps one of the 'guilts' incurred in Romsley is that of ungratefulness towards his relatives' involvement in the war (p. 74). (This would then help to explain the description of survival as 'unfair' in LXXVI.) Alternatively, the strange children might be those of Hill's generation who, unlike him, callously choose to ignore the events of World War II; James Wood argues that Hill 'needles us with our callousness'.[31] In 'Two Formal Elegies' from *For the Unfallen*, the ignorant are described as sunbathers with obscenely 'thickening bodies'; they are obscene – like the fattening vines in 'September Song' – when compared to the emaciated bodies of *Musulmänner* in the camps (p. 32). 'Is it good to remind' the tourists, the poet asks (punning on beach screens and sun-screen), 'on a brief screen/ Of what they have witnessed and not seen?' 'Sufficient men' (including Hill) 'confer' on the atrocities, but the adjective looks forward to its ironic deployment in 'September Song' ('Things marched,/ sufficient, to that end') from Hill's next collection, *King Log* (p. 19). Hill contrasts ineffective, erudite discussions about the Holocaust with 'midlanders' in 'Two Formal Elegies', the 'strange children' who witness atrocities on newsreel, but then promptly forget about them.

However, 'these children' could also denote that Hill directs his post-Holocaust resentment elsewhere. The demonstrative may indicate that some of the current generation of children have lost all ties with World War II, after the death of their grandparents. These might be the teenagers who, at a screening of Tony Harrison's *The Gaze of the Gorgon* in 1995, could laugh at newsreel images of the Holocaust, a laughter that might arise by being conditioned by movies to respond to horror with titters, or a technological gap that results in speeded-up motion of newsreel footage appearing, for them, inherently comical.³² In a more famous instance of this kind of reaction to atrocities on film, American students laughed at the killing of a Jewish prisoner in *Schindler's List*, and were expelled from the cinema. Some of them explained afterwards that it was '"not unusual for them to laugh at screen violence because they know it's not real'"; after all, this was 1994, the same year that *Pulp Fiction* was released, a film that encouraged the audience to smile at an adolescent's head being blown off in the back of a car.³³ However, the critic must be wary of writing off a whole generation of children attuned to respond to ironic violence on film. As Peter Robinson has noted, 'strange' is an elusive, strange and curiously abstract adjective.³⁴ If the children are strange as in section XXIX of *Mercian Hymns*, then they are 'staggeringly-gifted'; if they are so as in section IX of the same poem, then they are peculiar and unconventional, or possibly unhinged (the 'strange church' smells of 'censers/ and polish', and the 'strange curate' 'took off into the marriage-service'). In the context of *The Triumph of Love*, the adjective might anticipate the 'strange guild' of LXVI; if so, then it denotes a specific set of anti-Semites (p. 34). A 'guild' is a society for the mutual aid or prosecution of a common object. In this case, the object of vituperation is Hill's wife:

> But what strange guild is this
> that practises daily
> synchronized genuflection and takes pride
> in hazing my Jewish wife?

'To haze' means to insult or disconcert; who exactly perpetrates the harassment remains unclear. Whether these are religious bigots ('synchronized genuflection' may refer to an over-zealous service) or secular neo-Nazis, the phrase 'strange guild', with its elision of the individuals' identities within the crowd, certainly links with a fear of the 'mob' expressed elsewhere in *The Triumph of Love*. Compiling the 'crowd-demonry' of the 'Flemish tormentors' in LXXI, Jacques Callot's slaughterers (XXVIII) and the reference to the hired thugs in Rose Alley that battered John Dryden on 18 December 1679 (LXII), this is a para-Marxist poem that worries about the effects of the mob '*A se stesso*' ('To the self') (pp. 37, 32). Hill sounds not unlike the authors of *The Dialectic of Enlightenment* when he complains that 'Entertainment overkill . . . acts as the brain of the putsch': mass culture risks swamping the subject with the 'brute mass and detail of the world' in LXX (p. 37). Despite Hill's clear 'resentments' towards various manifestations of the 'mob', the phrase 'strange children' remains uncomfortably vague as a target of venom in *The Triumph of Love*. Logan indicates that these children may be the lesser mortals known as Hill's readers when he argues that the poem 'loathes its reader more than it loves him [*sic*]' (p. 219). For Logan, the denunciation is bound up with the wilful obscurity of *The Triumph of Love*: the 'strange children' may refer to readers who refuse to be patient. In the next section, I discuss this supposed 'difficulty' in relation to awkward poetics, and Hill's notion of democratic art.

## Awkward lyricism and the art of atrocity

Hill's post-Holocaust poetry cannot be understood separately from the charges of academicism that surround his work; the accusation of self-defeating erudition can be addressed to awkward poetics in general. As Hugh Haughton points out, 'This most sensuous English poet needs the mask of scholarship.'[35] The awkwardness of Hill's poetry arises precisely from the inextricability of his lyricism and learning. Hill's poems refuse to comply with the 'openly servile', as he terms undemocratic art that pretends to be democratic in *The Triumph of Love* (p. 21). Such resistance to an 'accommodating' art that appeals to the lowest common denominator has lead to accusations of élitism: Laurie Smith brands Hill a fascist in the poetry magazine *Magma* because of Hill's supposed predilection to subdue the reader with his learning.[36] Robert Potts retorts in the next issue of *Magma* that the slander arose out of a stubbornness to accept that the reader might be interested 'in anything she did not know already'; as Gervais succinctly puts it, Hill does not loathe his readers, but 'expects [them] to think harder than some of them want to'.[37] Smith's expectation recalls Philip Larkin's comment that a good poem should be understood immediately: when Harrison asks the reader in one of his early poems to look at one of Goya's paintings in the Prado, Larkin retorts in a letter, 'WHY THE FUCKING HELL SHOULD I?'[38] (Harrison himself would later remark that if he cannot understand Hill's poetry, then who can?)[39] Larkin and Hill's versions of democratic art clearly diverge: for Hill, it requires the reader's perseverance; for Larkin, it must be accessible, acceptable, and widely read.[40]

Hill's vision of awkward, resistant, yet democratic, art appears to be much closer to that which Adorno outlines in his essays 'Commitment' and 'On Lyric Poetry and Society'. In an interview for the *PBS Bulletin*, Hill argues that 'legitimate difficulty . . . is essentially democratic', and quotes the German philosopher Theodor Haecker: '"Tyrants always want a language that is easily understood."'[41] A previous interview for *Paris Review* elaborates on these points:

I would add that genuinely difficult art is truly democratic. And that tyranny requires simplification . . . Haecker argues, with specific reference to the Nazis, that one of the things the tyrant most cunningly engineers is the gross over-simplification of language, because propaganda requires that the minds of the collective respond primitively to slogans of incitement. Any complexity of language, any ambiguity, any ambivalence implies intelligence . . . resisting, therefore, tyrannical simplification.[42]

These comments link with Adorno's contention in 'Commitment' that committed literature, compromised by its concern to impart political messages, is comparable to propaganda. Autonomous art, as Adorno proposes in 'On Lyric Poetry and Society', is able instead to resist *'dem Getriebe'*, which Shierry Weber Nicholsen translates as the 'bustle and commotion' of society.[43] Whereas Hill endorses the friction Adorno outlines between art and what the poet refers to in interview as the destructive 'attrition of daily life', he does not share one aspect of the élitism that Adorno displays in *The Dialectic of Enlightenment*.[44] Adorno's dialectic between committed and autonomous art could be exposed as a restrictive utopian move. He wishes to bring Kafka and Joyce to the masses, but not mass culture to the élite. Harrison does not appear to follow this logic with his fusion of working-class subject matter and classical forms, but he also displays distaste for the 'pap', as he regards it, of popular culture; Jack Shepherd notes that he has a particular hatred of Country and Western music and jazz.[45]

In contrast, Hill's evaluation of supposedly 'low' art is more subtle: artistic sophistication for this poet does not only dwell in the realms of autonomous writing. In *The Triumph of Love*, he contends that the awkward poetics of truly democratic art resist 'tyrannical simplification' through extensive labour, and crafting: hence the appreciation in the long poem of both the prints of Callot, a seventeenth-century French engraver (more of which later in this chapter), and the films of Laurel and Hardy.[46] Hill's admiration for artistic labour in *The Triumph of Love* is encapsulated in the oxymoronic evaluation of the Laurel and Hardy films as a 'flawless shambles' (p. 57).[47] '[F]lawless shambles' also evokes the etymology of the word oxymoron itself, with its Greek root *oxumoros*, meaning 'pointedly foolish'. The crafting detected and condoned in 'pointedly' connects with Adorno's comments in 'On Lyric Poetry and Society' that the lyric should struggle to resist complacency, in the sense of giving in to artless *Getriebe* – as in ephemeral committed art. Labour can be wasted, however: Adorno argues against an avant-garde poetics that pretends to be purely autonomous, remaining in *'der bloßen abgespaltenen Existenz'* ('mere separate [or "divided"] existence'), and against the traditional binary between the 'pure' lyric and society.[48] The dialectic between the title's categories in 'On Lyric Poetry and Society' strives for Hill's sense of a 'purest apprehension', at the same time as admitting the impossibility of a truly autonomous art. Hill's term 'purest apprehension' comes from *The Triumph of Love* (p. 4), to describe wind visible as a 'roiling [disturbed] plug of sand': the phrase is reworked from his essay on A. E. Housman, 'Tacit Pledges', which refers to 'sensuous apprehension' in the other work of the Worcestershire poet.[49] A 'purest' apprehension mixes the intellect with the sensuous to achieve in poetry what Hill terms 'perfect pitch' in section CXLVIII (p. 82).[50]

At the same time as he desists from constructing an opposition between awkward poetics and a homogenised, 'mass' culture, Hill refuses to give in to what he calls – quoting from the 1802 Preface to the *Lyrical Ballads* – the potential 'savage torpor' of the reading public as a whole (p. 27), and their craving, as William Wordsworth sees it, for excitement and ephemeral stimulation.[51] Endorsing Hill's criticism of confessional poetry in *The Triumph of Love*, Jeffrey Wainwright refers to this 'craving for extraordinary incident' as 'cosmeticised anguish'.[52] For Hill, the avoidance of self-indulgence is bound up with artistic responsibility, and the requirement to respond to historical atrocities with committed lyricism, at the same time as accepting that these are events plainly resistant to artistic representation. Christopher Ricks responds to this paradox in '"The Tongue's Atrocities"', discussing it in terms of aesthetic culpability: '[A]trocity may get flattened down into the casually "atrocious", or it may get fattened up into that debased form of imagination which is prurience.'[53] Pybus notes that Hill's more recent work does not tend to agonise as much over the possible selfishness and inconsequence of the text – as in the oft-quoted '(I have made/ an elegy for myself it/ is true)' from 'September Song' – but to concede instead that the impossibility of attaining artistic perfection is one of the 'unavoidable aspects of human existence'.[54] Hill imagines, in a more impish manner than in 'September Song', the creation of poetry as wasteful (as, indeed, 'pissing in the wind') in section XXXVII of *The Triumph of Love*: 'Incontinent/ fury wetting the air. Impotently/ bereft satire' (p. 19).[55] As Hill contends in the *Paris Review* interview, 'the closest approximation of truth requires that the shortcomings of the self shall be admitted into the most intimate textures of the work': the potentially jarring effects of pitting self-criticism against moments of intense lyricism form one of the most noticeable manifestations of awkward poetics in *The Triumph of Love*.[56] In the following discussion, I explore the tension between lyrical moments in the long poem (focusing on the opening line), and the ensuing exposition of the art of atrocity, which encompasses newsreel of the Holocaust, and the prints of Jacques Callot.

In an edition of *Poetry and Audience* from 1957, Hill applauds the critique of aesthetic larceny in David Marno's 'The Temptress', in which the poet-figure, 'lacking scruple', has 'profited by another's pain'.[57] Awkwardness in *The Triumph of Love* similarly arises from the tension between the will to represent the dead and the impossibility of true representation. The poem meditates on mourning, memory and the simultaneous danger of commemorative art turning into a 'social salve'. In 'Poetry of the Committed Individual', Huk uses the phrase 'social salve' to explain Adorno's worries about elegiac art produced as a 'profitable commodity in market societies': her description of the theorist's plea for writers to manifest this process only 'through formal representation of such tendencies and contradictions within the artist's medium itself' cements the connections between Adorno and Hill (p. 179). Such contradictions are enacted in the words 'salving' and 'salvific' from section LVIII of *The Triumph of Love* (p. 31). They suggest that memory-work is a form of healing or soothing, calling on the archaic sense of salving to mean 'accounting for' and harmonising, and 'to salve' as in saving property from fire or loss at sea. At the same time, the phrase echoes the imperative of the Latin *salvere*, to hail: elegiac 'hailing' risks 'salving' in another archaic sense, of soothing wounded pride, or smoothing over a defect or disgrace. The self-conscious inability of Hill to produce the poetry of 'salving' only in the more positive sense is encapsulated in the very first line of *The Triumph of Love*: 'Sun-blazed, over Romsley, a livid rain-scarp' (p. 1). Shelley's rainbow from 'The Triumph of Life', Iris's 'many coloured scarf', might be expected after the first three feet instead of rain.[58] As with Wordsworth's 'spots of time' from *The Prelude*, the line may be meant to recapture an epiphanic (and possibly ambivalent) moment in Hill's youth: Romsley is a semi-rural community on the border of the Black Country in the West Midlands.[59] A 'rain-scarp' could be both a steep, rain-swept slope, and a deluge bent by the wind (like the 'plug of sand') to look like a scarp. '[L]ivid' invites the creative misreading 'vivid' – since the image is 'Sun-blazed' – as well as meaning 'livid' in the sense of angry (as with 'livid/ Thor' in *Mercian Hymns*); the second line refers to 'Guilts', which similarly puns on 'gilt', as in 'tinged with gold', recalling Wordsworth's description of youth as a 'golden gleam' in *The Prelude*.[60] However, 'livid' can also refer, less grandly, to a bluish leaden colour; to the mark left by a bruise.[61] For Adorno, poetry is *the* genre which records 'the sounds in which sufferings and dreams are welded': the conflation of contrasting emotions in Hill's first line links with the theorist's comments on Goethe's '*Wanderes Nachtlied*' in 'On Lyric Poetry and Society'. For Adorno, Goethe's '*Warte nur, balde/ ruhest du auch*' has '*die Gebärde des Trostes*', a dialectical air (or gesture) of consolation: 'its unfathomable beauty cannot be separated from some-thing it makes no reference to, the notion of a world that withholds peace'.[62] Whereas Adorno argues that this *'Pathos der Distanz'* ('pathos of detachment') in nineteenth-century German lyric poetry is paradoxi-cally a symptom of society's encroachment upon the individual, the 'unfathomable beauty' of the first line of *The Triumph of Love* inherently contains, in contrast, restlessness.[63]

Awkwardness here resides in both the ambivalent epiphany and the refusal of the poet to sustain it; the single line takes eighty-two pages of philosophical justification (the sections are reminiscent of the structure of Adorno's *Minima Moralia*), and is then returned to with the more affirming, and personal, *'the* livid rain-scarp' (p. 82).[64] Hill's specific use of colour as an aspect of an objective correlative also recalls Adorno's celebration of the poet Eduard Mörike's fusion of the 'classicistic ele-vated style' and 'the romantic private miniature' in lines such as *'Der Himmel wogt in purpurnem Gewühle'* ('The sky surges in purple turbu-lence') from *'Auf einer Wanderung'* ('On a Walking Tour').[65] Adorno defends the lyric here as offering not *Gemütlichkeit* or a romantic past, but the *idea* of a 'self-restoring immediacy', akin to Wordsworth's 'ren-ovating Virtue', something which 'more and more . . . flashes out abruptly' in lives compromised by the 'bustle of competing interests, a prosaic life'.[66] Mörike registers the impossibility of a truly 'self-restoring immediacy' in 'On a Walking Tour' with the memorable adjective *'lust-beklommen'*, meaning 'oppressed with pleasure'.[67] For Hill, however, the oppression in the poet's bright world does not remain unspoken – the pun contained in 'purest apprehension' denotes uneasiness as well as understanding – whereas in the German poet's work it is merely inti-mated. To deploy Mörike's 'pathos of detachment' would be an obscene lyrical strategy for a writer who has witnessed the history of twentieth-century Europe. Goethe's genius, for Adorno, resides in the withholding from the lyric of what is disturbing, but for Hill, writing an extensive philosophical poem at the end of the twentieth century, the notion of the aesthetic itself has been irreparably altered by the events of World War II. It bears comparison with the surviving German buildings in section XII of *The Triumph of Love*: after the war they are the same, but differ-ent ('Even the things that stood,/ stood in unlikeness') (p. 5). Throughout the poem, suspicions surrounding the aesthetic are explored via various artworks which engage with atrocity. These exemplars counterbalance the lyric moments throughout the poem, such as the 'moist woods/ full of wild garlic' in CI, the chips floating in the vinegar or river in LIII, and the coal fire's reflection 'planted in a circle/ of cut-back rose bushes' in VI (pp. 52, 2).

The Book of Daniel forms the starting point for this artistic equivalent of the 'car' or masque in Shelley's 'The Triumph of Life'. In *Tony Harrison and the Holocaust*, I argue that Hill offers a post-Holocaust reading of Thomas Hardy in 'September Song': 'Roses/ flake from the wall' echoes the line 'And the rotten rose is ript from the wall' from 'During Wind and Rain'.[68] Hardy's rose forms part of an elegiac lament for a dying aristocratic tradition: Hill transforms this into a metaphor for those murdered by the Nazi regime. The same process is afoot in *The Triumph of Love*: Wainwright illustrates that the 'fiery furnace of the Book of Daniel is covered by images of the Holocaust' (p. 14). Whereas the rose can denote a universal victim, however, the reference to Daniel (3:6) evokes specifically Jewish suffering (and triumph): when Nebuchadnezzar demanded that whoever did not worship his golden image be cast into the midst of a 'burning fiery furnace', four Jews were cast into the blaze; they were then seen miraculously 'walking in the midst of the fire'. By transforming the furnace into an image of the Holocaust, Hill simultaneously drains the narrative of any sense of triumph: Naomi Replansky's poem 'The Six Million' foregrounds Hill's implicit point about a post-Holocaust reading of Daniel when she states that 'They entered the fiery furnace/ And never one came forth.'[69] One such ensuing palimpsest – as Wainwright terms it – occurs when a burning Jew is set against the survival of the four in the furnace. '[D]ropping feet first' from a housetop (p. 10), this Jew is possibly a response to a particular (or imagined) photograph or newsreel of the Warsaw ghetto. Kirsch accuses Hill of self-righteously appropriating the image for his own gratuitous ends:

> to try to make one's own condemnation of [the Holocaust] louder and more sincere than everyone else's, to treat it as in some sense a personal affront, does not drive home its evil with greater force. Instead, it deflects attention from the crime to the judge, and demands admiration for his moral sensitivities . . . This tone – Hill as cicerone to the Holocaust, pointing out a particular grisly scene – is entirely unappealing.[70]

On the contrary, the poet's worries about the possibilities of aesthetic larceny begin in the fifth line of the section, as the man falls in a 'composed manner' (p. 10). He is 'composed' only in the sense of his captured position in the photograph or newsreel frame; the horrific irony contained in the adjective points to the unique agony of the victim, which is beyond representation. Of course, the Jew is also 'composed' in the sense of arranged artistically within the poem itself.

Wainwright interprets XX as a critique of Holocaust sensationalism, and 'aestheticised prurience' (p. 14): this propensity certainly appears to be embedded in the embittered command to the Shauspieler (cinema operator) to 'Run it through again' (p. 11). The Shauspieler and poet share the perspective of the perpetrator as they reflect on the footage of agony that fails to agonise. Since the Nazis produced much of the news-reel arising out of the Holocaust, the writer and cinema operator can only feign to be disinterested when viewing representations of the vicar-ious past; the Shauspieler is referred to ironically as '[*ein*] Hauptmann' (a military captain) (p. 10).[71] Hill, like Plath, is aware of the inextricabil-ity of representation and spectacle for a post-Holocaust generation that receives history primarily through visual media. In contrast to 'Lady Lazarus', however, awkward poetics express this conundrum more self-consciously: Plath's peanut-consuming crowd is replaced with the Shauspieler, who is complicit in offering up the 'exposed' agony of the victim for the 'world-exposure' of media attention. In a pun on the 'instant' camera, suffering becomes 'instantly' available for a potentially indifferent audience. Lyon interprets the critique of faux instantaneous-ness as an attack on the 'peremptory directness of the movie maker . . . words reach through the cinematic distortion of the visual to an unas-similable reality' (p. 18). However, despite Hill's wariness of the medium, Alain Resnais's self-conscious poetics in the film *Night and Fog* indicate that an opposition cannot be sustained between 'dogmatic' celluloid and the ambiguous machinations of literature. 'We are told of a film of obscenity,' Lyon argues, 'but we are also alerted to the potential obscen-ity of film': Hill extends his criticism to 'barbaric' poetry; he recognises that his poems ultimately cannot escape sensationalism, even as they display an awareness of spectacle. This undercuts Kirsch's criticism that Hill attempts to make his cicerone 'more sincere than everyone else's'. The paradox of Holocaust, and post-Holocaust, literature is that it moulds 'terminal agony' into the permanence of 'interminable' art (*The Triumph of Love*, p. 10); the worry is that the agony becomes not only 'endless' but also, to a desensitised audience, interminable in the sense of boring. Even as Hill seems to insist that the image offers 'instruction' to the post-Holocaust poet (p. 11), its precise nature remains ('for ever') obscure. Allusions to Icarus's foolishness in the 'wings of flame' apper-tain not to the Jew, but the post-Holocaust poet, who might insensitively 'compose' the image whilst hoping for some kind of easy apprehension.

The idea that this figure is paradoxically moving 'in suspension' links with one particular critique of aesthetic culpability in *The Triumph of Love*. Throughout the poem, Hill's awkward poetics focus on images of suffering in the art of atrocity – including *The Triumph of Love* itself – and interrogate the possibility of artistic complacency. In section XXIX, England is figured as a storm-tree 'turbulently at rest' (p. 17):

What is this strange tree that bears so well
such heavy fruit commingled with new blossom;
and who are these
hanging amid the branches,
in bonds of remonstrance,
like traitors like martyrs? (p. 16)

The primary references here appear to be to Abel Meeropol's protest
song 'Strange Fruit', and Alexander Pushkin's poem 'Anchar' (subtitled,
in Dylan Thomas's translation, 'The Poison-Tree'); a note to the text
explains that this is 'The exotic poison tree (or Upas-tree) of travellers'
tales.'[72] In an example of Hill's democratic response to artistic crafting,
Meeropol's popular lyrics are more resonant in this passage than
Pushkin's verse. They were a response to the lynch mobs still prevalent
in the American South in 1938: Billie Holliday famously recorded his
protest song in 1939. The 'strange and bitter crop' metamorphoses into
the 'strange tree' in *The Triumph of Love*: the history of slavery in Britain
and America is, for Hill, 'at rest' in the sense of in the past, 'laid to rest',
but also 'turbulently' present.[73] It is the 'transcendent shade' in the body
politic, a series of atrocities that should bear heavily on the national
psyche. However, Hill's palimpsest imagination is at work here again
beyond the primary references: as section XXVIII mentions Callot, these
lines must also refer to a particular print of the French artist's, entitled
'The Hanging' (1633) (Fig. 2.1), which forms part of the sequence entitled *Les Misères et les Mal-heurs de la Guerre*. Based on the Thirty Years'
War with Germany or France's invasion of northern Italy against the
Spanish Hapsburgs, the engravings overall depict a world 'turbulently at

Figure 2.1 Jacques Callot, 'A la fin ces Voleurs . . .' ('The Hanging') from
*Les Misères et les Mal-heurs de la Guerre* L.R.35.c.7, by permission of the British
Library

rest' by contrasting, within each 'frozen' frame, the unordered movement of tree leaves with the horizontal lines of the sky or the soldiers' weaponry. 'The Hanging' is the only print in which the curved lines of storm clouds appear to emanate from blown leaves. The lower branches have been stripped of all foliage, but not by the storm: they have been replaced with what the military historian Norman Chevers calls the 'strange fruit' of the hanged men.[74] Chevers's *Humanity in War* explains Hill's line 'like traitors like martyrs'. It is initially unclear why the soldiers are being punished. Chevers uncovers the significance of the drum and dice: if a corps was guilty of a crime, to prevent its obliteration, only a portion was executed; the unlucky soldiers are thus martyrs in the sense of ensuring the regiment's survival.

At this point the connections with Pushkin's poem become clearer: just as the king exploits the slave in 'Anchar' by demanding that he bring him the poison of the Upas-tree, ensuring his certain death, the commanders' rules for seventeenth-century warfare ensure that there will be scapegoats for the corps's guilt as a whole. Hill thus overlays the 'dead green' foliage of the Upas-tree, and the 'black bodies swinging' in Meeropol's southern breeze, with what Chevers refers to as Callot's 'foul crop of awful acorns'.[75] Any sympathy for the soldiers is tempered – if not extinguished – by Hill's reference in the previous section to antecedent plates in *Les Misères et les Mal-heurs de la Guerre*. Hill's 'hideously-festive-death's foragers' (p. 16) are both the clowns, jesters and players in the *commedia dell'arte* of Callot's *Balli di Sfessania* sequence (1621–2), and the pillaging soldiers in *Les Misères et les Mal-heurs de la Guerre*. In 'Plundering a Large Farmhouse' (Fig. 2.2), the depiction of murder, rape

Figure 2.2 Jacques Callot, 'Voyla les beaux . . .' ('Plundering a Large Farmhouse') from *Les Misères et les Mal-heurs de la Guerre* L.R.35.c.7, by permission of the British Library

and torture is epitomised by the horrific detail of a man tied upside down, burning above a makeshift fire; the detail is rendered more chilling because it does not form the centre of the frame, as if it were just another random instance of what Hill terms the slaughterers' 'work/ of sport'. This killing joins the chain of images connecting victims of burning throughout *The Triumph of Love* – not unlike Harrison's palimpsest of fire images in his work – which includes the frame possibly from the Warsaw ghetto. The specific connection here seems to be Hill's emphasis on an archaeology of civilians as victims: the man in the farmhouse and the Jew affect the poet with an 'uncouth terror' (p. 16) which is also akin to his, and the reader's. In section LXXXV, the seven-year old Hill experiences this fear as 'fiery dreams of houses' (p. 44), which the older poet recognises as photo-negatives of the Warsaw ghetto.[76] As always, though, Hill is wary of identification: the human flesh of the dying may be 'our own', but the fact that Callot's tree is done 'so well' suggests artistic manipulation as well as value. For the soldiers and Jew there can be no position of spectatorship, as opposed to the aesthetic culpability of the poet and engraver as both witness and voyeur.

Aesthetic culpability is summed up later in the poem as a process of infliction. Sections XCVII and XCVIII are typical of the shifts in *The Triumph of Love* between an effort, as Wainwright sees it, to 'do justice by all these unlived and unliveable lives', an ensuing suspicion that the poet may be compromising the dead, and assertions that it may be better to risk insensitivity than not speak at all, and avoid castigating the nation as a place with 'so many memorials, but no memory' (p. 40). These concerns are not new in Hill's *oeuvre*: in one of his first post-Holocaust poems, 'Two Formal Elegies' (from *For the Unfallen*), songs created out of the demise of others are predicated on an 'Arrogant acceptance'; the musicality of the two sonnets is likened to a flourishing wilderness, which 'Deceives with sweetness harshness' (p. 31).[77] In *The Triumph of Love*, however, written over forty years later, the arrogant benevolence of the subtitle to 'Two Formal Elegies' ('*For the Jews in Europe*') has been dropped: as he states in section XIX, 'the Jew is not beholden . . . of pity' (p. 10). As in 'September Song', in XCVII Hill deplores the economics of genocide ('they possess and destroy by numbers'), but admits that his poetics could be indistinguishable from this numbering (p. 50).[78] The victims of the 'graphs of . . . annihilation' are paradoxically numbered, in the senses of being 'given a number' as prisoners, and closer to death in that 'their number is up'; they are 'numberless' in death, but also numberless in the sense that the magnitude of the Holocaust reduces many of the 'numbered' to the anonymous. Any attempt to overcome this 'mass-solitariness' still endangers the dead with possible 'multiples of infliction' as the poet attempts to make them 'sensate'. Such paradoxes run throughout *The Triumph of Love*, and are, as usual, accompanied by the 'pointedly foolish' oxymoron.[79] Wise foolishness informs the statement that the yard in, and day on, which an anonymous victim dies is both 'particular' (as in 'unique'), and 'dull' (as both overcast and ordinary). Even the pronouns struggle to separate the general and the particular: 'this' face in a mass grave is then followed, after a single comma, by 'these' faces; the 'unique' visage is also 'indistinguishable'. Adorno's para-Marxist plight to celebrate the self at the end of a century so hell-bent on eliminating individuality finds an echo in Hill's railing against the 'graphs of totality' that 'pose annihilation'. '[P]ose' invites the mis-reading 'suppose' (or 'impose'), and the contradiction that the graphs both propound annihilation whilst at the same time 'posing' a pretence: they formulate deaths as well as pretending to reflect an uncomplicated relationship between cause and effect.

By the end of the section, when Hill imagines the mass grave as Sheol (the Semitic equivalent of classical Hades) leaking onto the surface of the Earth, it might appear that he has moved beyond any worries about aesthetic 'infliction', but the earlier 'posing' also suggests artistic manipulation. By placing a model in a specific position, the artist manipulates the object, which is akin here to a poet making a metaphorical leap between corpses and Sheol. This self-consciousness in *The Triumph of Love* is far from self-congratulatory, however: the following section denounces the previous one as the self-deluding work of a man who fancies himself 'a token Jew by marriage' (p. 51).[80] His long poem is then evaluated as a travesty of Robert Bridges's extensive philosophical reflections on the evolution of the human soul in *The Testament of Beauty*. False identification through 'token marriage' is compounded by the confusion of Ashkenazic and Sephardic Jews. This attack on a supposed lack of knowledge by an anonymous voice (the Ed.?) simultaneously demonstrates that Hill knows he should not confuse the traditions of German or East European with Spanish and Middle Eastern Jews.[81] This self-consciousness about self-consciousness counteracts Logan's criticism that this passage exudes the 'sweat of piety' (p. 210). In section C (representing the millennial concerns of the poet), another interposed voice cries '*I/ don't wish to know that*' (pp. 51–2) when Hill begins to discourse on the Blitzkrieg ('lightning war') in mid-century Europe. A wilful ignorance, when it comes to an acquaintance with mobile modern warfare, is akin to the deliberate 'desolation of learning' with which Hill upbraids his harshest critics elsewhere in *The Triumph of Love* (p. 63). This forms the final move in Hill's movement between representation, and an acknowledgement of the culpability of the aesthetic. Awkwardness may ensue when the millennial poet challenges his own work within *The Triumph of Love* itself, but this requires more courage than the imagined person who has a 'black-out' in 1940, and finds another oxymoron in post-war Europe 'irreparably repaired' (p. 52). As I discuss in the next section, artistic nerve is also mandatory when Hill begins to highlight flaws in his recollections, and, by extension, in the poem itself.

## Memory, memorials and the 'fascism of representation'

Awkward poetics fuse lyricism, scholarship and daring self-critique in *The Triumph of Love*, reflecting Adorno's criterion in 'On Lyric Poetry and Society' that a poem should be 'a philosophical sundial telling the time of history' (p. 46). Artistic risks invite compromise, however: 'telling the time' in poetry cannot, for Hill, enact an impartial 're-membering' of the past, as the narration of history is termed in Toni Morrison's *Beloved*.[82] In section CXXII, *Memoria*, 'the loan-shark', donates memories and then mercilessly takes them away (p. 65). This is demonstrated in CIII, where the poet struggles to invoke the memory of a particular detail of the Holocaust:

> . . . I do not recall which
> death-camp it was that sheltered Goethe's oak
> inside the perimeter. I cannot
> tell you who told me or in what footnote
> it sat hidden. (p. 53)

A footnote offers potentially important material that is nevertheless subordinate to the main argument. The post-Holocaust poet's sense of the obscenity of prose when a 'death-camp' is reduced to a footnote is registered in this passage. At the same time, the post-Holocaust writer who can only experience the 'hypermediated memory' of the past requires educating through conversation, and subordinate passages in such history books. The existence of the tree in a camp is – unusually in the context of *The Triumph of Love* in its entirety – not backed up with a named, or indicated, historical source. By recounting this flaw in his memory, Hill deploys a similar move to Harrison at the beginning of 'The Mother of the Muses'. Harrison struggles to recall lines from *Prometheus Bound* in a poem that stresses the fickle gift of Mnemosyne; Hill points out that only a fallible poet is collating the (albeit impressive) range of historical references in *The Triumph of Love*.[83] Both writers highlight the mediated nature of their engagement with history, as opposed to remembering inaccurately or improperly. Hill's enacted failure to remember is surely significant, since only a small amount of research would have uncovered the camp as Buchenwald: Resnais's *Night and Fog* mentions 'Goethe's oak tree at Buchenwald', and notes that the Nazis 'built the camp around it, because they respected the oak tree'.[84] The pathos of detachment that Adorno detects in Goethe's nature poetry – such as in '*Wanderes Nachtlied*' – is unavailable to this post-Holocaust poet who surely knows that Buchenwald was built on the site of Goethe's favourite forest retreat near Weimar; the tree in question was destroyed during an Allied bombing raid in 1944, but the Nazis preserved the stump. By (perhaps) pretending not to remember such details, Hill draws attention to 'This and other *disjecta membra*' (p. 53) in the poem as a whole: the proliferation of historical references produces, as the Latin phrase suggests, fragments and scattered remains rather than an unproblematic artistic 'whole'. The etymology of '*disjecta membra*' emphasises both the efforts of the toiling post-Holocaust poet and the pain of 'drawn' victims – as in delineated, distorted in agony, or metaphorically disembowelled – without merging the separate identities. '*Disjecta membra*' is a corruption of Horace's '*disjecti membra poetae*' from *Satires* (I: 4, 62), which the *OED* (2nd edn) translates as the 'limbs of a dismembered poet'. The inextricability of the flawed, remembering self from history is likened to an abuse of the object: the rupturing of the previous iambic lines occurs when the historical 'remains' in the poem are described as akin to the 'abused here drawn/ together with pain for their further dis-/ memberment' (p. 53).

Towards the end of CIII, Hill hints that it might be better to give in to awkward poetics and attempt to remember compromised '*disjecta membra*' than to produce poems comprising merely 'self-pleasured *Ironia*' (p. 53). Hence the negatives in the section ('I do not . . . I cannot') are counterbalanced by the line break 'dis-/ memberment'. As a nonce (and nonsense) antonym to 'dismemberment', to engage in 'memberment' suggests that the poet salvages historical details (recalling the earlier 'salving' in LVIII), at the same time as he risks amalgamating unrelated fragments in *The Triumph of Love*. A 'member' is a part or organ of the body ('*membrum*' means a 'limb'): for a poet as interested in etymology as Hill it is surely no coincidence that his use of 'memberment' and '*disjecta membra*' point to Horace's *Satires* as well as the contemporary usage of the latter phrase. Francis Howes's translation of the Horace passage from which '*disjecti membra poetae*' originates maintains that however a reader might rearrange the stylistics of the poet, the 'core' of true poetry remains untouched: 'Tho' piecemeal torn, you see the *Poet* still'.[85] Michael Brown's version similarly emphasises that the poet's 'limbs' are precisely these stylistic quirks: 'If you stripped away the pattern of

quantities and rhythm . . . you wouldn't find . . . the limbs of even a dis
membered poet.' Hill thus employs the etymological and literary context
of the phrase '*disjecta membra*' to connect the fragments of history in *The
Triumph of Love* with the dismembered limbs of Horace's poet. *Laus et
vituperatio*, 'praise and blame', the dictum that recurs throughout the
poem, connects with the ambiguity of '*disjecta membra*'. Contemporary
usage would suggest that Hill denounces his work as mere fragments, but
the context of the *Satires* suggests otherwise. 'Limbs' are also post-
Holocaust poetics, and successful ones at that: another reference here in
both Hill and Horace is to that most revered of poets, Orpheus, who was
torn from limb to limb by the jealous Ciconian women; 'The poet's limbs
were [then] scattered in different places, but the waters of the Hebrus
received his head and lyre.'[86] For Hill, these '*disjecta membra*' are also
those, specifically, of the modern writer: the phrase recalls the 'heap of
broken images' and the 'fragments . . . shored against my ruins' in *The
Waste Land*.[87] As in T. S. Eliot's poem, the role of the public poet in *The
Triumph of Love* is also partly that of the historian, sifting, in the mid-
1990s, through the detritus of twentieth-century Europe. With Hill's
gesture towards Horace, the role of satirist can be added. In *Satires*,
Horace explains that the satirist should point to his own flaws (as Hill
does throughout *The Triumph of Love*), instead of making malicious jibes
at contemporaries as well as the failings of the time.[88]

Hill's worry that *The Triumph of Love* might be a collection of unrelated historical fragments complements his suspicion that the poem
might be implicated in what Gillian Rose has referred to as the 'fascism
of representation'.[89] The culpability of the aesthetic encompasses the
elegiac: the Nazis' *Ordnungsliebe* might find an echo in the 'passion for
order' in an unreflective modern elegy. In section XIII, 'what was taken'
in conflict – such as the 'war-dead, picked/ off the sky's face' (LXXVIII)
– is later 'committed *in absentia* to solemn elevation' (pp. 6, 41).
Lugubrious 'funeral/ music' cannot be entirely disassociated from
*Ordnungsliebe* in that the hefted 'baroque trumpets' are also hefty (stal-
wart) 'inventions/ of supreme order' (pp. 6, 7).[90] The question mark after
'order' refers back sixteen lines to 'Who can now tell what was taken . . .'
(p. 6). Hill worries that the crafted nature of funeral music may provide
uncritical succour, and that *The Triumph of Love* as a whole might
appeal to a traditional elegiac convention that nudges the subject
towards unproblematic consolation. Awkwardness arises here out of
Rose's plea in *Mourning Becomes the Law* for artists to engage with 'the
representation of Fascism and the fascism of representation' (p. 41). Is
*The Triumph of Love* the equivalent of pompous, memorial music (akin
to the 'quasi-vatic self-importance' that Ian Hamilton detects in the

poem), or the self-conscious, '*sad and angry consolation*' of the tiny grave 'among the cold slabs of defunct pomp' in CXLVIII (p. 82)?[91] The moments of embarrassing self-flagellation throughout the poem imply an awareness of 'the fascism of representation': Hill makes the reader acutely aware of 'the indecency of his own status', as Rose argues Thomas Keneally does in *Schindler's Ark* when Schindler stares down at the dissolution of the ghetto 'from a safe position' (p. 45).

In contrast, in Steven Spielberg's *Schindler's List*, the character looks (to Rose) like 'a ludicrous saviour on a charger': as with Hill's readers who may gain succour from the 'inventions/ of supreme order', 'the audience is thereby spared the encounter with the indecency of their position'. *The Triumph of Love* is haunted by the possibility that the author has only printed indecent 'scabs': in section XLI, Hill admits that the 'insightfully caring' poet is uncomfortably akin to the 'pruriently intrusive' writer who replicates the viewpoint of the oppressor in his vainglorious attempts to represent the dead (p. 21). Hence the critical aside in XXXIX inquires how much time the 'Rancorous, narcissistic old sod' has left of 'injury time', in the sense of extra time in the football match of life, but also time to 'injure' others with his controversial subject matter (p. 20). (Hill registers an unsettling connection between inflicted 'wounds' and 'Poetry' in the half-rhyme from 'History as Poetry' in *King Log* (p. 41).) Such interjections constitute awkward poetics by leaving readers 'unsafe' – as Rose proposes *Schindler's List* should, but does not – pondering not only the representation of Fascism but also the possibility of their own prurience. Just as a sneaking suspicion of the prurient imagination remains in the 'sensate corpse' which 'excites/ multiples of infliction' in XCVII – as with the 'blue' wounds from 'History as Poetry' – in the section before the introduction of the 'inventions/ of supreme order', Hill discusses a Parisian artist who 'concluded . . . we must be brought/ hard up against the unlovely/ body of Aesthetics' (pp. 50, 6). No artwork can extract pleasure from the notion of aesthetics, from the funeral music in XIII – and Hill's own 'Funeral Music' – to the 'desolate/ masterwork' of Rouault's *Miserere*. This unseemly gratification might be injurious to those who perished during the creation of the 'Parisian oblation': 'then unknown' refers to the fact that Rouault began work on the *Miserere* at the outset of World War I, but it was not completed until 1948.

In section XXXII, the 'blatter of trumpets' similarly calls attention to the fascism of representation, but this time specifically in relation to memorials (p. 18). Rose contends in *Mourning Becomes the Law* that films such as *Schindler's List* should leave the audience 'unsafe' by making it 'discover and confront [its] own fascism' (p. 48). She illustrates this with the example of audiences made to identify all too easily with a gun-toting hero who despatches all around him in a manner not entirely dissimilar from that of the SS; this abstract man forms the contemporary equivalent of the fascistic anti-hero in film-noir that Adorno analyses in *Minima Moralia*.[92] Rose wishes that the recipients of post-Holocaust art might appreciate their 'mutual implication in the fascism of our cultural rites and rituals'; for Hill, this includes the construction of memorials. He is not specifically interested in the memorialisation of the Holocaust, as James E. Young is in *The Texture of Memory*, but he does share Young's suspicion of the 'well-groomed memorial'.[93] In 'Of Commerce and Society', Hill indicates this with the 'fatted marble' of an Auschwitz memorial (p. 51). Young worries that visitors 'will never know' the experiences of camp inmates, and only engage with the self-referentiality of memorials; the self-satisfied sculpture in Hill's poem makes the existence of the camp seem, obscenely, a 'fable/ Unbelievable'. In *The Triumph of Love*, the 'fatted marble' of London's Constitution Arch – designed by Decimus Burton, and erected in 1828 – is described as a 'Well-set imperial fixture' (p. 17). It is 'Well-set' in the sense of well-made and enduring; 'imperial' primarily means 'of the British empire', but the fascism of representation is alluded to in the other meanings of 'supreme in authority', magnificent, and august. Like Offa in *Mercian Hymns*, the monument is interpreted as an 'image of a tyrannical . . . order and beauty . . . an objective correlative for the inevitable feelings of love and hate which any man or woman must feel for the *patria*'.[94] Quadriga – the bronze statue on top of Constitution Arch – is meant to symbolise a huge figure of peace descending from heaven, but Hill also reads the rearing horses as an aggrandisement of military success, 'Victory's/ equestrian stone cancan': the monument was, after all, originally named after the Duke of Wellington. Young recognises the same contradiction in Berlin's Brandenburger Tor: 'A landmark celebrating Prussian might' is crowned with the Roman goddess of peace; hence Horst Hoheisel's proposal to demolish the monument to 'make room for the memory of Jewish victims of German might and peacelessness'.[95] Quadriga's complicity with violence is registered in Hill's poem as the city 'snarls' beneath the goddess, saluting her image of supreme authority. This collusion is then undercut with an allusion to Hardy: 'the noon guns' heavy ripple' which 'shakes the dead' in XXXII recalls the 'great guns' that 'Shook all our coffins as we lay' in 'Channel Firing'.[96]

Section XXXII continues to subvert the pomp of Constitution Arch with other references to World War I:

> What guns? Which dead? Haig, whom they justified
> in his self-image to the tune of thousands?

The luckless stop-press vacancies? The regiments
rehiring by the week,
hoisting the dead-beat with galvanic
blatter of trumpets? (p. 18)

Conscripts are 'luckless' in that they respond to the adverts and die on
Haig's battlefield; the dead are also 'luckless' here as 'stop-press vacancies'. '[D]ead-beat' appertains to the tired troops and blaring trumpets,
evoking God's Judgement-Day trumpet in 'Channel Firing'; the irony is
that the music will not help them 'beat' death, but is complicit in allow-
ing them to die. '[B]latter' of trumpets – which is amended in XXXIII to
the more historically accurate 'Wavering bugles' – attacks the inseparability of aesthetics from Haig's self-glorification, but the worry remains
in *The Triumph of Love* that the attempts to remember the dead cannot
entirely escape from the self-congratulatory pomp displayed by
Constitution Arch. Hence Hill tries throughout the poem to distinguish
between the 'well-groomed' public memorial and private graves: in
CXXVIII the pomposity of the 'towers of remembrance', complemented
by the awkward Latinate phrasing ('bore to inaugurate'), contrasts with
the 'fields of the dead' (p. 70). The hope is that the 'scratch' of a private
memorial in CXLVIII might prove equivalent to the elegy itself: even if
the public poem does not gain a huge audience, it might still be an appropriate arena for memory to be 'cared for' (XCII), unlike the 'bustle and
commotion' of everyday, 'prosaic life', which does not allow for such
activity (pp. 81, 47). Elegies therefore provide, as Hill argues poems in
general do in the Haffenden interview, a 'constructive scepticism as one
of the instruments of resistance to the drift of the age' (p. 88). As the self-
referential CXXXIX states: 'I am saying (simply) [simply?!]/ what is to
become of memory? Yes – I know –/ I've asked that before' (p. 75).
Section XCII is hardly simple in that the last semi-colon actually makes
it unclear whether memory has 'gone/ under' like the common elm and
shires, or is 'cared for' like the 'rare white cattle'; this recalls the scold-
ing of Britain in LXXVI as a nation 'with so many memorials [like
Constitution Arch] but no memory' (p. 40). Elegiac poems might thus be,
like the gravestones in CXXVII, 'conjurations of triumphs', in the sense
of celebrating the lives of the deceased, and preserving their memory (p.
70). '[F]ields of preservation' in CXXVII denote war cemeteries,
however: section XXXII has already pointed out the dangers of glorious
war memorials; these might apply to the elegy as much as public sculpture. Triumphant Quadriga, and the *Triumph* in the title of the poem
itself, could be regarded as fascistic in Rose's sense of fascism as 'the
triumph of civil society, the triumph of enraged particular interests' (p.

58). Hill's title refers primarily to Petrarch's *Trionfo d'Amore*, but it must surely be read as ironic, given the poem's acknowledgement throughout 'of what is owed the dead' (p. 63), and its evocation of Leni Riefenstahl's Nazi propaganda film, *Triumph of the Will*.

As well as displaying Hill's awareness of the 'fascism of representation', awkward poetics in *The Triumph of Love* self-consciously discuss the difficulties of forging a post-Holocaust poetry attentive to history, at the same time as celebrating the beauty of the '"brief gasp between one cliché and another"'. Despite this attentiveness, the 'two or three' critics that Hill mentions in the *Paris Review* interview still regard Hill himself as pitiless in his cicerone tone when he describes the image of the burning Jew, and gestures beyond the Holocaust to a wider history of twentieth-century atrocities. I discuss the charge of Holocaust relativism against Harrison in the next chapter: both writers are not especially interested in Holocaust literature (despite Hill's familiarity with Radnóti and Desnos), but rather in the awkward challenges that beset poetry when it tries to engage with atrocity. Hence Ricks argues that the 'dignified force' of poems such as 'Of Commerce and Society' arises from Hill's grasping that the Holocaust 'both is and is not unique . . . Hill does not permit the Jews' sufferings to be separated from or aloof from the other hideous sufferings which fill the air of the past and the present' (p. 58). One reason for Hill and Harrison's insistence on analysing a wider history of atrocity can be adduced from the interest in war poetry in general at the University of Leeds in the 1950s and the 1960s, an institution with which both writers are associated: Harrison was a classics undergraduate, an MA student (in Latin) and then a Ph.D. student there until 1970; Hill was appointed as an associate lecturer in 1954, and did not leave the university until 1980. Levi alerts a school pupil to the danger of merging different narratives surrounding Holocaust, and war, literature when he points out that 'Escape as a moral duty was the fantasy of POW adventure movies . . . Even if we prisoners had managed to get beyond the electrically charged fences, our wooden clogs would have made stealthy walking impossible.'[97] For a post-Holocaust poet such as Hill, blessed with the luxury of living in ordinary times – as the echo of the Chinese saying in section XCVI of *The Triumph of Love* suggests – the task is not to copy the stylistics of Holocaust poets such as Różewicz (as Paulin intimates he should), but to produce awkward poetics that highlight his own status as a non-combatant in the war, and other 'shortcomings of the self'.[98] By admitting such concerns into 'the most intimate textures of the work', *The Triumph of Love* achieves a necessarily awkward balance between lyricism and an ethical response to history. 'Balance' is an unfashionable word in literary criticism: John Barrell associates it with mannered, bourgeois complacency.[99] By balance here I mean achieving a dialectic between autonomous and committed literature. Hill's achievement comprises a self-conscious exposition of his own techniques and shortcomings – as Adorno desired – in the poetry itself.

## Notes

1. William Logan, 'The Triumph of Geoffrey Hill', *Parnassus*, 24: 2 (May 2000), pp. 201–20, p. 208. Hill quotes from Ezra Pound's 'Envoi (1919)' ('Beauty Remains . . .') in his collection of essays entitled *The Enemy's Country: Words, Contexture, and other Circumstances of Language* (Oxford: Clarendon Press, 1991), pp. 83–102, pp. 93, 102. John Whale used the phrase 'an ethical response to history' to describe one link between the Leeds poets in the 1950s and 1960s at the 'Poetry at Leeds' conference (12–13 September 2003 at the University of Leeds).
2. Geoffrey Hill, *Tenebrae* (London: André Deutsch Ltd, 1978), p. 35. My emphasis.
3. Paul Celan, *Selected Poems*, trans. Michael Hamburger (London: Penguin, 1996 [1988]), pp. 176, 177, 206, 207. Both the German lines are quoted as epigraphs to '1. Ave Regina Coelorum' and '2. Te Lucis Ante Terminum'; the first poem translates the German as 'There is a land called lost' (*Tenebrae*, p. 35).
4. Tom Paulin, 'A Visionary Nationalist: Geoffrey Hill', in *Minotaur: Poetry and the Nation State* (London: Faber, 1992), pp. 276–84, p. 280.
5. Tadeusz Różewicz, *Conversations with the Prince and Other Poems*, trans. Adam Czerniawski (London: Anvil, 1982), pp. 44, 43.
6. Geoffrey Hill, *For the Unfallen* (London: André Deutsch Ltd., 1959), p. 51.
7. John Haffenden, *Viewpoints: Poets in Conversation* (London: Faber, 1981), p. 93. Here, Hill comments that 'If one writes lyrics of which nostalgia is an essential element, naïve or malicious critics will say that the nostalgia must be one's own . . . To be accused of exhibiting a symptom when, to the best of my ability, I'm offering a diagnosis appears to be one of the numerous injustices which one must suffer with as much equanimity as possible.'
8. James Wood, 'Too Many Alibis' (rev. of *Canaan* and *The Triumph of Love*), *London Review of Books*, 1 July 1999, pp. 24–6, p. 24.
9. Geoffrey Hill, *The Triumph of Love* (London and New York: Penguin, 1999 [1998]), p. 70.
10. Jon Harris, 'An Elegy for Myself: British Poetry and the Holocaust', *English*, 41:171 (1992), pp. 213–33.
11. Miklós Radnóti, *Camp Notebook*, trans. Francis Jones (Todmorden: Arc, 2000), p. 71.
12. Geoffrey Hill, *King Log* (London: André Deutsch, 1968), p. 25.
13. Theodor Adorno, 'Commitment', in *Literature in the Modern World*, ed. Dennis Walder (Oxford: Oxford University Press, 1990), pp. 89–99, p. 96.
14. Mary Ann Caws, *The Surrealist Voice of Robert Desnos* (Amherst: University of Massachusetts Press, 1977), p. 10.
15. In '"How Fit a Title . . .": Title and Authority in the Work of Geoffrey Hill',

Hugh Haughton argues that 'We hear nothing . . . of the energetic surrealism of Desnos', and refers to the baroque images in Hill's poem as 'tortured pastiche' (*Geoffrey Hill: Essays on his Work* ed. Peter Robinson (Milton Keynes: Open University Press, 1985), pp. 128–48), pp. 135, 142. Curiously, Hill notes in *Preghiere* (Leeds: Northern House Pamphlet Poets, 1964) that 'Domaine Public' forms the 'title of Robert Desnos' Collected Poems, published posthumously in *1947*' (p. 2, my italics). Desnos's *Oeuvres Posthumes* was published in 1947, whereas *Domaine Public* (1953) includes extra texts such as 'The Night of Loveless Nights', 'Corps et Biens' and 'Fortunes' (Caws, p. 216). The version of 'Domaine Public' in *King Log* replaces 'blood' with 'spleen', perhaps to emphasise the poem's macabre humour: a spleen can refer to 'the seat of melancholy or morose feelings' as well as 'the seat of laughter or mirth' (*OED*, 2nd edn).

16. The title originates from Book XI of *Paradise Lost* (*Poems of John Milton*, London: Thomas Nelson and Sons Ltd, npd., pp. 272–3): 'I had hope,/ When violence was ceased, and war on earth,/ All would have then gone well; peace would have crowned/ With length of happy days the race of man' (ll.778–81). The last line of Hill's poem may contain an echo of lines from Job (19: 7–10), such as 'He . . . hath stripped me of my glory, and taken the crown from my head', but the more obvious references are to Shakespeare and *The Prelude* (V: 23–5), where 'Man . . . Might almost "weep to have" what he may lose' (*The Oxford Authors: William Wordsworth*, ed. Stephen Gill (Oxford and New York: Oxford University Press, 1986 [1984]), p. 435). Wordsworth quotes from Shakespeare's sonnet number 64: 'But weep to have that which it fears to lose' (*The Sonnets*, ed. M. R. Ridley (London: J. M. Dent and Sons, 1976), p. 34). 'That which is taken from me is not mine' suggests that, unlike in Shakespeare's and Wordsworth's poems, there is no point in even thinking about weeping for potential lost property in the camps, but the ambiguous line makes it unclear whether 'That' 'is not mine' because it did not belong to the person in question anyway, or because it is 'not mine' only when taken from them. As with the demonstratives in *The Triumph of Love*, 'That' creates further ambiguity: it could refer to abstract property, or to 'Our flesh' in line three.

17. Radnóti, p. 57. Francis Jones does not use an accent for 'Bor'.

18. Dan Pagis, 'Europe, Late', trans. Stephen Mitchell, in Schiff, *Holocaust Poetry*, p. 6.

19. Combs Pit refers either to the pit in West Yorkshire, near Dewsbury, or the mining disaster at Thornhill in Durham (1893).

20. As in *Mercian Hymns*, in which the identities of the child and Offa become enmeshed, history and mythology merge at the beginning of *The Triumph of Love*. Saint Kenelm (or Cenelm, or Cynchelm) is mentioned, who, according to local legend, died in Romsley in 821. Logan argues that Cynchelm's death 'was retrospective, eleventh-century fantasy for William of Malmesbury and others. The real ninth-century Cynchelm died in manhood, probably fighting the Welsh, and never succeeded to his father's throne' (p. 202). Born in 814, his head was cut off in another local legend by Askbert, the hired assassin of Cenelm's sister, who thought she might become queen if her brother was safely dispatched. A pillar of light then reputedly shone over the thicket in Worcestershire where Cenelm was secretly buried. This pillar fuses with the

image of 'Coventry ablaze' in VII (p. 3). In his paper at the 'Poetry at Leeds' conference, Hugh Haughton argued that the line 'Kenelm, his mouth full of blood and toffee' refers to W. B. Yeats's comment in a letter to Dorothy Wellesley (21 December 1936) that Wilfred Owen's poetry was 'all blood, dirt and sucked sugar-stick' (*The Letters of W. B. Yeats*, ed. Allan Wade (London: Rupert Hart-Davis, 1954), p. 874).

21. James Joyce, *Ulysses* (London: Minerva, 1992 [1922]), p. 120.
22. Peter McDonald, '"*Violent Hefts*": Geoffrey Hill's *The Triumph of Love*', *Metre*, 10 (autumn 2001), pp. 65–78, p. 72.
23. Edna Longley, 'All you Need is Love' (rev. of *The Triumph of Love*), *Metre*, 6 (summer 1999), pp. 70–4, p. 72.
24. James Young, *At Memory's Edge: After-Images of the Holocaust in Contemporary Art and Architecture* (New Haven and London: Yale University Press, 2000), p. 1.
25. Rodney Pybus, 'What Fun . . . and Strange Beauty', *Stand*, 3 (4) and 4 (1): 712 (2002), pp. 30–6, p. 31.
26. Igor Webb, 'Speaking of the Holocaust: The Poetry of Geoffrey Hill', *The Denver Quarterly*, 12: 1 (spring 1977), pp. 114–24, p. 118; Geoffrey Hill, 'The Art of Poetry LXXX', *Paris Review*, 154 (spring 2000), pp. 270–99, p. 285.
27. Ian Thomson, *Primo Levi* (London: Vintage 2003 [2002]), p. 396.
28. In 'An "Exemplary Poet": Geoffrey Hill's Wordsworth', David Gervais notes that Hill is 'obsessed with the Holocaust' (*Agenda: A Tribute to Geoffrey Hill*, ed. William Cookson and Peter Dale, 34: 2 [summer 1996], pp. 88–103, p. 101).
29. Hill, 'The Art of Poetry LXXX', pp. 284, 285.
30. Boyd Tonkin, 'Hard Lines from the Bitter Bard', *The Independent*, 6 February 1999, no p.n. (article held in the Geoffrey Hill folder, The Poetry Library, Royal Festival Hall).
31. Wood, p. 25.
32. This incident is discussed in Antony Rowland, *Tony Harrison and the Holocaust* (Liverpool: Liverpool University Press, 2001), p. 64.
33. Quoted in Dora Apel, *Memory Effects: The Holocaust and the Art of Secondary Witnessing* (New Brunswick, New Jersey and London: Rutgers University Press, 2002), p. 33.
34. Peter Robinson discussed this passage in his paper at the 'Poetry at Leeds' conference, entitled 'Jeffrey Wainwright: Debt to the Dead'. He commented that if Hill is referring to a current generation of youths, then he ignores the demonstrations that many of them attended against, for example, the war in Iraq in 2003. It could also be argued that many of these, and millions of others besides, might *still* be ignorant about numerous details of twentieth-century history. 'Strange', in the context of *The Triumph of Love*, may deliberately recall the 'strange fruit' of the trees depicted by Meeropol, Pushkin and Callot, which I discuss later in this chapter.
35. Hugh Haughton, '"How Fit a Title . . .": Title and Authority in the Work of Geoffrey Hill', p. 135 (see Note 15).
36. Laurie Smith's comments are alluded to in 'Subduing the Reader (2)', *Magma*, 24 (autumn 2002), pp. 53–62. David Boll and Robert Potts respond to Smith's claim that Hill, 'like Pound, is fascist' (p. 53).

37. Boll and Potts, above, p. 59; David Gervais, 'Geoffrey Hill: A New Direction?' (rev. of *Speech! Speech!*), in *The Reader*, 11 (autumn/winter 2002), pp. 77–88, p. 78.

38. Philip Larkin comments 'I don't want to transcend the commonplace' in the John Haffenden interview (p. 125), and 'poets write for people with the same background and experiences as themselves' in *Required Writing: Miscellaneous Pieces 1955–1982* (London: Faber, 1983), p. 69. The quotation is from a letter to Kingsley Amis (21 November 1982), in *Selected Letters of Philip Larkin 1940–1985*, ed. Anthony Thwaite (London: Faber, 1992), p. 682. Larkin is referring to *The Penguin Book of Contemporary British Poetry*, and comments 'see that note on p. 46: "(See the picture *A Dog Buried in the Sand* among the Black Paintings of Goya in the Prado)" – WHY THE FUCKING HELL SHOULD I??? See the picture *Kilroy was Here* in the Gents in The Black Horse.' The Harrison poem in question is 'The Ballad of Babelabour', in *The Penguin Book of Contemporary British Poetry*, ed. Blake Morrison and Andrew Motion (London: Penguin, 1982), pp. 45–6, p. 46.

39. Michael Alexander, 'Tony Harrison in Conversation with Michael Alexander', *Verse*, 8: 2 (1991), pp. 84–93. Harrison states: '[Hill] sort of gets quite difficult, and I think, if I can't understand somebody's work then who can? I think I'm a fairly intelligent reader of poetry' (p. 90).

40. In an extensive (and vituperative) footnote in *Style and Faith* (New York: Counterpoint, 2003), Hill attacks Larkin's dismissal of a modernist triumvirate (Pound, Picasso, Parker) as 'postprandial' (p. 203). He interprets Larkin's reflex anti-modernism as a sign of 'narrow English possessiveness, with regard to "good sense" and "generous common humanity"' (p. 204). Hill argues that the right-wing politics of the letters are evident in the poetry; their publication should have only surprised those who presumed that Larkin was writing about '"human life as we know it"': 'The notion of accessibility of his work acknowledged the ease with which readers could overlay it with transparencies of their own preference.'

41. Geoffrey Hill, 'Gold Out of Loss', *PBS Bulletin*, 194 (autumn 2002), p. 5.

42. Geoffrey Hill, 'The Art of Poetry LXXX', p. 277.

43. Theodor Adorno, 'Rede über Lyrik und Gesellschaft', in *Gesammelte Schriften II: Noten Zur Literatur* (Frankfurt am Main: Suhrkamp Verlag, 1974), pp. 49–68, p. 49; 'On Lyric Poetry and Society', in *Notes to Literature*, trans. Shierry Weber Nicholsen (New York: Columbia University Press, 1991), pp. 37–54, p. 37. 'Rede über Lyrik und Gesellschaft', originally a talk for RIAS Berlin, was revised several times, and first published in *Akzente* in 1957.

44. Haffenden, p. 83.

45. Jack Shepherd, 'The "Scholar Me": An Actor's View', in *Critical Anthologies. 1. Tony Harrison*, ed. Neil Astley (Newcastle: Bloodaxe, 1991), pp. 423–8, p. 424.

46. In an interview in *The Guardian* (2 July 2003, p. 3), Hill reputedly lauded Puff Daddy's poetic diction as juicing up the imagination. Sadly, this turned out to be a spoof quotation in response to Seamus Heaney's admiration for Eminem's verbal energy.

47. This recalls Olly's famous oxymoron of a 'fine mess'.

48.  '*Rede über Lyrik und Gesellschaft*', p. 50; 'On Lyric Poetry and Society', p. 38.

49.  Geoffrey Hill, 'Tacit Pledges', in *A.E. Housman: A Reassessment*, ed. Alan W. Holden and J. Roy Birch (London: Palgrave, 1999), pp. 53–75, p. 56. '[S]ensuous apprehension' refers here to the quality of Housman's phrasing. This takes three forms: the depiction of the particular as if it arose from direct observation; the ability to choose 'what Yeats called "the intellectually surprising word which is also the correct word"'; and the 'logopoeic form of grammar and syntax'. Hill's deployment of logopoeia draws on Ezra Pound's description of this poetic technique in *ABC of Reading*. The appeal to the visual imagination constitutes phanopoeia; emotions evoked through the sound and rhythms of speech react to melopoeia. Logopoeia occurs with the fusion of phanopoeia and melopoeia, 'thus stimulating the intellectual or emotional associations which have remained in the receiver's consciousness in relation to the actual words or groups of words employed' (J. A. Cuddon, *A Dictionary of Literary Terms* (London: Penguin, 1982 [1977]), pp. 369–70). Hill's phrase 'sensuous apprehension' stresses that Housman's verse comprises, and provokes, intellectual *and* emotional responses.

50.  Peter McDonald eloquently discusses the differences between Hill's notions of 'pitch' and 'tone' in '"*Violent Hefts*": Geoffrey Hill's *The Triumph of Love*', *Metre* 10 (autumn 2001), p. 68. 'Pitch' refers to a 'deliberated alertness' in the deployment of language, where the intended meaning takes stock of potential misconstructions. In contrast, 'tone' alludes to a more complacent collusion between the writer and audience, 'where words and phrases are employed to mark and confirm the degree of that practical and mutually accepted relationship'.

51.  *The Oxford Authors: William Wordsworth*, p. 599 (see Note 16). In 'An "Exemplary Poet": Geoffrey Hill's Wordsworth', David Gervais argues that 'What makes Wordsworth a touchstone for Hill is . . . his verse-music and the way he deals with tragedy' (p. 91) (see Note 28).

52.  Jeffrey Wainwright, 'Geoffrey Hill: *The Triumph of Love*', *P. N. Review*, 26: 5 (May/June 2000), pp. 13–21, p. 18.

53.  Christopher Ricks, '"The Tongue's Atrocities"', in *Modern Critical Views: Geoffrey Hill*, ed. Harold Bloom (New York: Chelsea House, 1986), pp. 55–68, p. 55. Ricks illustrates that remonstrations in poetry over exploitative aesthetics are not, of course, new: in the *Agenda* essay Gervais quotes Wordsworth's 'soothing thoughts that spring out of human suffering' at the beginning of his essay on Hill; in 'Nutting', 'pain and pleasure are very close and violence also ushers in a kind of aesthetic benignity' (p. 97). Nevertheless, Ricks argues that, with the advent of the Holocaust, 'upon this ancient dubiety . . . there has been urged in the last forty years a unique and hideous modern intensification' (p. 56). Gervais recognises this when he states that Hill could not have ended a post-Holocaust poem in the same way as Wordsworth's 'Elegiac Stanzas Suggested by a Picture of Peele Castle': 'Not without hope we suffer and we mourn' (p. 101). This is debatable, but the logic does follow Lawrence Langer's denunciation of humanist discourse in *Admitting the Holocaust* (Oxford: Oxford University Press, 1995). For Langer, the 'persisting myth about the triumph of the spirit'

includes the ideas that hope springs eternal, and mourning might be finite (p. 3).

54. I discuss 'September Song' at length in *Tony Harrison and the Holocaust*, pp. 23–6.

55. Does Romana Huk's delineation of a '"Leeds Renaissance"' (*Critical Anthologies. 1. Tony Harrison*, p. 75) help to explicate this awkward 'pissing'; this fusion of, and frisson between, aesthetics, history and politics in *The Triumph of Love* and Hill's work as a whole? Hill certainly participated, as Huk argues, in an 'upsurge of interest in the international world of art and politics' at the University of Leeds in the 1950s and 1960s. Huk admits that she devised the term 'Leeds Renaissance' only half-seriously; in 'Writing at Leeds 1950–2003', John Barnard adds that it risks homogenising a diverse set of writers into a retrospective construct (*Stand*, 175, 5: 2 [2003], pp. 56–8, p. 57). However, he illustrates that there were shared attitudes between poets such as Harrison, Hill and Silkin, including a commitment to the morality, but also potential inauthenticity, of art, and a dislike of what was perceived as the London establishment. Huk argues in a later essay, 'Poetry of the Committed Individual: Jon Silkin, Tony Harrison, Geoffrey Hill, and the Poets of Postwar Leeds', that '*negotiations* with the vexed idea of commitment' connect the Leeds poets (in *Contemporary British Poetry: Essays in Theory and Criticism*, ed. James Acheson and Romana Huk (New York: State University of New York Press, 1996) pp. 175–220, p. 176). A self-conscious interplay between aesthetics, history and politics is certainly evident in early *Poetry and Audience* poems such as Thomas Blackburn's 'The Clockwork' (17 February 1956, pp. 6–7) – which elegises Sophie Scholl and other German students executed by the Nazi regime – and Silkin's 'Furnished Lives' (2 November 1956, pp. 4–6) about homeless children in London. Harrison, Hill, Silkin, Blackburn and Soyinka's ruminations over the agony of the aesthetic are inevitably influenced by academic debates, given the Leeds poets' association with the university in the 1950s and 1960s, unlike comparable 'Renaissances' such the Hull scene of the 1970s and 1980s. (Hull poets such as Sean O'Brien and Peter Didsbury spent time in pubs such as The Polar Bear and restaurants like Trios, having only had a tangential relationship with the University of Hull due to fleeting meetings with Douglas Dunn – Larkin was a distant figure.) However, many of the Leeds poets and academics whose work featured in *Poetry and Audience* in the 1950s and early 1960s appear to eschew political poetry, such as Keith Waddams, R. C. Cunningham, George Campbell and Edward Morgan. A pseudonymous A. Bludgeon complains (11 May 1956, pp. 6–8) that the magazine printed verse influenced by, not Yeats, Eliot or Auden, but, 'horror of horrors, the Georgians!' The generalisation, at that time, was valid, if only in the pejorative sense of the term. Even Tony Harrison is wary of committed writing: in an editorial from *Poetry and Audience* 7 (1959–60), he writes that if poets are 'socially committed' then they should 'join a welfare organisation and be practical', and that if their ensuing 'Blank Despair is so full of Horror and Torture', then they should kill themselves (p. 2). In contrast, as early as 1955, Hill, in an edition of *Poetry and Audience* devoted entirely to his work (11 November 1955), was displaying a less dismissive awareness of the perils of commit-

ted art in poems such as 'The Distant Fury of Battle', with its ironic reference to the 'profits' of the graves' 'Combine of doves and witnesses' (p. 4).

56. Geoffrey Hill, 'The Art of Poetry LXXX', p. 284.

57. In an editorial (8 November 1957), James Simmons writes: 'My gratitude is due to Mr. Geoffrey Hill for drawing my attention particularly to the last verse of THE TEMPTRESS' (pp. 1–2). It discusses the publication of David Marno's collection *Mandrake Me.*

58. *Shelley's Poetry and Prose*, ed. Donald H. Reiman and Neil Fraistat (London and New York: W.W. Norton and Co., 2002), p. 494.

59. *The Oxford Authors: William Wordsworth*, p. 565 (see Note 16).

60. *The Oxford Authors: William Wordsworth*, p. 567; Geoffrey Hill, *Mercian Hymns* (London: André Deutsch Ltd, 1971). There are no page numbers in *Mercian Hymns*: 'livid/ Thor' is from XXVII. The term 'creative misreadings' comes from Rodney Pybus's article on Hill in *Stand* (p. 33).

61. In 'Quotidian Epic: Geoffrey Hill's *The Triumph of Love*' (*The Yale Journal of Criticism*, 13: 1 [2000], pp. 167–76), Michael Edwards similarly argues that in Hill's opening image there is a 'conflict between the [sun] and compact rain, and, in lividity, the color of wounds and of unhealthy flesh' (p. 168).

62. 'Rede über Lyrik und Gesellschaft', p. 53; 'On Lyric Poetry and Society', p. 41.

63. 'Rede über Lyrik und Gesellschaft', p. 49; 'On Lyric Poetry and Society', pp. 37, 41. Adorno notes, quite simply, that 'the substance of a poem is not merely an expression of individual impulses and experiences'; instead, the lyric is the 'aesthetic test' of Hegel's dialectical proposition that the individual is mediated by the universal, and vice versa ('On Lyric Poetry and Society', pp. 38, 44). The apparent harmoniousness of the lyric thus actually records 'the mutual accord of . . . suffering and love' (p. 40). As opposed to a social analysis of the lyric's 'pathos of detachment', and the critical demand that it be 'virginal', Hill's self-conscious engagement with history in *The Triumph of Love* makes it much easier, of course, to avoid Adorno's critical admonishment that 'Social concepts should not be applied to the works from without but rather drawn from an exacting examination of the works themselves' (pp. 38–9). This self-consciousness risks the charge of solipsism, however, and the fact that the perhaps unseemly attacks on contemporary critics might be anathema to Adorno's vision of autonomous art. Such apparently detrimental tactics can be partly explicated by the fact that Adorno's essay is specific to nineteenth-century German and French poetry, as opposed to a late twentieth-century poet responding to the dangers of narcissism in poetry, the media, and an increasingly philistine culture, as Hill sees it, that luxuriates in a 'desolation of learning' (p. 63).

64. My italics.

65. 'On Lyric Poetry and Society', pp. 47, 49.

66. 'On Lyric Poetry and Society', p. 50; *The Oxford Authors: William Wordsworth*, p. 565. Adorno's 'prosaic life' recalls Wordsworth's disparaging references to 'ordinary intercourse' and 'trivial occupations' in *The Prelude* (p. 565).

67. 'On Lyric Poetry and Society', p. 47.

68. Rowland, p. 26.

69. Naomi Replansky, *The Dangerous World: New and Selected Poems, 1934–1994* (Chicago: Another Chicago Press, 1994), p. 7.

70. Adam Kirsch, 'A Stick to Beat the Century With', *Times Literary Supplement*, 29 January 1999, p. 8.

71. In '"Pardon?" Our Problem with Difficulty (and Geoffrey Hill)', John Lyon reads 'Hauptmann' as referring specifically to Gerhart Hauptmann (1862–1946), a naturalistic playwright, poet and novelist (*Thumbscrew*, 13 [spring/summer 1999], pp. 11–19, p. 18). Hauptmann privately denounced Nazis, but stayed in Germany, and was denigrated by émigrés. Lyon contends that Hill evokes the tragedian because 'an awareness of the naivety of naturalism and of the compromised nature of any art in attempting to treat the Holocaust is present . . . Art is never more suspect than when it claims to be loud and direct.'

72. *The Bronze Horseman: Selected Poems of Alexander Pushkin*, trans. D. M. Thomas (London: Secker and Warburg, 1982), pp. 62–3 (the note is located on p. 259).

73. Lewis Allen (Abel Meeropol), 'Strange Fruit', www.pbs.org/jazz/video/audio_strangefruit.html.

74. Norman Chevers, MD, *Humanity in War* (Calcutta: Baptist Mission Press, 1869), p. 113.

75. *The Bronze Horseman: Selected Poems of Alexander Pushkin*, p. 62; Chevers, p. 115.

76. The reference to '*The Franchise Affair*' helps to unpack the significance of the 'Centrally-placed small round window' which opens the section. In Josephine Tey's *The Franchise Affair* (London: Arrow, 2003 [1949]) – later turned into a film directed by Lawrence Hall in 1950 – Marion Sharpe and her mother lead an unremarkable life at their country home, The Franchise, until the police call with a demure young woman, Betty Kane, who accuses them of kidnap and abuse. She provides a detailed description of the attic room in which she was kept, down to the crack in its round window. Her testimony is disproved by the end of the novel: during her supposed imprisonment in the house, she was actually conducting an affair with a married man.

77. As I argue in relation to 'September Song' in *Tony Harrison and the Holocaust*, 'Like a smug sculptor fashioning the "fatted marble" of Holocaust memorials . . . [the poet] might appear "quietly confident" that they have created a "true" sonnet commensurate to the horror of the atrocity . . . Christopher Ricks complies with this potential obscenity . . . when he contends that Hill "has written the deepest and truest poems"' about the Holocaust (p. 26). Whereas Hill is fully aware of the dangers of artistic complacency in 'September Song' and 'Two Formal Elegies', in 'On Geoffrey Hill' Calvin Bedient counters that this leads to an 'overplayed fastidiousness' in the sonnets; 'too formal-bookish', they mince 'with obscurity' (*Modern Critical Views: Geoffrey Hill*, pp. 101–11), p. 103 (see Note 53).

78. This recalls Paul Celan's '"He who counted our hours/ counts on./ What is he counting, tell me?/ He counts and counts . . ."' (quoted at the end of Władysław Szpilman, *The Pianist*, trans. Anthea Bell (London: Victor Gollancz, 1999 (1946)), p. 212). Wolf Biermann's epilogue attacks (but then uses) 'Numbers. More numbers. Of all the three and a half million Jews who

once lived in Poland, two hundred and forty thousand survived the Nazi period' (p. 212). As Biermann intimates, an appreciation of numbers does not necessarily lead to enlightenment, as Hill argues elsewhere in *The Triumph of Love*. The lines 'African new-old/ holocaust suffers up against/ the all-time Hebrew *shoah*' highlight the debasing propensities of historical comparison when directed by computation alone (p. 65). Possibly referring to Rwanda, the journalistic phrase 'all-time' emphasises the insincerity of creating a league table of atrocity.

79. Adorno contends in 'On Lyric Poetry and Society' that the essence of 'great works of art . . . consists in giving form to the crucial contradictions in real existence' (p. 39). Paradox and oxymoron thus prove critical to the 'great work' of art entitled *The Triumph of Love*. The two terms can be distinguished: paradox refers to an apparent contradiction in a general concept (or concepts), whereas 'oxymoron' is usually applied to two particular words which set up an apparent paradox. Oxymorons in *The Triumph of Love* increase towards the closure, and include 'perfectly imperfected' cadence (p. 60), the 'new-old/ holocaust' (p. 61), 'obtuse wisdom' (p. 62), 'uncommitted writing' (p. 72) and 'unsecured security' (p. 75).

80. Logan detects a 'clumsy echo of Plath' in this line: the reference is to 'Daddy', where the narrator contends that she may well be a Jew (p. 210). Hill's verse 'is embarrassed' at this point, Logan argues, and espouses a 'superiority drenched in the sweat of piety'. The intertextual link may actually be to a possible literary antecedent to Plath's poem: John Berryman's short story 'The Imaginary Jew'. In 'The Imaginary Jew and the American Poet', Hilene Flanzbaum outlines Berryman's position: 'the Jew has become a symbol for the alienated American poet – the symbol for himself' (*The Americanization of the Holocaust*, ed. Hilene Flanzbaum (Baltimore and London: The John Hopkins University Press, 1999), p. 19). Plath's poem may actually be subverting the identity politics of Berryman's short story, in which an Irishman says to the (non-Jewish) protagonist, '"You look like a Jew. You talk like a Jew. You *are* a Jew"' (quoted in Flanzbaum, p. 28). Hill's reference to Berryman or Plath (or both poets) in *The Triumph of Love* constitutes a retort to Longley's implicit suggestion that good poetry can only arise out of personal experience. Hill's marriage might seem to provide him with a personal insight into Jewish history and culture, but he self-consciously undercuts such a potentially crass supposition.

81. To over-differentiate between Ashkenazic and Sephardic Jews would also be problematic: Thomson mentions George Segre, a medical student, who met Jewish refugees from occupied Europe at Turin railway station in summer 1939. Thomson states that, as opposed to the pious Segre, who was familiar with Hebrew, 'Levi showed little interest in helping these East European transients; indeed, he kept a conscious distance from them.' Segre explains: '"To most assimilated Jews these low-classed ragged Ashkenazim were unsavoury – no anti-Semitism is more corrosive than Jewish anti-Semitism"' (p. 97).

82. Toni Morrison, *Beloved* (London: Picador, 1988 [1987]).

83. Tony Harrison, 'The Mother of the Muses', in *The Gaze of the Gorgon* (Newcastle: Bloodaxe, 1992), pp. 38–45.

84. *(Nuit et Brouillard) Night and Fog*, dir. Alain Resnais (1955).

85. The lines from Horace are:

> . . . *quod prius ordine verbum est,*
> *posterius facias, praepones ultima primis,*
> *non, ut si solvas, 'postquam Discordia taetra*
> *belli ferratos postis portasque refregit,'*
> *invenias etiam disjecti membra poetae.*

These are quoted from *The Satires of Horace*, ed. Arthur Palmer (London: Macmillan, 1968), pp. 20–1. Francis Howes's translation is included in *Horace in English*, ed. D. S. Carne-Ross and Kenneth Haynes (London: Penguin, 1996). The full passage is as follows:

> Let every line's arrangement be reversed,
> And place the first word last – the last word first;
> What's the result? – 'Tis poetry no more,
> And therefore was not poetry before.
> Not so – *When Discord brake the ponderous bar*
> *And oped the adamantine gates of War:*
> Here dislocate – distort him, as you will; –
> Tho' piecemeal torn, you see the *Poet* still. (p. 376)

Michael Brown's translation, from *Horace: Satires I* (Warminster: Aris and Phillips, 1993), differs:

> if you stripped away the pattern of quantities and rhythm and put the earlier words later, interchanging the first and last, you wouldn't find – as you would if you broke up 'when once War's iron-clad posts and portals dread Discord broke ope' – the limbs of even a dismembered poet. (p. 47)

86. Ovid, *Metamorphoses*, trans. Mary Innes (London: Penguin, 1955), p. 247.
87. T. S. Eliot, *Selected Poems* (London: Faber, 1961 [1954]), pp. 51, 67.
88. In section X, Hill points to the 'failings' of his time whilst echoing the Horace passage: the 'slow haul' to forgive the shortcomings of Chamberlain is described as placing a 'last' thing 'first'. Both translators of Horace agree that if a good poem's last word is placed first, and vice versa, then the result may be a dismembering of the text, but the core of the poetry still remains. In *The Triumph of Love*, this move leads precisely to the completion of the section. Hill recounts that the phrase 'nation shall rise up against nation' is an example of 'a telling figure out of rhetoric,/ epanalepsis, the same word first and last': section X has the 'same word first and last'; the word in question is, naturally – given the puns throughout the poem – 'last' (p. 4).
89. Gillian Rose, *Mourning Becomes the Law: Philosophy and Representation* (Cambridge: Cambridge University Press, 1996), p. 41.
90. The link between aesthetics, in the form of music, and atrocity lies at the heart of the *The Pianist* (see Note 78), the testimony of Władysław Szpilman, which was filmed by Roman Polanski. In both the book and the film, music and the historical events unfolding outside the studio are initially set at loggerheads: when the Germans invade Warsaw, Szpilman is giving a

Chopin recital at the radio station (p. 38). They gradually intertwine in the narrative as the Germans advance, such as when Szpilman compares the march towards the Marne as culminating in 'the fermata of the second section of Chopin's B minor scherzo' (p. 57). By Chapter 7 he begrudgingly concedes that a jazz band comprising Jewish policemen 'was excellent' (p. 77). His attempts to recall his compositions while starving in a flat towards the end of the war nevertheless echoes the famous passage from *If This Is A Man* when Primo Levi tries to remember a passage from Dante. Civilised art still distinguishes the human from barbaric conduct in both texts; it must also be noted that the references to classical music provide Polanski with an excellent opportunity for a film score in *The Pianist*. Unlike in Levi's book, art betrays the class consciousness of the narrator in Szpilman's testimony: references are made throughout the book to the poorer parts of the ghetto, his connections with the upper echelons of Warsaw society, and the more unfortunate wretches living in Gęsia, Smocza and Zamenhof Streets. His cultured background saves his life: the music-loving Captain Wilm Hosenfeld allows Szpilman to live after he plays Chopin's Nocturne in C sharp minor, whereas a labourer from Smocza may not have sparked such generosity. This highlights Levi's point that the survivors are not the true witnesses of the Holocaust: the survival of Szpilman means that his book necessarily translates into a film account of the Warsaw ghetto better than the imaginary testimony of a labourer shot on the first day of the occupation.

91. Ian Hamilton, 'Between Me and We' (rev. of *The Triumph of Love*), *Sunday Telegraph*, 21 February 1999, p. 12.
92. Theodor Adorno, *Minima Moralia*, trans. E. F. N. Jephcott (London: Verso, 1978 [1951]), pp. 45–6. Rose distinguishes between Fascism, a historically specific phenomenon, and fascism, the triumph of authority, the display of power and 'enraged particular interests' (p. 58); hence my analysis of Constitution Arch as fascistic is not, in this sense, anachronistic.
93. James E. Young, *The Texture of Memory* (Yale: Yale University Press, 1993), p. 70.
94. Hill in interview with Haffenden (p. 94).
95. James E. Young, *At Memory's Edge*, pp. 92–3.
96. *Selected Poems of Thomas Hardy*, ed. P. N. Furbank (London: Macmillan, 1967), p. 61.
97. Thomson, p. 345 (see Note 27).
98. The popularisation of the curse 'May you live in interesting times' may be a corruption of a Chinese saying about not wanting to be 'a man in turbulent times' (see the discussion of Chinese proverbs at www.open-face.ca/~dstephen/chprov.htm).
99. John Barrell, 'Close Reading', in *Literature in the Modern World*, ed. Dennis Walder (Oxford: Oxford University Press, 1990), pp. 131–7.

# Chapter 3

# 'There's something for everyone in a myth': Auschwitz-Birkenau and the Classics in Tony Harrison's *Prometheus*

Melvyn Bragg: 'It was said, I think, by Adorno that there, er, there can be, is no, can be no poetry after Auschwitz, and your response was that there can be only poetry after Auschwitz.'

Tony Harrison: 'I would turn it on its head, yes. I think, I think there is only poetry.'

The exchange above took place during an episode of *The South Bank Show* in 1999. Bragg recognises that Harrison has already responded to Theodor Adorno's warning about 'barbaric' art: references to the Holocaust occur frequently in the poet's work, from the encounter with the survivor of Auschwitz and Buchenwald in the early poem 'Allotments', to the frames of Birkenau in the film/poem *Prometheus*.[1] One of the reasons for this recurrence of Holocaust imagery is repeated during the interview with Bragg. The poet remarks that his grand-dad or school took him to see newsreel of the camps when he was eight years old: the images 'always weighed' on him, and he felt 'the whole idea of life had been blighted'. Susan Sontag experienced a similar shock when she first saw photographs of Bergen-Belsen and Dachau: '"Nothing I have seen – in photographs or in real life – ever cut me as sharply, deeply . . . it seems plausible to me to divide my life into two parts, before I saw those photographs (I was twelve) and after."'[2] Both responses are symptomatic of the secondary witnessing that Dora Apel explores in relation to photography and artwork in *Memory Effects*. In this chapter, I examine the ways in which Harrison, as a secondary witness, represents Auschwitz-Birkenau in *Prometheus*: self-critical, awkward poetics arise when the poet juxtaposes a redemptive scene in the death camp with its subsequent dismissal by one of the film/poem's characters. Harrison's self-conscious critique of his fire metaphor is contrasted with the cinematography, which – with its replication of Holocaust icons – adheres to what Apel terms the 'sacrilized aura' of modernist representations of the camps in photography (p. 117). This chapter then explores the charge of relativism that has been made against *Prometheus*: close readings of the miners' and Io's death scenes illustrate that Harrison draws metaphorical connections (or 'chains') between these sequences and the Auschwitz scene, rather than conflating separate events.

Despite his recognition that secondary witnessing has the potential to 'blight' experience, and 'cut . . . deeply' into the writers' psyches, Harrison replies to the popularisation of Adorno's statement ('there . . . can be no poetry after Auschwitz') with the bold retort that there 'is only poetry' after the advent of the Holocaust. This self-assurance diverges from Harrison's more tentative statement in 1987 that poetry is only '*maybe . . . one* medium which could concentrate our attention on our worst experiences without leaving us with the feeling . . . that life . . . has had its affirmative spirit burnt out'.[3] His confidence in the genre partly derives from the influence of classical myth and drama on his work: Harrison has always celebrated the ability of Greek tragedy to discuss atrocities in full daylight, with the open eyes of the tragic mask. The classics have also determined his agonised humanism (which I discuss in *Tony Harrison and the Holocaust*), and its desire to register 'the seismic events of the twentieth century, which we're still quaking from', without negating the hope that 'creative memory' might 'allow the suffering to be shared and made bearable across great gaps of time'.[4] The last comment puts Harrison at odds with critics such as Lawrence Langer who argue that proper reflection on the events of 1933 to 1945 should cancel out any possibility of a humanist 'triumph of the spirit' in the post-Holocaust era.[5] In this chapter, I investigate the tensions between Harrison's classical influences in *Prometheus* (including humanism and the deployment of myth), and the representation of Auschwitz on three occasions in the film/poem. The film includes several shots of Auschwitz-Birkenau taken on location, but there are also two other, metaphorical connections with the camp: firstly, in the disturbing scene in which miners are melted into bullion; secondly, in the equally unsettling sequence where several cows, and the character Io, are killed in a slaughterhouse.

Problems surrounding commemorations of the human spirit in the context of the Holocaust are not limited to post-Holocaust literature. In *The Periodic Table*, Primo Levi demonstrates how his faith in humanism is challenged when he begins to correspond with Doktor L. Müller, a former employee at the Buna plant at Auschwitz. Levi is wary of meeting Müller because he distracts him, and interests him 'more *as a man* than as an opponent'.[6] On the same page of the 'Vanadium' section, however, Levi is disgruntled that the German chemist attributes 'the events at

Auschwitz to Man, without differentiation'. Levi is tempted to think about Müller as a human specimen rather than a pawn of Nazism, but he is also unsettled by the idea that the latter specificity might be elided by the chemist's attempt to blame the human race for Auschwitz. Hence Levi can correspond with the chemist 'man to man', yet he is also appalled that Müller attempts to cancel the distance between Germans employed at Buna and the Jewish prisoners. Müller notes that 'In May of 1944 he had been able . . . to have his status as a chemist recognised', as Levi does in Buna; the former inmate's disapproval of the comparison between them is registered with his ironic, parenthetical interjection, 'like me!' His correspondent's Christian humanism argues for the retention of 'precious human values' in the midst of brutality: Levi sends him a German copy of *If This Is A Man*; Müller perceives in the book 'a fulfil-ment of the Christian precept to love one's enemies, and a testimony of faith in Man' (p. 185). Levi counteracts the misreadings with an asser-tion that 'every German must answer for Auschwitz, indeed every man' (p. 187). The main difference between the two ideological perspectives is that Müller's Christian humanism attempts to exculpate both him, and Germans in general, whereas Levi blames Müller and all the other 'unarmed' who 'clear the road' for dictators. Nevertheless, there remains an uneasy slippage between 'every German' and 'every man' for a writer whose faith in humanism tempts him to think about enemies as humans first, and opponents afterwards.

In many of the post-Holocaust poems I analyse in *Tony Harrison and the Holocaust*, awkward poetics arise out of the friction between the poet's humanist desire to celebrate the 'spirit', and the difficulties of rep-resenting twentieth-century atrocities. *Prometheus* continues this process by attempting to forge a humanist dialectic in which redemptive sequences are integrated with reminders of 'seismic events'. Awkward poetics then arise out of the self-conscious juxtaposition, and subversion, of individual scenes. An unremittingly pessimistic undercurrent unsettles the narrative: the Birkenau sequence initially celebrates 'creative memory' in the form of redemptive candles and, by proxy, the film/poem itself, but this idealist impetus is then undercut by the subsequent scene – which indicates that ideological might always triumph over humanist niceties – and the film's overall recognition of art's inability to avert 'seismic events'. Steve Padley registers Harrison's struggle with the humanist dialectic when he comments that *Prometheus* is '[Harrison's] most ambitious and complex exploration of the role of art as a means of affirmation and commemoration of the human spirit at the end of a century of mass destruction and suffering on an unimaginable scale'.[7] However, several reviewers of the film/poem disagree with Padley's ref-

erence to the film's complexity in engaging with the 'spirit': Wally
Hammond is critical of the film/poem's 'creaky' visuals, and regards it as
'Dramatically . . . turgid'; Mark Ford evaluates it as 'not nearly as powerful as earlier Harrison theatre and film scripts . . . as a cinematic experience the film is rather dull'; Herbert Lomas insists that it is 'plotless,
storyless', and reiterates 'banalities'.[8]

*Prometheus* is not without its faults – the second half of the film/poem,
for example, is over-long – but I argue nevertheless in this chapter that
Harrison's re-imagining of classical myth is astonishingly ambitious.
Awkward poetics figure differently – and more implicitly – in the
film/poem, however, than in the open splenetic of *The Triumph of Love*.
Like Sylvia Plath's camp poetics, representations of the Holocaust in
*Prometheus* are bound up with the voice of an intermediary. Harrison's
workbooks for the film/poem numbered 3 and 4 illustrate that Hermes
– whose voice dominates the final cut – became a much more prominent
character in *Prometheus* as the drafts developed. In contrast, workbook
2 explores the possibility of a multivocal *Prometheus*, which might have
included 'interviews with miners on [their] last day at [the] mine' (p.
263), 'THE VOICE OF AESCHYLUS PROMPTING' the miners (p.
314) and 'Voices inside the Head of PROMETHEUS' (p. 362); in workbook 3, the Boy '"interprets" for the statue and Aeschylus comes out
Yorkshire', as in '"tell Zeus to go and fuck 'issen!"' (p. 599). Although
the characters in the final cut are self-conscious about their tribulations
– Hermes often addresses the audience directly – they do not (unlike the
voices in *The Triumph of Love*) comment on aesthetic risks in the production of the text itself. Hermes's vicious verbal attacks on the subju-
gated characters in *Prometheus* would be unlikely, of course, to
encompass ruminations on the exploitative nature of art, in contrast to
the earlier Harrison play *The Trackers of Oxyrhynchus*, with its satyr
refrain that 'Summat's been flayed/ for this sweet serenade'.[9] The alter-
cation between Hermes and the Old Man in the cinema calls attention to
the medium, but – unlike the splenetic voice in *The Triumph of Love* –
the characters do not explore the film's potential 'barbarism' in its
deployment of Auschwitz to demonstrate the applicability of the
Promethean metaphor.[10] This is not to suggest that film/poems are necessarily inferior to narrative poems, or that *Prometheus* is devoid of self-
critique: Harrison implicitly registers the film's 'barbarism' with the
juxtaposition of scenes in the Auschwitz sequence, rather than through
the characters' dialogue. Workbook 2 reveals that Harrison was originally toying with the idea of directly engaging with art's exploitation of
suffering in his rendition of Aeschylus, since he has circled, and marked,
a handwritten note: 'the cruelty underlying all ART' (p. 358). Workbook

4 critiques 'HARMONY', the title Zeus 'prefers to give his reign', but Harrison simply chooses not to stress a connection in the final cut – as he does in *The Trackers of Oxyrhynchus* – with the concept of artistic 'harmony', that might similarly veil 'a multitude of wrongs' (p. 753).

Harrison's decision not to engage self-consciously with art's exploitation of suffering in *Prometheus* nevertheless leaves the film/poem open to the (incorrect) charge of relativism. Levi's refusal to attribute Auschwitz 'to Man' in *The Periodic Table* – even though 'every man' must 'answer' for it – indicates the dangers of one relativist approach to the Holocaust, in which various atrocities are regarded equally as temporary aberrations from humanity's advance. In his introduction to *Theoretical Interpretations of the Holocaust*, Dan Stone is adamant that his authors do not 'use the Holocaust as a "topic" on to which they can attach their particular hobby horse'. This statement arises just after a quotation from an article on environmental damage, where the writer connects '"the burnt bodies of Jews . . . unavoidably not only to the vaporized bodies of children in Hiroshima, but also to the bleeding bodies of the American Indian and the corpses of hundreds of millions of buffalo, bears, and wolves"'.[11] The adverb 'unavoidably' hides a contentious slippage between different phenomena. An unsympathetic critic might similarly charge Harrison with insensitivity towards historical contingencies, since the poet has a tendency to connect such events as the Holocaust, the dropping of the atom bomb, and the fire bombing of Dresden and Hamburg under the auspices of the fire metaphor that extends throughout his work. However, Harrison's post-Holocaust poems, whilst risking inappropriate linkages, usually outline differences, as well as similarities, between historical and mythical events. *Prometheus* is no exception; a fruitful tension develops between the mythic method and historical specificity. A deliberately provocative slippage between the latter categories is illustrated when Harrison comments in interview that '"I've always been obsessed with Dresden, that a place destroyed by fire has all these Promethean images. For me, that's why Zeus had it destroyed."' Nicholas Lezard, the interviewer, points out that 'Those who have other, more conventional explanations for Dresden's destruction might raise an eyebrow.'[12] The intertwining of myth and history in *Prometheus* results in an ingenious, but extensive, metaphorical chain which envelops the Titan's theft of fire from Zeus, the mining industry, pollution, smoking, a foundry, factories, poetic inspiration, Auschwitz, Dresden, steelworks, crematoria and cavemen. The dizzying ingenuity with which these connections are made in the screenplay, dialogue and digital editing also leaves the film/poem open to the charge of relativism: Keith Miller detects arrogance in Harrison's conflation of all '"the big themes of the past 100 years into one enormous supermyth: Orgreave to Auschwitz via Dresden, all aboard!"'.[13]

Hill's insistence in *The Triumph of Love* that the Holocaust can be contextualised in relation to other twentieth-century atrocities provides one defence for Harrison's inclusive fire metaphor. Hill's imaginative 'palimpsests' in his long poem are also similar to the metaphorical chains that Harrison draws on in his work; *Prometheus* forms the apotheosis of this artistic method. Defending the individual – here in the guise of the Titan – against a chain of injustices, and atrocities, also forms one impetus for the 'committed' Leeds poetry of the 1950s and 1960s, which includes Hill's and Harrison's early work: Jon Silkin reveals that the journal *Stand* began in 1952 because he 'lived in a society marked by its casual indifference to the individual and his [sic] suffering . . . For some the victim is seen in focus most sharply in the context of the concentration camp.'[14] The critic Lorna Hardwick exculpates Harrison's metaphorical comparisons in the context of the film/poem's main classical intertext, Aeschylus's play *Prometheus Bound*, rather than the Leeds poets' sense of the increasing dissolution of the particular. Hardwick discusses various versions of the Prometheus myth and Aeschylus: she notes that Richard Schechner's staging of *The Prometheus Project* in 1985 was criticised for the 'attempted moral conflation of the bombing of Hiroshima and sexual abuse', but points out that in Aeschylus's play 'the treatment of Prometheus and Io is structurally and metaphorically linked in that both cases stem from Zeus's misuse of power.' If Aeschylus deploys metaphor so inclusively, the argument goes, then Schechner and Harrison should be allowed to do the same. A critic such as Elie Wiesel, who insists on the non-comparability of the Holocaust, might retort that the events of 1933 to 1945 are different from those of the fourth century BC. In contrast, *Prometheus* revels in a myth's ability to incite ingenious comparisons, challenging the notion of the 'Holocaust sublime' with its provocative connections between Io, miners and Auschwitz inmates.

The coterminous possibilities of metaphorical inclusiveness and relativism are ingrained into Harrison's working methods. In the introduction to the screenplay, Harrison eulogises digital editing, and its ability to call up clusters of poetic images, feeding his 'deep-rooted way of letting disparate images grow together' (p.xxiv). Michael Kustow, the executive producer for *Prometheus*, reports that the poet set off on a lone '"recce"' of Europe before the filming began, and recalls Harrison's excitement at returning with 'trophies' of Promethean iconography; their London office contains 'a Prometheus cigarette lighter from Japan, and issues of a bondage magazine called *Prometheus*, presumably because he was bound to a rock'.[15] Hence workbook 3 contains four pages of pictures of Prometheus lighters (pp. 572–5), and three pages of Prometheus cigars (pp. 576–9). A box of Titan matches (p. 994), and 'Black Cat' safety matches 'Found at Auschwitz 96' (p. 812), are pasted into workbook 4. (The former 'trophy' finds its visual equivalent in the film/poem when the Boy chooses between 'Eagle' and 'Titan' matches.) Kustow's recalling of the 'recce' is followed by his statement that 'There's something for everyone in a myth', which confirms the democratic nature of the story of Prometheus that Hans Blumenberg investigates so exhaustively in *Work on Myth*.[16] However, collated iconography does not necessarily translate into cogent metaphor, as Padley contends in a review of Harrison's collection *Laureate's Block*, which contains poems with a 'litany of metaphors . . . too many variations on a flimsy theme'.[17] The possibility that the ingenious fire metaphor might similarly provide 'too many variations' in *Prometheus* links with Neil Corcoran's assertion that Harrison's later poetry lacks sufficient '"inwardness"'.[18] *Prometheus* certainly risks presenting an indiscriminate list of Promethean metaphors as the film detours 'through some of [Europe's] blackest black spots, like a package deal sold by a demonic travel agent', but the film/poem does display 'inwardness' in its self-critique of the fire metaphor in the context of Auschwitz, the excision of a song which was originally part of the sequence in the camp, and the overall sense of art's inefficacy.[19] This chapter also defends Harrison against the charge of relativism, since that charge suggests that the poet completely elides historical specificities: both *The Triumph of Love* and *Prometheus* indicate that although history's 'black spots' can be conjoined with imaginative palimpsests or metaphorical chains, these 'seismic events' also maintain exclusivity.

Holocaust poets and novelists such as Levi, Tadeusz Borowski, Jerzy Ficowski, Miklós Radnóti and Zbigniew Herbert have also had to confront the dangers of there being 'something for everyone in a myth'.[20] *The Odyssey* provides a framework for Levi to illustrate his exploits on his return from Auschwitz in *The Truce*: Russian soldiers are 'like Ulysses' companions after the ships had been pulled ashore'; the Soviet Union has 'a Homeric capacity for joy and abandon'.[21] The classics provide appropriate comparisons, but also initiate a distancing effect that both explains, and does not explain, the significance of Levi's Homeric journey. One of the first classical references in *If This Is A Man* illustrates this paradox. After his arrival at Auschwitz, Levi is loaded onto a lorry with thirty other prisoners: a 'strange guard' asks if they have any money or watches to give to him in a 'small private initiative of our Charon' (p. 27). This courteous pillaging transposes the booty with the fare of one silver obol that the mythical Charon demanded to transport the soul across the Acheron and Styx. The reference accrues resonance through an understanding of other aspects of the myth. Charon steers his boat, but does not row it, 'as this task was given to the souls of the dead': this reflects the prisoners' inevitable compliance as they reach the end of a tortuous journey, and are deposited into a confusing world of 'strange individuals' with 'comic berets' (p. 26).[22] At the same time, other characteristics of Charon limit Levi's comparison. The inmates are surprised that the German soldier does not shout 'threats of damnation', but asks for the treasure 'courteously': this grates against the mythical Charon, named after his bright eyes ('chara', meaning joy or delight, and 'ops', 'eye'), who revels in his macabre work.[23] Problems are thus evident in the malleability of classical references: whereas Levi compares a Nazi to the mythical boatman, the poet Jerzy Ficowski alludes to Charon in relation to a Jewish figure in '5.8.1942, In Memory of Janusz Korczak'. Korczak ran orphanages in Warsaw, and accompanied his staff and children to Treblinka. He refused opportunities to be smuggled into the 'Ayran' part of Warsaw: Ficowski likens Korczak's heroism to a 'Charon of his own free will', as he directs his orphans during the deportation.[24] The allusion is apt in its image of Korczak leading the children to their death, but also inappropriate in terms of his selfless bravery, as opposed to the boatman who delights in his services to the dead, and requires recompense with the obol.

The fact that Charon can be deployed to describe both a Jewish hero and a strange Nazi demonstrates the freedom, and trappings, of classical iconography. As Daniel R. Schwarz argues, the classics and other epic antecedents – such as *The Divine Comedy* – place the *Lager* experience 'in a Western context' in *The Truce*, but Levi 'cannot sustain the effort to use mythic methods to give shape and significance to the moral anarchy he observes'.[25] Awkwardness arises when the confusions of his post-Auschwitz experience are related through mythological signs, as in the passage from *The Truce* I analyse in *Tony Harrison and the Holocaust*, where the world returns 'to primeval Chaos', and everyone searches anxiously for 'his own place . . . as the particles of the four elements are described as doing in the verse-cosmogonies of the Ancients' (p. 208).[26] The language is strained, embarrassing and paradoxical, as Levi attempts to make sense of his experiences with the detritus of humanism and the classics. At the beginning of this paragraph from *The Truce*, Levi notes that he 'cannot remember exactly how and when my Greek sprang up from nowhere': the translation is ambiguous, and could refer to the mythological references to follow, or the introduction of 'the Greek' a page later, Mordo Nahum, with whom he spent 'an unforgettable week of vagabondage' (p. 209). In *If This Is A Man*, the Greek characters are inseparable from Levi's faith in civilisation, humanism and the

classics: 'their aversion to gratuitous brutality, their amazing consciousness of the survival of at least a potential human dignity made of the
Greeks the most coherent national nucleus in [the] Lager, and in this
respect, the most civilised' (p. 85). Classical references function in the
same way as the Greek characters in *If This Is A Man*, since they signal
that fragments of civilisation do survive in the midst of the camp. They
also provide a rejoinder to the Nazis' appropriation of classical imagery
for their own purposes. This links with Herbert's contention that the
classics exude 'human dignity', seriousness, strict objectivity, and universal appeal; however, this potential universality was precisely exploited by
the Nazis' appropriation of myth.[27] Adorno criticises the idea that the
classics might be 'innocent' as an adherence to 'epic naiveté', and appeals
to their supratemporal applicability as 'sloppy' transcendentalism.[28]
Nevertheless, in 'Why the Classics?', Herbert argues that attention to
myth alongside history in poetry means that 'even the shriek of terror is
transformed into a cry of hope'.[29] This reflects Levi's refusal to eschew
his humanism on even the 'darkest days' in Auschwitz, by always recognising 'in my companions and in myself, men, not things' (p. 398).
Harrison, like Levi and Herbert, stubbornly preserves humanist beliefs
in his art, despite any dangers of relativism that might arise in the deployment of classical references. This preservation bolsters his confidence
that poetry can allow suffering 'to be shared and made bearable across
great gaps of time'. However, Harrison's retort to Adorno ('only poetry')
is tempered when the poet and film crew enter the gates of Auschwitz-
Birkenau.

## Redemption, Christ and Auschwitz-Birkenau

Miller's detection of relativism in *Prometheus* ('Orgreave to Auschwitz
via Dresden') refers to different locations in the film/poem, which begins
in Yorkshire and then follows a golden statue of the Titan hero on its
journey from the Humber to Greece. Miller suggests that the fire metaphor encourages a lack of specificity: the decline of the coal industry
equates with the fire bombing of the German city, and the crematoria in
the Polish camp. A detailed analysis of the Auschwitz scene demonstrates
that there is no 'equation' at this point in the film: the awkward striving
towards redemption is subverted in the subsequent scenes, which emphasise the triumph of ideological will over moments of humanist remembrance. Harrison's attempt to forge a humanist dialectic in the midst of
Birkenau is compromised, as the director himself admits when he says he
could not find a reason to 'sing' in Auschwitz. 'Inwardness' occurred

during the editing of the film in relation to a scene in which an actor sang on the rail tracks of Birkenau: this footage was cut from the final version of *Prometheus* (along with another thirty-six hours of film in total), and substituted with a moving scene in which a Jewish visitor walks through the camp, accompanied by classical music; this culminates in an astonishing crane shot in which candles of remembrance are placed beneath the statue of Prometheus, and reflected in its golden sheen.[30] The candles can be read – in the context of the rest of the film – as symbols of redemption, and as referring outwards to other historical phenomena. Awkward poetics arise out of the juxtaposition of this scene with Hermes's subsequent diatribe, followed by a controversial, anti-redemptive image of Christ. The latter frames encompass the pessimistic side of Harrison's agonised humanism: they then reflect back on the preceding scenes in Auschwitz, making the celebration of redemption appear desperate almost to the point of self-parody.

In contrast with the frame of Christ, the lingering shot of the 'Yohrzeit' ('remembrance') candles may seem uncontroversial. Like the emotive John Williams scores in the relevant Steven Spielberg films, the crescendo of strings indicates exactly how the viewer should respond emotionally to the crane shot. However, if the frame is read in the context of the subsequent scenes, the music seems almost ironic in its fraught attempt to celebrate a 'triumph of the spirit' in the context of the Holocaust. The score's initial bid to incite emotion, and its subsequent subversion, links with the use of extradiegetic music in Alain Resnais's film *Night and Fog*: André Pierre Colombat argues that this director 'refuses to impose upon his spectator any sentimental or lyrical attitude traditionally conveyed by the easy use of affective adjectives, pathetic music, a linear chronology or the domination of only one significant series'. Initially, it appears that, unlike *Prometheus*, the awkward poetics of *Night and Fog* encourage frequent 'Inversions, encounters, distancing, constant interpretation and ruptures of signifying series'.[31] However, Hermes's dialogue deliberately undercuts Harrison's score: the subsequent scenes rupture the attempt at redemption, making the initial celebration of the 'spirit' appear even more desperate. Rather than encountering 'ruptures of signifying series' in Harrison's metaphorical chains as a whole, though, the inclusiveness of the fire metaphor in *Prometheus* encourages the critic to look beyond Auschwitz, and connect the frame to other instances of candles and fires of remembrance. The crane shot links with previous adaptations of Aeschylus's play: Hardwick discusses Tom Paulin's *Seize the Fire*, commissioned by the BBC in 1989, which ends with a fade to a dark background, 'relieved only by pinpoints of light – candles, the touch of the director, Tony Coe'. Hardwick argues that this conclusion 'creates an unforgettable resonance with the candle-carrying protestors in Wenceslas Square before the fall of the Soviet-dominated regime in the former Czechoslovakia'. As Harrison points out in the introduction to the screenplay for *Prometheus*, 'images of torches in procession, the destructive element as a redemptive symbol, is paralleled in the way Jewish Pilgrims to Auschwitz place *Yohrzeit* (Remembrance) candles in the ovens' (p. xxi). The viewer shifts between thinking about the frame as specific to the camp, and the 'obsessional function' of the fire metaphor in the film/poem as a whole.[32]

In *At Memory's Edge*, James E. Young argues that postmemory artists share a 'categorical rejection of art's traditional redemptory function' because the notion that 'suffering might be redeemed by its aesthetic reflection . . . is simply intolerable'.[33] Harrison's initial attempt to celebrate the 'triumph of the spirit' in the form of the 'Remembrance' candles would appear – if taken out of the context of the subsequent scenes – to be at odds with what Young terms our 'decidedly antiredemptory age'. An unsympathetic critic might then summarise the 'Yohrzeit' scene as a 'disconcertingly self-satisfied' appropriation of history.[34] The scene interprets remembrance as redemption, and appears symptomatic of Harrison's bold response ('only poetry') to Adorno's supposed maxim that there 'can be no poetry after Auschwitz'. The reduction of the philosopher's statement to a binary (poems or no poems) seems to result in the elision of Adorno's critique of 'barbaric' poetry. Unlike *The Triumph of Love*, *Prometheus* does not seem, initially, to display an awareness of its own aesthetic dilemma, the possibility that it might be an instance of 'barbaric' art which squeezes 'beauty or pleasure' out of Auschwitz as an 'extension' of Nazi crimes.[35] However, the subsequent scenes do demonstrate Harrison's awareness of the limitations of his own classical model. This wariness is immediately demonstrated in Hermes's speech after the crane shot: awkward poetics arise at the moment Hermes offers the gods' counterpoint to Harrison's humanist impetus; the messenger announces that 'Fuhrer [*sic*] Zeus' hates 'Jews flaunting' fire's 'sacramental use' and that every '"human rights abuse"'/ had its proud origin in Zeus'.[36] Workbook 4 includes the first draft of this scene, with a close-up on Hermes's '"fascist" caduceus snuffing one candle': the messenger 'has a snuffing frenzy', while Kratos and Bia 'stamp on' the candles, and 'kick them off the trailer' (p. 811). Hermes's monologue in the final cut counts as 'inwardness' in that it refers self-consciously to the previous frame, adding that the murders at Auschwitz compare with all instances of Zeus's power. As opposed to Harrison's self-conscious critique of remembrance and redemption in the context of Auschwitz, Hermes encourages relativism by proposing that all atrocities can be subsumed under the mantle of Zeus's violation of human rights. Following Müller's shift between the particular ('Auschwitz') and general ('Man') in Levi's *The Periodic Table*, the specific camp becomes an illustration of Zeus's wider plan to dump humanity 'in a mass pit', and create a less rebellious race of beings.

Awkward poetics – in the form of this precarious balance between remembrance, and the recognition of 'seismic events' – highlight the 'inwardness' that Harrison displays when he attempts to bring the humanist tenets of hope and redemption inside Auschwitz-Birkenau. *Prometheus Bound* celebrates the first tenet with the Titan's gift of 'blind hopefulness' – before fire – to humankind (p. 28). Aeschylus's original trilogy of plays also looks forward to the redemptive moment when Io's child, Heracles, will free Prometheus from the rock, and initiate the demise of Zeus's power. In *Prometheus Unbound*, Shelley draws on the revolutionary connotations of Aeschylus's play (it was, allegedly, Marx's favourite drama): Demogorgon implores the audience at the end of the fourth act to 'defy Power which seems Omnipotent;/ To love, and bear; to hope, till Hope creates/ From its own wreck the thing it contemplates' (p. 286). Harrison registers Shelley's influence on *Prometheus* in the introduction to his screenplay, noting that the Prometheus myth seems to be reworked more frequently during periods of social upheaval: the repercussions of the French Revolution are compared to the decline of the coal industry and socialism.[37] The introduction also appears to replicate Aeschylus and Shelley's hopefulness in its appeal to allow 'suffering to be shared and made bearable across great gaps of time'. In contrast, the film itself is resistant to this idealism. *Prometheus* ends on a much bleaker note than much of Harrison's earlier poetry and film/poems. Harrison's humanist dialectic is illustrated in the balancing of doves and hawks at the end of *The Shadow of Hiroshima*, whereas *Prometheus* concludes with self-critique, questioning art's impact on society (rather than the possibility of prurient piety in the film/poem itself). A fire engine stands outside a decrepit cinema; inside, the Old Man is about to be consumed by flames. Miraculously, the defunct fire engine has moved from the scrap yard to the cinema: whereas this demonstrates the powers of artifice, it is immediately undermined by the fact that it cannot put out the flames. As with Bia's use of string quartet music to tranquillise him during his murderous journey across Europe, the inference is that art is helpless to avert historical atrocities; moreover, it can be manipulated by those that initiate them. The Old Man's grandchild runs off down the street: he may wish his 'suffering to be shared', but this cannot hide the fact that, by the end of the film, his family has been almost entirely wiped out. His grandfather is burnt in the cinema, his mother has been executed in a slaughterhouse, and his father has been 'killed' twice; once, by being melted in a furnace, and secondly, in the recycled form of the Prometheus statue destroyed in Greece.

This pessimistic ending is compounded by Harrison's (correct) decision to excise the song from the Auschwitz-Birkenau scene: the precarious balance between the candle shot and subsequent scenes may well have tipped into self-parody if the song had been included alongside the crescendo of strings. Kustow suggests in *The Observer* article that the singing would have accompanied shots of Birkenau: Auschwitz 'seems almost a kindly environment', he writes, compared 'with this vast windswept field wrapped in barbed wire and lined with shacks. There is such hopelessness it stops your heart.' Kustow and Harrison react to this bleak atmosphere, in contrast with the museum and 'Austro-Hungarian brick barracks' at Auschwitz:

> Tony sets up to film an emotional song about death-fire and remembrance-fire, which Robert Tear has pre-recorded. The crew collects around the actor Richard Blackford, who composed the song. Richard treads the railway lines towards the retreating Steadicam, lip-synching to Tear's voice. In the dank air we do it three, five, seven times, as if to keep doing it so intently was to keep at bay the despair of the place. Eventually, Tony takes out the song altogether. 'I couldn't find a reason to break into song in Auschwitz,' he says.

Shots of the 'Jewish Pilgrim' and rail tracks remain, but the song has gone: the crane shot of the candles is left to provide the only remnant of hope with its depiction of 'remembrance-fire'. Inwardness in the form of editing produces instead a wordless sequence in which the Pilgrim moves, it seems, towards Birkenau, accompanied by a classical score. This scene appears to capture the self-evident 'hopelessness' of the 'vast windswept' camp; however, in a sense, the score's crescendo – as the camera pans down the statue towards the candles – offers the redemptive equivalent of breaking 'into song at Auschwitz'. Harrison's comment that he could not 'break into song' suggests his recognition of a tension between aesthetics and atrocity: the juxtaposition of the strained crescendo of strings with the subsequent scenes then fulfils Adorno's notion of self-critical, 'barbaric' art.[38]

Workbook 4 contains a draft of the missing song, which eventually became part of Richard Blackford's major choral work *Voices of Exile*.[39] This workbook twice presents the Pilgrim as, alternatively, a cantor, someone who directs the singing of a congregation in church, or prayers in a synagogue (pp. 811, 858). Although the critic has to be wary of evaluating the song out of the context of the excised footage (and its score), the cantor's diction indicates that awkwardness would have arisen in the form of heightened rhetoric: the first verse refers to '[the candles'] burning, yes, but to invoke/ the souls who passed along these tracks/ to a destiny of smoke' (p. 858). Composed in the ballad form of iambic tetrameters and trimeter, the stanzas ruminate on the connections between the redemptive candles and crematoria ovens: Wordsworth's daffodils are replaced with the 'dancing eyes of candle flame' that 'reclaim/ the souls trapped in the blaze'. The redemptive moments are carefully qualified in the song, as in the scene in the final cut: the candles' flickering is 'frail', as are, by insinuation, aesthetic attempts at remembrance. Nevertheless, to 'reclaim' – to win back something – sounds hopelessly idealist in this context; a subjunctive would have registered a tentative attempt at reclamation (but upset the tetrameter), whereas the infinitive suggests the possibility of what Young terms an 'intolerable' act of redemption. The 'burning flickering' in the second verse is also meant to 'reclaim' lost souls, and, in addition, 'redeem': murdered inmates are 'saved', or 'compensated for' – the usual meanings of 'redeemed' – with the candles, which salve the 'rusted heart of Man'. Similarly, in the penultimate stanza, 'souls are lost' in the 'cooled blaze' (of the crematoria?), 'unless a hand pluck a brief candle/ from the hell of Holocaust' (p. 859). The conjunction indicates that 'so many millions' who 'left as smoke' will be forgotten unless acts of remembrance are repeated, as in the placing of candles in the crematorium in Auschwitz, or, by proxy, in the form of artworks such as the song, and the film/poem itself. The sentimentality evident in these lyrics is evidence of a (deliberately) desperate attempt to redeem the 'rusted heart of Man' (p. 858) in a post-Holocaust context. Awkward poetics, if the song had been included, would have counterbalanced the song's heightened rhetoric with Hermes's subsequent action and dialogue: a candle is 'suddenly snuffed by the <u>caduceus</u> of Hermes' in workbook 4 (p. 861); in the final cut, he rages against the foolhardiness of redemptive acts.

If awkward poetics skilfully balance the strained attempts at redemption in the Auschwitz scene with Hermes's diatribe, the frame that follows his monologue displays the metaphorical chain's ability to court controversy. This shot depicts a factory chimney in Nowa Huta (Poland); the camera pans down to a crucifix of Christ. Simultaneously, the statue is superimposed onto the chimney, so that smoke seems to be emanating from the crucifix; this is followed by a shot of a 'Non Stop' sign. The frame invites multiple readings. Perhaps it is meant to comprise a POV (Point of View) shot from Hermes's perspective, following on from his previous monologue; in the subsequent shot, he is seated in the 'Non Stop' bar. Hermes's voiceover before the Auschwitz scene ends with the sentiment that 'Zeus approved . . . and endorsed/ the Führer's flames of

. . . Holocaust': the last word lingers in the sound mix with the next shot of the Jewish Pilgrim; this suggests that the entire sequence may be figured from the messenger's perspective, just as, in workbook 1, 'the [original] play takes place as if bugged by ZED [Zeus]' (p. 54). According to this reading, the chimney represents ongoing atrocities, and Zeus's violation of humanity; its denotation of pollution resonates with Hermes's dream of a 'universal emphesyma [*sic*]' (p. 63). A subtle visual linkage is established during Hermes's following speech: a shot of the factory through net curtains connects with an earlier, fleeting shot of a similar curtain casting shadows in the Old Man's house, as a symbol of his lung disease caused by smoking, and (possibly) a life spent down the mines. (The actor Walter Sparrow, who played this character, 'died of lung cancer soon after the film was made'.[40]) One of Harrison's photograph albums, entitled 'Poland 1', anticipates this subtlety with two photographs of net curtains, and the smoking chimney underneath the latter.

The framing device of the Prometheus myth indicates that Harrison, rather than portraying Hermes's perspective, may primarily be drawing parallels between Christ and the Titan in this controversial frame. Shelley's version of the myth adheres to this parallelism in *Prometheus Unbound*: the Titan is enveloped in 'A robe of envenomed agony' and a 'crown of pain'; this fuses a reference to Nessus's shirt of fire with Christ's 'gorgeous robe' and crown of thorns.[41] Philip Vellacott's translation of Aeschylus also draws attention to the links between Christ and Prometheus in his use of the word 'crucified' to describe the Titan's plight.[42] A passage in workbook 4 establishes these connections at an early stage in the planning of the film/poem: Harrison notes that Christ is 'nailed to a cross', 'not a rock', but the planned shot at Nowa Huta 'just might/ be Prometheus in disguise'; both figures are described as 'usurpers' (p. 815). A drawing with the note 'P. betwixt crucifix & smoke' indicates that the link could have been made more blatantly than in the final cut; one character (presumably Hermes) on p. 814 'pokes Christ in side – (spear) with caduceus'. The sketches on page 815 arise out of the 'recce' pictures in the photograph album 'Poland 1': this includes six photographs of the crucifix with the chimney on the right hand side of the frame, followed by two shots of the partially obscured chimney, so that the smoke appears to emanate from Christ's head. Despite this clear metaphorical connection, the absence of awkward poetics in the silent frame of Christ is disquieting, since, as Bryan Cheyette points out in relation to George Steiner's work, 'For Steiner, the Judaic rejection of Christ led directly to the death camps.'[43] If the frame comprises a POV shot from Hermes's perspective, the anti-Semitic *mise en scène* may suggest that the murders at Auschwitz were a reprisal for the crucifixion. Like Marc Chagall's painting *White Crucifixion*, the controversial frame could also be read as forcing Christians 'to witness the Holocaust and be found wanting'.[44] Awkward poetics could then be regarded as arising, not in the frame itself, but in its juxtaposition with the earlier attempt at redemption in Birkenau: Harrison's humanist dialectic encompasses the sacred image of 'a redemptive figure' who 'has been overwhelmed'; this counterpoint to the candle shot suggests that the Holocaust comprises 'the beginning of a disastrous period in history'.[45]

The image of the crucifix may also be read as a reclamation of Christ as a murdered Jew – Chagall inscribes INRI on the cross, abbreviating the Latin for 'Jesus of Nazareth King of the Jews' – or suggest that the Son of God provides a symbol for the destruction – following Müller – of 'Man' at Auschwitz.[46] Then again, the frame could be interpreted as an ironic comment on the attempted appropriation of Auschwitz for Christian purposes. Originally, the museum at Auschwitz celebrated Polish nationalism, and subsumed the fact that around 90 per cent of the victims of the camp were Jewish by emphasising only general victims of Fascism. A monument to the Jewish victims arose in the form of a barracks at Auschwitz; the visitor could easily mistake this part of the camp for Birkenau a few kilometres away, where the majority of inmates perished. There have been several attempts to appropriate the camp for a Christian context over the years: in 1984 a furore arose over the establishment of a Carmelite convent against the walls of Auschwitz; in 1998 radical Catholic nationalist groups placed crosses outside the camp's southern perimeter, which undermined already fragile Polish–Jewish relations. Unlike *Night and Fog*, which has been criticised for failing to 'present the assault against the Jews as an essential pillar of the Nazi phenomenon', the screenplay for *Prometheus* displays an eagerness to establish Auschwitz-Birkenau as a site mainly for Jewish remembrance: hence the description of 'Jewish nightlights', and the 'Jewish Pilgrim' (played by a Jewish actor, Richard Blackford) (p. 60); workbook 4 illustrates the plan to surround the statue with 'nightlights with [the] Star of David' (p. 811).[47] This precision suggests that the director would be attuned to the sensitivities surrounding the introduction of Christian iconography immediately after the visit to the camp.

All these different readings of the metaphorical 'chain' surrounding the Christ figure indicate the ability of the visual image to resist definitive interpretation. This resistance, in other contexts, can be interpreted as symptomatic of postmodern filmmaking. Harrison's attempt to forge a 'cinema of poetry' in the screenplay (p.xxvi) can be compared to Hans-Jürgen Syberberg's *Hitler – A Film from Germany*, where the director 'offers no single interpretation' for the rise of Nazism; instead, he 'constructs spectacles that allow several readings simultaneously', and creates 'incongruities, tensions, contradictions, ambivalences'. Anton Kaes argues that 'any recourse to statements by the filmmaker that would constrain the potential meaning of the film' would do 'injustice to the textual multivalence of the film's collage principle.' Syberberg's stylistic 'multivalence' in *Hitler – A Film from Germany* encompasses photographs, chants, speeches, dolls, puppets, re-enactments, superimpositions, news reports, projections, and – most importantly – ironic interjections, and disjunctions between the extradiegetic music and *mise en scène*. As with Sue Vice's appraisal of postmodern novels in *Holocaust Fiction*, monologic discourses are dismissed in *Hitler – A Film from Germany*; the 'burden is placed on the spectator [or reader] to engage in a dialogue with the film and create his or her own version' of Nazism.[48] Harrison's metaphorical chain similarly indicates that there is 'no single interpretation' of the Christ image – just as there is no fixed reading of Prometheus – since the frame allows 'several readings simultaneously'. Repeated poetic motifs in Harrison's text, such as the images of cooling towers, also suggest a similarity to Syberberg's 'collage principle', but *Prometheus* – unlike the German director's film – relies on linear narrative, competing ideologies and (as I shall discuss) modernist cinematography, techniques that *Hitler – A Film from Germany* rejects.

The crucifix shot in *Prometheus* comprises an instance of controversial spectacle in the film/poem, rather than a postmodernist celebration of dialogism that dominates the narrative. Instead of constructing 'spectacles that allow several readings simultaneously', Lomas accuses *Prometheus* in 'Rhyming Film' of 'a mess of imprecision and propaganda' (p. 53); Ford argues in 'Missing the Vital Spark' that the ideological contest between the Old Man and Hermes 'is so obviously set up in the [former's] favour that it never manages to generate any convincing intellectual tension or dramatic suspense' (p. 26). Postmodernist films allow for multiple reader responses to narratives emptied of didacticism, whereas – in contrast with the multiple readings encouraged by the Christ image – *Prometheus* clearly sides, overall, with the socialist Old Man (despite the odd criticism) against the imperious Hermes, and Communism, Stalinism, Fascism and free trade embodied in the figure of Zeus. The film is not as didactic as Ford suggests, however, since the depiction of environmental damage implies a critique of the miner's unreflective celebration of socialism and industrialisation. In workbook 1 the poet notes, 'Let's be honest to the ambivalence' of Prometheus's gift of fire (p. 38), and, 'The daughters of Ocean recognize the ambiguity' of the Titan's offer (p. 52); newspaper articles – and extracts from books – on environmental concerns are pasted throughout the workbooks. Workbook 1 contains a typed quotation from Jeremy Rifkin's *Entropy: A New World View* with the (handwritten) heading 'The case against Prometheus' (p. 90), and a photograph of a factory with the handwritten caption 'The Temples of Prometheus' (p. 107). These environmental concerns – central to the original plan to stage Aeschylus's play on a Ferrybridge slagheap – are still prevalent in the film/poem, which was produced several years later. Ford also underplays Hermes's occasionally ambiguous character: the polyglot Harrison may be siding with the messenger when Hermes chides the audience for their lack of linguistic skills. Indeed, Hermes's description of himself as 'slumming it in Hull or Leeds' (p. 21) with a few 'by 'eckers like's' (p. 18) – mixed with classical iambs – forms an ironic comment on the author-figure himself.[49]

The bold 'cinema of poetry' outlined in Harrison's introduction to his screenplay links with postmodernist films' celebration of the 'obsessional function of the image', here in the guise of the metaphorical chains that dominate the film/poem's narrative. However, the absence of Syberberg's self-conscious 'mosaic of stylistic quotations' in *Prometheus* indicates that the film/poem resists the label of a postmodernist text.[50] The cinematography also demonstrates the film/poem's resistance to the critical label 'postmodernism'. In *Memory Effects*, Apel contrasts the 'somber, aestheticized modernist compositions' of traditional photographs of the camps, 'devoid of people', with James Friedman's critique of an approach that makes the pictures seem like 'transparently timeless windows into history' (pp. 111–12). Erich Hartmann takes the latter stance by replicating 'the oft-repeated icons of Holocaust imagery', whereas Friedman reveals the camps 'as the tourist sites they are today' (pp. 112, 117). Resnais adheres to Friedman's strategy in *Night and Fog* by cutting between black and white, and colour, shots of gas chambers: the narrator notes that 'A crematorium may look as pretty as a picture postcard . . . Today, tourists are photographed standing in front of them.' In contrast, Hartmann 'carefully effaces the present, producing images that effectively continue the look and feel of postwar archival imagery, projecting a view of "the way it was then"'; Friedman counteracts the invisibility of the modernist photographer (in Apel's terms), and highlights his position as a secondary witness (p. 117). *Prometheus* primarily follows the traditional approach with its 'somber, aestheticized' version of Auschwitz-Birkenau, in keeping with the director's final decision not to 'sing' in the camp. The scene is not entirely devoid of people, but the long shot of the 'Jewish Pilgrim' presents him as a lone visitor into a 'window' of history.

Apel lists the icons that Hartmann regurgitates (Bernhard Schlink calls them clichés in *The Reader*): 'worm's-eye and bird's-eye views of train tracks, entrance gates with the sign *Arbeit Macht Frei*, guard towers, barracks, mounds of shoes, mounds of suitcases, artificial limbs, barbed wire, and crematoria ovens' (pp. 112–13). These icons are prevalent in the photograph album 'Poland 1': there are six shots of the *Arbeit Macht Frei* gates, three pictures of the approach to Birkenau, two photographs of the barracks, and one each of the barbed wire and a bombed crematorium. The final cut of *Prometheus* contains six of these icons; a shot of a shimmering reflection of barbed wire in a puddle is emblematic of Birkenau's apparently effortless ability to register its own misery. As Young argues in *At Memory's Edge*, the problem is that these icons can turn 'mythic, hard and impenetrable' (p. 50), hindering secondary witnesses' understanding of the past. Auschwitz-Birkenau's function as a museum in *Prometheus* is indicated with the lone figure of the Jewish Pilgrim. In contrast, the photograph album 'Poland 1' indicates the fascinating possibility of the film/poem directly addressing this issue of secondary witnessing: it contains two shots of a 'city sightseeing' bus in Auschwitz, offering tours 'every day'; a separate plastic folder contains a colour photograph of tourists, flanked by a black and white still of a selection on the right-hand side of the frame. In contrast, Friedman photographs cafés, deliveries and toys in the car parks of the camps: shots of the phallic gnomes on the German-Czech border earlier in *Prometheus* (see Phil Hunt's photograph in Fig. 3.1) are attuned to Friedman's determination to record the effects of tourism, but not within the 'sacralized aura' of Auschwitz-Birkenau. Images are left to speak for themselves, replicating the 'feel of postwar archival imagery', whilst projecting a vision of '"the way it was then"'. Whereas Friedman often appears in his own photographs to emphasise his position as a secondary witness, the third-person narrative in the Auschwitz scene presents a seemingly 'objective' view of the camp until Hermes's intervention, and his subsequent POV shot (possibly) of the Christ figure. As Hill demonstrates in *The Triumph of Love* with his self-critique of aesthetic prurience in relation to newsreels of the Holocaust, there can be no objective representation of the camps. Harrison's 'inwardness' in the scene did result in the excision of the song, and the subversion of the redemptive candle shot, but it does not produce a self-critical approach to the representation of Birkenau in terms of the cinematography, as opposed to the self-conscious, awkward poetics in the form of the humanist dialectic, and the juxtaposition of scenes.

Paradoxically, at the same time as the replication of Holocaust icons appears to present Auschwitz-Birkenau '"the way it was then"', the editing plays with the geography of the camp. It is unclear throughout

Figure 3.1 Phil Hunt, photograph of gnomes on the German-Czech border ©
Phil Hunt

the sequence – particularly for viewers who have not visited the camps –
whether the action takes place in Auschwitz or Birkenau: this has repercussions for historical as well as geographical accuracy, and the ambiguous status of the Prometheus statue. In contrast, the screenplay stresses
the differences between Auschwitz and Birkenau: it moves from the interior of the 'crematorium ovens, Auschwitz' to the exterior railtrack at
Birkenau (pp. 59–60). In the film, when the Pilgrim leaves the crematorium, a continuity cut appears to be followed by shots of him moving
towards Birkenau; the synchronized sound mix also suggests that these
are match cuts. The screenplay counteracts this possibility: it indicates
that a subsequent crane shot of the huts depicts Birkenau as the Jewish
man leaves the camp; a missing frame in the film picks him up *'leaving
through the entrance of Birkenau'* (p. 60). It also notes that *'He leaves
the crematorium, and we find him at the end of the railtrack.'* In workbook 4, the Pilgrim/Cantor is also found 'at the end of the rail track that
leads through the gateway of Birkenau' (p. 858): to 'find' the Pilgrim suggests the existence of unused footage, or a switch in location. In the crane
shot, the position of the barbed wire and pylons – and the windows and
chimneys on the entrance building to the camp – suggest that the Pilgrim
cannot be walking towards Birkenau. At first, the wire and pylons are on

the right-hand side of the frame; in the matching crane shot of the camp, they are, therefore, on the left. As the Jewish man approaches the entrance, the chimneys are on the inside of the building; in the crane shot looking towards him, windows face the camera, and the chimneys are only partially visible on the other side of the building. The fleeting shot of the statue of Prometheus in the middle of this sequence thus passes on the outside of the Birkenau entrance: it forms an instance of eyeline matching from the perspective of the Jewish Pilgrim moving away from the camp. In conversation, Harrison supported this reading of the shot, commenting that he did not take the statue inside Birkenau, although the lorry's hydraulics would have made this possible.

This fusion of space is caused by the insertion of a jump cut where a continuity cut is expected. It takes place when the Pilgrim leaves the crematorium at Auschwitz: the footage from Auschwitz and Birkenau has been spliced together, so it only seems as if the Pilgrim is moving towards Birkenau. Jump cuts are an integral aspect of artistic licence, but this editorial decision connects with the drawbacks of postmodernist versions of camp interiors in *Memory Effects*. Viewers without access to the screenplay might assume that the action in *Prometheus* takes place entirely within Auschwitz, as opposed to the (less frequently visited) Birkenau camp. Similarly, a photograph of a toy in a car park may form a rejoinder to modernist representations of the camps, but Friedman's *Parking lot, Dachau concentration camp* offers limited information about the camp to the viewer with little or no knowledge about the interior of Dachau (p. 111). The jump cut in *Prometheus* similarly has the ability to obscure historical details of Auschwitz-Birkenau for viewers unfamiliar with the layout of the camps. If a disorientated viewer were to assume that all the sequence occurs in Birkenau, the fact that the retreating Nazis destroyed Birkenau crematoria would be glossed over. The screenplay refers specifically to the Pilgrim placing a candle in '*the dark mouth of a crematorium oven in Auschwitz*' (p. 59); the photograph album 'Poland 1' contains a shot of crematorium rubble in Birkenau. Young comments on the ability of film to displace historical truth in relation to *Schindler's List*: ghetto scenes at Zgoda Square were filmed in Kazimierz across the river, so Spielberg 'had to reverse the direction of the march of ghetto Jews, so that they flowed over the bridge *into* his filmic ghetto . . . and not out of Kazimierz over the Vistula River into Podogórze, as they had originally'. '[I]t is a short step towards confusing the history made in this film,' Young argues, 'for history itself' (p. 86). In *Prometheus*, there is similarly a thin line between the viewer's – but not the director or screenplay's – possible confusion between the geography of the camp as depicted in the film, and the dimensions of Auschwitz-Birkenau in reality.

Figure 3.2  Phil Hunt, photograph of the Prometheus statue in Auschwitz © Phil Hunt

Spliced footage of the interior and exterior of Birkenau also has reper-cussions for the status of the Prometheus statue. Like the image of Christ at the end of the sequence, the statue invites multiple readings in the film as a whole: its metaphorical chain encompasses the miners, the father-figure, the Old Man, humanity, the classical framework, the Allies, the coal industry, socialism, humanism, poetry, the author-figure, and Harrison himself. Once it has been established that the shot of the statue on the lorry depicts it moving outside Birkenau, Phil Hunt's striking photograph of Prometheus inserted into the text of the screenplay (see cover/Fig. 3.2) can be located as outside the camp (p. 60). The position of the windows, chim-neys and sleepers in the picture compared to the crane shot of Birkenau in the film supports this reading. If the statue were inside the camp looking outwards, it could be interpreted as a positive symbol of defiance on behalf of the previous inmates (even if this would risk eliding them with a figure primarily representative of miners in *Prometheus*, or 'Man'). Prometheus's stance could also be interpreted positively as an example of what André Pierre Colombat calls 'inversion' in *Night and Fog*: whereas Resnais counteracts the Nazis' misuse of Haydn's 'Deutschland über Alles' by attaching extracts to deportation scenes, Harrison subverts the Nazi appropriation of classical imagery by escorting the statue to the Birkenau entrance.[51] However, it is disconcerting to contemplate Prometheus gazing into Birkenau, since the raised arm – which primarily represents the miners' defiance, as well as the idealised, Stalinist worker – is uncomfortably reminiscent of a Nazi salute. Again, this could be an instance of 'inversion', but it also highlights the slipperiness of classical references, if, like Charon, Prometheus can function as a symbol for both the prisoners and Nazis. Of course, the latter was certainly not Harrison's intention – the figure merely points to the misuse of fire in Auschwitz – but the publication of the photograph does betray the ability of controversial frames with multiple interpretations (as with the image of Christ) to resist authorial control. Elsewhere, the poet displays an acute awareness of the semiotics of statues in relation to Fascism: in his presidential address to the Virgil Society, published as 'The Tears and the Trumpets', Harrison comments that a Fascistic statue of Virgil in Mantua constitutes a monument more appropriate to Mussolini or any other 'conqueror than to a poet'.[52] However, as opposed to Hill's suspicions surrounding the aesthetics of Quadriga in *The Triumph of Love*, Harrison chooses not to stress the fact that the huge edifice of 'Goldenballs' could be mistaken for a 'dominating Fascistic statue' in the midst of Auschwitz. This links with the connection between Prometheus and the candles in the crane shot: the statue is associated with 'remembrance-fire' throughout this scene. In contrast, earlier in the film, an angry crowd of the ghosts of those killed in the fire bombing of Dresden berates the classical fire-giver for providing the human race with the means of mass destruction. This extraordinary scene self-consciously echoes a sequence in *The Shadow of Hiroshima*, where the ghosts of those killed by the atom bomb collect in a baseball stadium. In *Prometheus*, a montage of empty seats in a Dresden football stadium is juxtaposed with an image of the Old Man crying as he begins to understand the Allies' complicity in atrocity. A close-up on a reflection of Prometheus's fist, which faces downwards, indicates the temporary defeat of the fire-stealing hero. Harrison cannot afford the same linkage between the statue and the perpetrators in Auschwitz, since this would mean allying Prometheus with Nazis. The photograph of the raised arm of the statue outside the entrance to Birkenau demonstrates that, within the context of the inclusive fire metaphor that dominates the film, this possibility exists, but is occluded.

## Metaphorical chains and the death of the miners

Problems surrounding the replication of Holocaust icons, and the ability of the metaphorical chain surrounding Prometheus to encompass Nazis as well as 'Jewish nightlights', need to be counterbalanced with

Harrison's self-conscious subversion of his humanist dialectic in the midst of Auschwitz-Birkenau. In the next two sections, I analyse the ramifications of the fire metaphor in relation to the scenes in which the miners and Io are killed. The poems I discuss in Chapter five of *Tony Harrison and the Holocaust* draw attention to associated – but not identical – problems surrounding dialectics of articulacy, and the ethics of representation, in relation to working-class characters and victims of atrocity. *Prometheus* continues this process, linking – but not conflating – the miners' demise with that of the camp inmates. Prometheus, the miners and murdered inmates stand for Zeus's dream of the destruction of humankind: Hermes refers to the statue as 'part scrap metal, part scrap man' (p. 37). These linkages necessarily risk controversial connections between mythic material and different historical phenomena.

The Open Symposium essays focus instead on Harrison's skilful manipulation of the Prometheus myth and Aeschylus's play: for example, MacKinnon argues that the recycling of the miners ingeniously solves the problem of Prometheus's immobility. The sequence could also be interpreted positively as a critique of links between industrialisation and the Holocaust. MacKinnon contends that the furnace has a particular symbolic resonance: 'Fire and the fuels that produce and sustain it are explored in their relevance to key industrial processes'; for example, in their 'prominent place in the abominations of Auschwitz'.[53] Since the scene is set somewhere in Germany (unnamed in the screenplay) near the Berlin–Dresden road, it could be read more specifically as a diatribe against German firms who exploited slave labour during the war, including Krupp, Junkers, Messerschmitt, Heinkel and Dynamit Nobel. Harrison follows writers such as Zygmunt Bauman who explore the inextricability of industrialisation and the Holocaust. Bauman's investigation of the ramifications of the political state's monopoly of the means of violence and 'audacious engineering ambitions' is mirrored in German manufacturing industries' exploitation of slave labour during Hitler's reign. However, this section argues that the scene specifically explores the concept of '"industrial genocide"' that Harrison draws from the work of the author and photographer Nick Danziger (p. xix). Harrison takes the phrase – in his introduction to the screenplay – from the chapter on South Wales in *Danziger's Britain*: in Penrhys, 'People felt bereaved by the industrial genocide as if they had lost yet another father or son'.[54] Danziger's passage alludes in particular to the deaths of miners from pneumoconiosis in previous generations; unhealthy employment is replaced with what Harrison refers to as a 'frightening picture of . . . unemployment, vandalised inner cities, children without hope turning to drugs and then to crime to maintain their habit' (p.xix). Whole families have been driven from the Penrhys estate: Danziger likens the 'Horror' of 'empty houses steel-shuttered and the hulks of stolen cars' to 'a ruin as great as any after a battle or siege' (p. 323). Hence the apocalyptic sequence when the pit closes in *Prometheus* is akin to the confusing montage of a battle scene. The word 'genocide' usually denotes, however, the extermination of a race or nation, not a class of people: the fire metaphor's evocation of Auschwitz risks an inappropriate connection between the destruction of the coal industry and mass murder.

MacKinnon, in 'Film Adaptation and the Myth of Textual Fidelity', (see Note 13) demonstrates that introspection in this scene is directed towards, not a self-critique of the metaphorical chain in the context of the miners/inmates connection, but an 'awareness of the difficulties in transposing [Aeschylus's] ancient drama to film'. Harrison has 'solved some of these difficulties with ingenuity':

> An outstanding example is his conversion of unemployed steel workers into a golden statue of Prometheus so that it may be transported across Europe. The genius of the latter strategy is that the immobility of the play's hero, pinioned by Force and Violence to the rock at its beginning and forced to remain unmoving, is ensured in his rendering as statue. Yet, this possibly dramatic but defiantly anti-filmic immobility, more thoroughly achieved than in the play through the use of the smelted image, is countered by the device of the lorry.

The lorry does indeed form the imaginative locus for the movement in the film, as the statue, cattle-truck, Hermes, Io and the fire engine head towards Greece. Their frenetic activity conveys a sense of dramatic urgency, which is mirrored in Hermes's earlier monologue by the spoil heaps, delivered whilst moving purposefully towards the camera. This contrasts with the static Prometheus in classical drama: Vellacott notes that the hero in *Prometheus Bound* may have been represented 'by a dummy figure with a mask-head through which, once it was fixed in position, an invisible actor spoke from behind' (p. 153) (see Note 42). Harrison's ingenious re-imagining of Aeschylus's dummy is therefore undisputed; but what, exactly, does the 'smelted image' mean? Edith Hall lauds the scene as a visual representation of the relationship between concrete and abstract labour. Hall argues that *Prometheus*, 'the most important adaptation of classical myth for a radical political purpose in years', points out the 'relationship between the Prometheus myth and the history of Marxist politics' (pp. 129, 132) (see Note 40). In the foundry scene, 'miners' bodies are transformed visually into bullion – a horrific metamorphosis from concrete to abstract labor and thence to Symbolic Capital' (p. 132). This is perceptive criticism, tempered only by the fact that – as MacKinnon notes – the men (miners, not steel workers) are unemployed by this point in the film.[55] The furnace symbolises the disappearance of concrete labour in the coal industry: unlike many other British films about the decline of manufacturing industries, such as *The Full Monty* (in which Steve Huison, the actor playing Miner 4, appeared), *Prometheus* does not promise re-employment. Harrison's workers are disposed of before they have a chance to take their clothes off, or witness the decline of inner-city communities delineated in *Danziger's Britain*.

If *Prometheus* were simply a critique of Krupp et al., and the decline of the coal industry, the scene in the foundry would not be contentious, but controversy arises out of the visual concretion of 'industrial genocide': the overarching metaphorical chain links the sufferings of the miners to murdered inmates. In a sense, the two groups are represented simultaneously: the actors primarily represent miners, but the deployment of the fire metaphor cannot help but connect them with camp inmates. The montage of apocalyptic images portraying the destruction of the Yorkshire pit includes a shot in which Hermes traps six miners in a cattle-truck: Kratos and Bia proceed to drive them towards the German foundry. When they are deposited into the furnace, an extreme close-up on scraping fingers makes a visual connection between the miners' deaths and the scratches of murdered inmates in the gas chambers. A 'limit has been overstepped' here, but this is not an example of Saul Friedlander's 'new discourse': the inclusiveness of the fire metaphor results instead in, not a fascination with Nazism, but simply an ingenious, but controversial, metaphorical connection.[56] Like classical myth, the scene relies on the double meaning of signs: as soon the miners enter the cattle-truck, they begin to represent those who were transported to the camps, as well as unemployed pit-workers; the connection is subtly emphasised by the word 'TRANSPORT', which speeds past as Miner 5 looks through the slats. Miner 3 acts as the equivalent of the Steinlauf character in *If This Is A Man*, the former soldier who berates Levi for not washing, and trying to preserve remnants of civilised behaviour in Auschwitz. '[T]aking charge', Miner 3 demands that 'Anyone who has to go/ has to use his helmet as a po [chamber-pot]', then 'shove it peak first through t'truck slat'; 'Show some discipline', he intones (p. 38). Levi wonders if it might not be better to admit one's lack of a system amongst the chaos; the failure of the miner's 'civilized' appeal is registered in the next scene, as a helmet's contents '*slop over*'. Unlike many of the post-Holocaust novels explored in Vice's *Holocaust Fiction*, there are no definitive intertexts explored in Harrison's allegorical representation of a deportation. Workbook 2 mentions the intertext of Theodore Géricault's painting *The Raft of the Medusa*: the miners replace the survivors of the shipwreck

(p. 255); Harrison undermines the gravity of the image with the draft direction, '<u>They pee through the truck slats</u>', as viewers 'HEAR THE VOICE OF AESCHYLUS PROMPTING' the miners (p. 314). The poet's notes to this scene emphasise his wish to represent the miners as satyrs at this point in the narrative, and representatives of the Titan hero: the truck is 'full of captured miners like a [urinating] satyr chorus'; their 'passports' all contain the name 'Prometheus' (p. 255). These notes also contain the first (inspired) proposal to 'melt [the miners] all down into one giant statue'.

In the screenplay, the vocabulary deployed to emphasise the link between camp inmates and miners betrays a worry that the connection may be incommensurate. After the establishing shot of the sun rising between two cooling towers (the equivalent of the 'towering summit' in *Prometheus Bound*), a close-up depicts a '*flame logo*' (see Fig. 3.3): '*its black, white and red* [are] *rather reminiscent of Nazi insignia*' (p. 3).[57] '[R]*ather*' indicates a subtlety (and uneasiness) that the adverb 'unavoidably' in Dan Stone's critique of Holocaust relativism avoids; however, the sign may be '*reminiscent*' of Nazi iconography for the poet, but not for a viewer of the film without access to the screenplay. This tentativeness nevertheless renders the double meaning of the subsequent scenes clearer. Whereas the cattle-truck and foundry scenes establish a clear, and discomforting, link between miners and camp inmates, the previous action

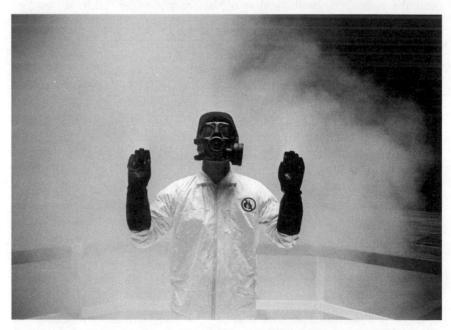

Figure 3.3  Phil Hunt, photograph of Kratos in the cooling tower © Phil Hunt

can be read, with recourse to the screenplay, as a subtle, allegorical representation of a roundup. Since Violence and Force connote (amongst other things) Nazis, the scene 'doubles' as a roundup: travelling from the towers to the estate, they form an anachronistic equivalent of Blind Joe in *Love on the Dole*, with his 'long pole tipped with a bunch of wires', rattling the windows to wake up the workers; they then return to the colliery in order to prepare to trap the unemployed men in the cattle-truck, and then murder them in Germany.[58] Shots of the brass band, which on one level appear to draw on familiar scenes about the demise of the coal industry in films such as *Brassed Off*, can be read in the light of this allegory as '*rather reminiscent*' of camp orchestras that accompanied inmates to, and from, work in camps such as Mauthausen.[59]

However, metaphorical ingenuity in the opening scenes is tempered by an uneasiness caused by the double meaning of the transportation sequence: the lack of awkward poetics at this point in the narrative make it unclear whether the viewer is meant to laugh at Miner 3's advice re the disposal of 'Turds' – a gallows humour that the miners do not recognise as such – or solemnly empathise with the miners' plight. The dialogue is self-conscious in that it refers to Harrison's previous work: Miner 4 comically derides Miner 3 for 'Making poetry out of stuff like this!/ Tha's t'bloody Shakespeare of puke and piss'; he simultaneously evokes the critical furore which has surrounded Harrison's deployment of the demotic, particularly in relation to *V*. Workbook 2 compounds the connection with *V*: the Old Man echoes Isaac Watts ('Time like an ever-rolling bloody stream,/ time like them shadows of t'cooling tower steam') to lambast 'theme park' Britain 'without a bloody theme' (p. 382); the hymn writer is also quoted towards the end of *V* as the poet elegises the decline of the working-class community in Beeston.[60] Graffiti – which forms the metaphorical locus for *V* – was originally meant to figure much more prominently in *Prometheus*: page 821 of workbook 4 outlines a plan to deface the statue with 'neo-Nazi, anti-Gypsy' signs; Harrison also pondered whether to 'add NF graffiti' to the derelict cinema in Knottingley (p. 777). These references to *V* indicate that the miners' scene – like the self-referentiality in *The Triumph of Love* – forms an ironic commentary on the artist's previous work; indeed, as a whole, the film/poem self-consciously situates itself as a culmination of the fire metaphor prevalent throughout Harrison's *oeuvre*. The narrative also mirrors Harrison's poetic trajectory: the first half of the film – as in the 'School of Eloquence' sonnets – focuses on the representation of working-class characters, whereas the second half concentrates on Europe's 'black spots', as with Harrison's work from *The Gaze of the Gorgon* onwards.

This self-consciousness does not extend, however – as in the Auschwitz sequence – to a critique of the fire metaphor. The metaphorical chain's elusiveness at this point in the film/poem is symptomatic of both its ingenuity, and limitations, in the overall narrative: the metaphors entice the viewer into following Harrison's remarkable connections, but sometimes it is unclear when the comparisons are being encouraged, or suspended. In a sense, the allegory renders the following murders in the furnace more disturbing: visually, the miners do not appear akin to deportees, which offers first-time viewers the possibility that an allegorical Auschwitz might not form the unknown destination. The screams that accompany the extreme close-up of the scraping fingers then subvert this hope. However, the metaphorical link between the miners and deportees means that any viewer with knowledge of what Apel calls 'modernist' Holocaust icons must fear for their future as soon as they enter the cattle-truck. In a later scene, Hermes raises his eyebrows as the fire engine follows Prometheus towards Dresden: this action performs a similar function for the post-Holocaust audience as the moment in *Schindler's List* when the women enter a shower room. Viewers of Spielberg's film are put on the edge of their seats as they dread to see what no mainstream director has yet dared to visualise: the death of inmates in a gas chamber. Hermes's eyebrows similarly indicate to a post-war audience that they are about to be shown the site of an infamous Allied atrocity: both films rely – as with the allegory of the miners – on a presumed knowledge of atrocities for the purposes of dramatic tension. *Schindler's List* is, however, different from *Prometheus* in that it purports – on the whole – to dramatise history, whereas Harrison's film operates at the level of classical allegory as soon as the miners' wives turn into Aeschylus's Daughters of Oceanus. In the cattle-truck and foundry scenes, the metaphorical chain encourages alternative readings, but the viewer is unsure whether they are witnessing the death of miners, satyrs, Géricault's survivors, the allegorical murder of deportees, the demise of humanity, the decline of the coal industry, or all of these at once in an outstanding example of the 'obsessional function' of Harrison's fire metaphor.

## Environmentalism and the 'female principle': the death of Io

The scenes in the cattle truck and foundry illustrate the moments in *Prometheus* where the film demonstrates its metaphorical ingenuity, and simultaneously risks over-extending its central conceit. Awkward poetics arise in the self-critique of the fire metaphor in the context of Auschwitz: the candle shot attempts a sentimental celebration of redemption, which

Hermes promptly subverts. In contrast, the miners' scene deploys the metaphorical chain to create a controversial connection – but not conflation – between the Holocaust and the demise of the coal industry. In this section, I analyse how Io's death similarly draws the viewer into making uncomfortable, metaphorical associations, in this instance between Aeschylus's play, cows, gypsies, environmentalism, the 'female principle' in classical drama, victims of fire, passivity, murdered inmates and Harrison's mother.[61] Tentative linkages – as in the miners' scene – continue in the screenplay when Io is killed, but, in contrast with the subtlety of the opening scenes in *Prometheus*, the visual metaphor of the slaughterhouse makes it clear that this sequence comprises a displaced representation of the gas chambers and crematoria. In this sense, Harrison goes a step further than Spielberg in *Schindler's List* by illustrating what happens beyond the door of the gas chamber; however, the double meaning of the scene means that the viewer both is, and is not, witnessing the murder of inmates. In a response to a question about why he depicted Jews as mice in his two *Maus* books, Art Spiegelman answered that he needed to '"show the events and memory of the Holocaust without showing them"'.[62] In Io's death scene, Harrison daringly attempts to depict the moment when inmates entered the gas chambers, but without actually showing it. On the one hand, the metaphorical displacement of Auschwitz with an abattoir could be read as insensitive. On the other hand, Harrison's stated intention was to make the viewer appreciate what it meant to be turned into an object due for extermination. As in *Night and Fog*, Harrison calls attention to the viewer's status as a potential perpetrator: this filmic equivalent of awkward poetics results in what Colombat calls a 'supplementary uneasiness' in *The Holocaust in French Film* (p. 128). As in the Io scene in *Prometheus*, the viewer of Resnais's film is forced to contemplate the perspective of the perpetrator: the camera pans around the camp from a guard tower in *Night and Fog*; the narrator warns of 'new executioners', and asks, 'Are their faces really different from ours?'

Harrison told Hall that in this scene 'he wanted his viewers to see, with brutal literalness, what it means to be turned into a cow (or into a human being treated like a cow) destined for a death chamber' (p. 137). In an interview with Peter Lennon, the poet comments that 'The turning of people into animals and mass killing is one of the things that haunts' the twentieth century.[63] The workbooks reveal that the figure of Io originally represented victimised gypsies. In workbook 2, an underlined, typed quotation from Misha Glenny's *The Rebirth of History: Eastern Europe in the Age of Democracy* argues that 'to enter the home of one of Hungary's 350,000 Gypsies is to encounter conditions comparable with some of the worst in the developing world' (p. 436); Harrison notes that a monument of Spartacus is inscribed with the graffiti '"Death to Gypsies"' (p. 414); workbook 4 figures 'Io as [a] Gypsy' with the dialogue '[fuck off, Gypsy in all appropriate tongues]', and imagines 'Fly posters "Death to Gypsies" "Hang the Gypsies" and, in Oswieçim "Gas the Gypsies"' (p. 761); Io then 'becomes more and more Gypsy'. The metaphorical connection between Io and murdered gypsies is played down in the final cut (the fly posters do not feature), and when Io walks towards a 'gypsy village' in Romania, '*the villagers . . . begin to chase her and throw stones at her*' (p. 69). Workbook 2 indicates that Io was originally to be 'Caught like a Friesian', and then, like the miners, 'crated, trucked and melted down' (p. 447); the comparison with the miners is compounded when a nameless character 'turns [the] gold with [a] stun gun' as they are melted into bullion (p. 256). (Workbook 1 reveals that, in the original play, a miner was to be transformed into Io, distracted by 'a bell, a buzzer a warning light' rather than the gadfly in classical myth (p. 54).) In contrast, in the final cut of the film/poem Io is meant to figure as a more abstract victim of oppression, encompassing camp inmates, cows and women, rather than, specifically, gypsies or miners.

Connections with the earlier Auschwitz sequence are established in the Lennon interview and screenplay. Harrison tells Lennon that the reprisal of the music (by Richard Blackford) in the Auschwitz scenes – when Io is burnt in the crematorium – 'makes the connection with the Auschwitz oven sequence'; in the screenplay, 'The colours of rust and metal and brick [in the abattoir] are close to those of Auschwitz'; 'Carcasses are scooped up and incinerated in an oven not unlike that of Auschwitz' (p. 79). The linking of colours is too subtle for the first-time viewer, but the depiction of the 'cattle-burning place' – which is meant to connect with the earlier frame of the crematorium oven in the camp – certainly makes it clear that the death of Io forms the second specific metaphorical connection with Auschwitz-Birkenau in *Prometheus*. Harrison's intention works in terms of the three POV shots from Io's, and the cows', perspective: a low-angle shot of a '"*guillotine*"' door emphasises the animals' entrapment; two other low-angle shots feature a worker about to dispose of Io with a stun gun. More frequently, however, the 'brutal literalness' of the scene works from the POV shots of the workers, Pasolini's '"free indirect subjective"', and – by allegorical association – Nazis: the most disturbing example of this is the lingering shot of a cow as it struggles to escape, with a worker holding a stun gun in the left-hand corner of the frame.[64] After the gun misses its target once, the cow momentarily relaxes, and is immediately dispatched; when the cow hits the floor, the diegetic sound is the same as when Io crumples. Shots from the perspective of the workers, 'indirect subjective' and (by proxy) Nazis then depict the cow resisting as it is hoisted in the air; Io's legs similarly twitch as a pitched hum, *'almost like that of . . . Io's cello'*, accompanies the hoist. The influence of classical myth is registered in the screenplay: the Boy's mother in Yorkshire completes her transformation into Io when she becomes *'half-black from carbon and half-white from chemicals, so that she has the brindled appearance of a Friesian cow'* (p. 78); the scene is anticipated before the visit to Dresden, when Hermes reveals that Kratos and Bia, who 'miss the swastikas of yesteryear', will keep 'the poor cow on the run' (p. 45). (In workbook 3, Hermes registers Force and Violence's participation in mass murder when he contends that 'we don't need gods, we simply choose/ men like you to gas the Jews/ bomb Dresden or create/ a gulag-ridden prison state' (p. 621).) In Aeschylus's play, Prometheus anticipates the birth of Heracles, and Zeus's downfall; this is referred to in *Prometheus* when Io noses an engraving of her future child. Ford argues that the film 'attempts to update the story of Io', and that the implication is, perhaps, that her son will liberate Prometheus; he concludes that 'these episodes seem irrelevant and confusing'.[65] On the contrary, the abattoir scene deliberately subverts the classical myth and Aeschylus's trilogy by disposing of Io: following the pessimistic undercurrent (and ending) of the film – which includes the burning of Prometheus – the inference is that there will be no Greek hero to save the world from free trade, environmental disaster and carnivores.

As with the miners' demise, the director skilfully redeploys classical myth – here to illustrate the ramifications of the mother's metamorphosis – but it is similarly controversial in its allegorical correlation between cows (instead of workers) and those murdered in the gas chambers. The scene draws on an early Harrison poem, 'Allotments', in which the younger poet includes the imagined, or reported, speech of an Auschwitz survivor. Whilst cuddling his lover by a slaughterhouse, where the 'odd glimpsed spark/ From hooves on concrete stalls scratched at the dark', a Pole, who 'had smelt/ Far worse at Auschwitz and at Buchenwald' points to the chimneys and says, *'Meat! Zat is vere zey murder vat you eat'*.[66] These metaphorical connections might be fine, one may argue, from the perspective of an adolescent struggling to come to terms with genocide, his burgeoning sexuality, and a corned beef sandwich, but not in relation to the adult poet's chain of images illustrating the Io myth. Yet the Holocaust poet Tadeusz Różewicz also likens his experiences as a partisan during the German occupation of Poland to being 'led to slaughter': 'man and beast' are 'empty synonyms', he contends in 'The Survivor', and 'The way of killing men and beasts is the same'.[67] Both Różewicz's poem and *Prometheus* are genuine attempts to illustrate 'what it means to be turned into a cow (or into a human being treated like a cow)', but they also court controversy through a 'brutal literalness' that risks replicating the perspective of the perpetrator, for whom the victims are indeed 'animals', or 'vermin'. In contrast, Władysław Szlengel's poem about the Warsaw uprising exploits this paradox. 'Counterattack' duplicates the perspective of the Nazis, who 'see their victims as cattle on their way to the slaughter house', but then subverts it, as the 'bovinized victims' fight back: 'the cattle awakened/ And/ Bared its teeth . . . Bullets whirl in a joyous song,/ REVOLT OF THE MEAT,/ REVOLT OF THE MEAT,/ REVOLT OF THE MEAT!'.[68] Whereas Szlengel's ironic commentary celebrates the Jews' heroic, but ultimately doomed, revolt, Io's death scene – with its daring attempt to visualise 'what it means to be turned into a cow' – risks being interpreted (against the director's intention) as endorsing the myth of Jewish passivity during the Holocaust.[69]

The death of Io is not just an allegory of Auschwitz set in an abattoir: various possible interpretations of the scene associate the classical character with phenomena as diverse as global pollution, and the religious persecution of women. These are conjoined with the classical concept of the 'female principle'. Oliver Taplin notes that Eva and Angelos Sikelianos's 'Delphic Idea' included the notion – forged with ideas drawn from Orphism, Buddhism, Dionysus, Pindar and Aeschylus – that the 'female principle' would save the world from rationalism and industrialisation.[70] Io's demise in *Prometheus* thus undermines the Sikelianos's idealism, but the classical character also provides an alternative to the masculinity of Zeus, Hermes, Nazis, the miner-father, Kratos and Bia.[71] As well as allegorising murdered inmates, Io is representative of a Hughesian 'Mother Earth': her death symbolises the environmental damage encountered in Romania in particular.[72] After being doused with chemicals, Io is dragged down a railway track in a visual reminder of the tracks inside Birkenau: this subtle connection nevertheless recalls Stone's diatribe against the likening of the 'burnt bodies of Jews' to environmental damage. The scene's extradiegetic music indicates yet another reference encompassed by the 'female principle'. The religious persecution of women is registered in the sequence in a Romanian monastery; when Io steals a candle, a monk beats a huge tuaca; when she is finally captured by Force and Violence, the monk's percussive beat returns. Monks, Kratos and Bia are opposed to two females in the film who are empathetic towards Io's plight: a woman gives her a loaf in Bulgaria; a male passenger shouts at her when she boards a tram in the Czech Republic, whereas a woman punches one of her own tickets for Io. These concrete examples of the 'female principle' are undermined by Io's capture: at the end of the film, the apocalyptic images of the destroyed cooling towers are accompanied by the sound of the Boy wandering across the post-industrial landscape, shouting 'mam'. This cry is subtly anticipated in the foundry scene, and is emitted just as the father dies in the furnace. Io and the mother's evocation at the film's closure recall the first word of the film ('Zeus'): the masculine, persecutory rituals of Zeus, Hermes, Kratos, Bia and Nazis are triumphant throughout *Prometheus*.

This outline of the 'female principle' demonstrates its skilful integration into the film's narrative.[73] However, Harrison's manipulation of the classical character of Io risks (as with Prometheus) using the Holocaust as an associated '"topic"' onto which the writer can 'attach their particular hobby horse' (see Note 11). Rather than forming an instance of relativism, though, the metaphorical chains in *Prometheus* point, overall, to differences, as well as similarities, between various mythical and historical phenomena. This process is exemplified in the scenes in Auschwitz-Birkenau, where the fire metaphor finds its limit point: awkward poetics arise in the form of juxtaposition and inversion; Hermes's diatribe and the Christ image undercut the excruciating sentimentality of the opening sequence, and its struggle to celebrate a humanist 'triumph of the spirit'. Throughout this chapter, I have demonstrated how *Prometheus* – a flawed classic – deploys ingenious metaphorical chains that are simultaneously in danger of making inappropriate connections. This risk is inextricable from Harrison's (industrious) working methods in his later poetry, which comprise a fascination with collecting multiple references to classical figures, and collating diverse images using, for example, digital editing. This process of collation continues in his next film/poem, *Crossings*, in relation to the mythical figure of Orpheus. In Harrison's earlier work, awkward poetics, in the form of, for example, subversive metrics, register the difficulties of representing atrocities, whereas in *Prometheus* the emphasis is on the inclusiveness of classical myth, 'something for everyone', rather than the dangers of relativism. Classical influences nevertheless result in a complex narrative that draws together the various manifestations of the fire metaphor through the interaction of the *mise en scène*, digital editing, music, dialogue, and poetry. However, the absence of awkward poetics in the miners' scene – as opposed to the self-critical subversion of the redemptive sequence in Auschwitz – demonstrates that the central conceit of Promethean fire sometimes strives for inclusiveness at the expense of a self-conscious exploration of potentially 'barbaric' art.

## Notes

1. Theodor Adorno, 'Cultural Criticism and Society', in *Prisms*, trans. S. and S. Weber (London: Neville Spearman, 1967), pp. 17–34, p. 34.
2. Quoted in Dora Apel, *Memory Effects: The Holocaust and the Art of Secondary Witnessing* (New Brunswick, New Jersey, and London: Rutgers University Press, 2002), pp. 118–19.
3. *Bloodaxe Critical Anthologies. 1. Tony Harrison*, ed. Neil Astley (Newcastle: Bloodaxe, 1991), p. 9. My italics.
4. These quotations from Harrison are taken from the interview with Bragg, and the introduction to the screenplay for *Prometheus* (London: Faber, 1998), entitled 'Fire and Poetry' (pp. vii–xxix, p. vii). For a fuller discussion of the poet's 'agonised humanism' see my introduction to *Tony Harrison and the Holocaust* (Liverpool: Liverpool University Press, 2001), pp. 1–26.
5. Lawrence Langer, *Admitting the Holocaust* (Oxford: Oxford University Press, 1995), p. 3.
6. Primo Levi, *The Periodic Table*, trans. Raymond Rosenthal (London: Penguin, 2000 [1975]), pp. 177–87. My italics. In *Is the Holocaust Unique? Perspectives on Comparative Genocide* (Oxford and Boulder, CO: Westview Press, 1996), the editor Alan Rosenbaum concurs with Levi's disagreement with Müller's reading of history, and argues that some reflections on the Holocaust are 'sterile' because they 'trade in some unnecessarily vacuous abstractions . . . [which] confuse, undermine, and prevent a full and accurate grasp of the realities in question. Typical . . . is the tendency to attribute . . . [the Holocaust] to "Man's inhumanity to Man"' (p. 3).
7. Steve Padley, 'Poetry and Atrocity' (rev. of *Tony Harrison and the Holocaust*), *English*, 52: 204 (autumn 2003), pp. 278–82, p. 282.
8. Wally Hammond, '"Prometheus"', *Time Out*, 14–21 April 1999, p. 77; Mark Ford, 'Missing the Vital Spark', *London Review of Books*, 13 May 1999, pp. 25–6, p. 26; Herbert Lomas, 'Rhyming Film', *Thumbscrew*, 13 (spring/summer 1999), pp. 52–5, p. 55.
9. Tony Harrison, *The Trackers of Oxyrhynchus* (London: Faber, 1991 [1990]), p. 44.
10. The image of the defunct fire engine – which I discuss later in the chapter – does challenge art's ability to represent atrocities, but this pessimism does not encompass the concept of aesthetic culpability in relation to representations of the Holocaust.
11. *Theoretical Interpretations of the Holocaust*, ed. Dan Stone (Amsterdam: Rodopi, 2001), p. 6.
12. Nicholas Lezard, 'Fire in his Belly', *The Independent on Sunday*, 11 April 1999, pp. 5–6, p. 5.
13. Quoted in Lorna Hardwick, 'Placing Prometheus', The Department of Classical Studies Open Colloquium 1999, http://www.open.ac.uk/Arts/Colq99/hardwick.htm. The Battle of Orgreave was the climactic skirmish of the 1984 miners' strike. As well as Hardwick's piece, papers were given at the Colloquium by Kenneth MacKinnon ('Film Adaptation and the Myth of Textual Fidelity'), Steve Woodward, ('Voices in the Past and in the Present: Tony Harrison's Reworking of the Prometheus Myth'), Peter Robinson ('Facing Up to the Unbearable: The Mythical Method in Tony

Harrison's Film/Poems'), Adrian Poole ('Harrison and Marsyas'), Stephen Regan ('Fire and Poetry: The Genesis of Prometheus') and Kai Merten ('Margin and Centre: Tony Harrison's Classical Positionings'). All but the last two papers are published at the website address above.

14. Jon Silkin, 'Editorial', *Stand*, 4: 1 (1958), pp. 3–4. Liberal relativism could be detected in Silkin's 'Jaffa, and Other Places' from *Amana Grass* (London: Chatto & Windus, 1971) where diasporic Jews are compared to former English rulers in the British Mandate Palestine. However, the poem immediately undercuts the comparison with the assertion that the rulers' shoes are 'Done with in worse places' (p. 29); the ensuing list of shoes, crutches, irons, teeth, ash, hair and dust must refer to Auschwitz.

15. 'Burning Ambition: The Producer Michael Kustow Relives the Making of Tony Harrison's *Prometheus*', *The Observer* (11 April 1999), http://film. guardian.co.uk/Feature_Story/Observer/0,4120,41473,00.html

16. In *Work on Myth* (trans. Robert M. Wallace), Blumenberg investigates how Prometheus 'presents an incredible variety of aspects and interpretations in the course of these two and a half millenniums' (London and Cambridge: The MIT Press, 1985 [1979], p. xxxi). For example, he contrasts Hesiod's version of the myth, in which the Titan does not escape, with Aeschylus's play, where, perhaps due to local 'Attic legend', he is freed from his bonds (p. 306).

17. Steve Padley, 'Fruitility', *PN Review*, 27: 1 (September/October 2000), pp. 56–7, p. 57.

18. Quoted in Nicholas Wroe, 'Tony Harrison: Man of Mysteries', in *The Guardian* (1 April 2000), pp. 6–7, p. 7.

19. Glyn Maxwell, (rev. of *Prometheus*) *Sight and Sound*, April 1999, pp. 55–6, p. 56.

20. Levi, Ficowski and Herbert are discussed in the following paragraphs. In 'Night over Birkenau', Borowski describes 'blue Orion' as 'like a shield abandoned in battle' as the 'transports growl in darkness' and the 'eyes of the crematorium blaze' (in *Holocaust Poetry*, ed. Hilda Schiff [London: HarperCollins, 1995], p. 55). The reference to the virile hunter's shield registers Borowski's feelings of guilt and abandonment, but also the inappropriateness of the prodigiously strong Orion as an Auschwitz figure. Like Borowski, Radnóti recognises the possibility of confronting contemporaneous scenarios with the baggage of antiquity. His use of the eclogue form and hexameters arose out of a classical revival movement in Hungary in the 1930s: in 1937 he was asked by Trencsényi-Waldapfel to translate a section of Virgil's *Eclogues*; in the same year, Anna Hajnal asked him to translate a Tibullus elegy. In *The Poetry of Miklós Radnóti: A Comparative Study*, Emery George argues that this marked 'a major turn in his career as a poet' (New York: Karz-Cohl, 1986, p. 351). Radnóti's reading of the *Eclogues* instilled him with a firm belief that poetry could confront the problems of the age through Virgilian tact and restraint; he was particularly drawn to Virgil's narrative of dispossession, and the interaction of poetics and politics.

21. Primo Levi, *If This Is A Man/The Truce*, trans. Stuart Woolf (London: Penguin, 1987 [1958]), pp. 232, 260.

22. Pierre Grimal, *The Dictionary of Classical Mythology* (London: Blackwell, 1986), p. 99.

23. Adrian Room, *Room's Classical Dictionary* (London: Routledge, 1983), p. 91.
24. *Holocaust Poetry*, pp. 62–3, p. 62.
25. Daniel R. Schwarz, *Imagining the Holocaust* (Basingstoke: Palgrave, 2000 [1999]), p. 96.
26. Rowland, pp. 15–16.
27. Zbigniew Herbert, 'Why the Classics?', and 'A Poet of Exact Meaning: A Conversation with Marek Oramus', in *The Poetry of Survival: Post-War Poets of Central and Eastern Europe*, ed. Daniel Weissbort (London: Penguin, 1993 [1991]), pp. 330–5, p. 334 and pp. 322–9, p. 327.
28. Theodor W. Adorno, 'On Epic Naiveté', in *Notes to Literature*, vol. 1, trans. Shierry Weber Nicholsen (New York and Chichester: Columbia University Press, 1991), pp. 24–9; 'On the Classicism of Goethe's *Iphigenie*', in *Notes to Literature*, vol. 2, trans. Shierry Weber Nicholsen (New York and Chichester: Columbia University Press, 1992), pp. 153–70, p. 153.
29. Herbert, 'Why the Classics?', p. 335. Herbert echoes Adorno's statement in *Negative Dialectics* – adding a redemptive note – (trans. E. B. Ashton) that 'suffering has as much right to expression as a tortured man has to scream' (Frankfurt: Suhrkamp, 1973 [1966]), p. 362.
30. In conversation with Jim Greenhalf, Harrison notes that '"At the end there were 36 hours of film to look at and edit down to two-and-a-quarter hours – it's the longest film I've ever made. I'd spend 12 hours a day going through the film. After one session I went back to where I was staying and just threw up"' ('Making Poetry an Open Book', *Telegraph & Argus*, 18 December 1998, p. 25).
31. André Pierre Colombat, *The Holocaust in French Film* (Metuchan and London: Scarecrow Press, 1993), pp. 162, 131.
32. The phrase 'obsessional function of the image' is taken from the Holocaust poet Jean Cayrol's interview with Raymond Bellour in *Les Lettres françaises*, 967: 28 (February 1963), pp. 17–18, p. 17. 'What I am seeking', Cayrol argues, 'is a lyrical poetry . . . In one single image we must be able to perceive the whole world.' Harrison's fire metaphor attempts the same artistic *coup de grâce* in *Prometheus*. Max Silverman discussed this passage in his paper on 'Art, Horror and Everyday Life' at the 'Remembering the Holocaust' symposium at the University of Manchester (7 May 2004).
33. James E. Young, *At Memory's Edge: After-Images of the Holocaust in Contemporary Art and Architecture* (New Haven and London: Yale University Press, 2000), p. 2.
34. In 'He Makes it Rhyme', Tim Kendall asks whether Harrison's poetry is self-satisfied in its appropriation of Bosnia and Iraq in a review of Sandie Byrne's *Tony Harrison: Loiner* in the *Times Literary Supplement* (30 January 1998), p. 13.
35. Young, p. 3.
36. Tony Harrison, *Prometheus*, p. 61. Zeus is figured as a Nazi throughout the workbooks. In workbook 3, Hermes argues that 'ZEUS was the first to set the style/ of variations on <u>Sieg Heil!</u> . . . to teach the cowed cunts to kowtow' (p. 587).
37. In the Introduction, Harrison includes a passage from H. H. Anniah Gowda's *Dramatic Poetry from Medieval to Modern Times* (Madras:

Macmillan, 1972), which describes *Prometheus Unbound* as providing 'the seeds of a future burgeoning'; this gave the poet 'a nudge in the direction' of his own version of the Prometheus myth (p.xiv). Just before the extracted section, Anniah Gowda criticises Shelley's 'insufferably wordy and abstract' language; despite these 'embarrassments', the drama 'soars . . . into the empyrean of a transcendental doctrine projected for what may be called a transcendental theatre not as yet created, still in gestation within the soul of the Western World' (p. 166). '[E]mbarrassments' have been detected in Harrison's poetry surrounding, for example, the representation of historical phenomena, and metrical deficiencies. Tim Kendall asks whether the iambic pentameter is 'skilfully handled', and whether there is 'anything disconcertingly self-satisfied about the appropriation' of sites of atrocity (see Note 34). Byrne has defended Harrison's intentional use of 'stonking doggerel' (Wroe, p. 7) (see Note 18); this is particularly applicable to some of the poems in *Laureate's Block*, such as 'A Celebratory Ode on the Abdication of King Charles III'. Similarly, *Prometheus* is mainly composed of iambic tetrameters after the prosaic opening scenes: the short lines of dialogue, developed in earlier film/poems such as *The Gaze of the Gorgon*, fit particularly well with the twenty-four or twenty-five frames per second of film (although the miners, for example, do slip into pentameter sometimes in the cattle-truck scenes). As Robinson notes, most critics respond to the film/poems as if they presented poetry on the page, whereas Harrison is attuned to the relationship between iambs and the 'telecined rushes' called up with Avid or Lightwords editing programmes (introduction, p. xxiv). Harrison's use of tetrameters, and relatively simple diction, in *Prometheus* – as opposed to Shelley's highfalutin language in *Prometheus Unbound* – allows the viewer to follow the verse narrative at the pace of the digital editing: as Greenhalf argues, the film is not 'an arty art-house movie obsessed with its own technique at the expense of the viewer's comprehension'.

38. In conversation, Harrison commented that the song was excised, not due to a recognition of the Holocaust sublime ('"I couldn't find a reason to break into song in Auschwitz"'), but because it did not fit, stylistically, into the overall sequence; more (non-musical) footage would have had to have been added in order to insert it seamlessly into the narrative.

39. *Voices of Exile* was first performed at Pool Arts Centre on 17 November 2001, with Robert Tear taking the solo tenor role.

40. Edith Hall, 'Tony Harrison's *Prometheus*: A View from the Left', *Arion*, 10: 1 (spring/summer 2002), pp. 129–40, p. 131.

41. *Shelley's Poetry and Prose*, ed. Donald H. Reiman and Neil Fraistat, 2nd edn (London and New York: W.W. Norton & Co. Ltd, 2002 [1977]), p. 218.

42. Aeschylus, *Prometheus and Other Plays*, trans. Philip Vellacott (London: Penguin, 1961), p. 38.

43. Bryan Cheyette, 'Between Repulsion and Attraction: George Steiner's Post-Holocaust Fiction', in *The Holocaust and the Text: Speaking the Unspeakable*, ed. Andrew Leak and George Paizis (London: Macmillan, 2000), pp. 67–82, p. 79.

44. Susan Gubar, *Poetry after Auschwitz: Remembering What One Never Knew* (Bloomington: Indiana University Press, 2003), p. 59.

45. Gubar, pp. 59, 60.
46. Gubar, p. 59.
47. Ilan Avisar, *Screening the Holocaust: Cinema's Images of the Unimaginable* (Bloomington: Indiana University Press, 1988), p. 16. By doing this, of course, Harrison cannot help but marginalise the 10 per cent of prisoners killed at Auschwitz who were not Jews, including Romanies, Poles and Soviet POWs. Also, the fact that the Jewish man is described as a religious Pilgrim, along with his traditional clothes, inevitably presents Jewish remembrance as primarily a non-secular activity. Films often rely on the semiotics of clothes, of course: the visibility of the shawl and kippah informs the audience that he is probably a religious Jew. As Apel notes in relation to Shimon Attie's installations and photographs entitled *The Writing on the Wall*, however, these semiotics are double-edged, since 'The atypical Orthodox Jew', as opposed to the 'parvenu' or assimilated Jew, becomes 'a stand-in for all Jews' (p. 48).
48. Anton Kaes, 'Holocaust and the End of History: Postmodern Historiography in Cinema', in *Probing the Limits of Representation: Nazism and the "Final Solution"*, ed. Saul Friedlander (Cambridge, MA and London: Harvard University Press, 1992), pp. 206–22, 212.
49. These ambiguities illustrate the impossibility of identifying a main character with Harrison: Zeus's 'lickspittle', as Vellacott's translation of Aeschylus has it, clearly offends the poet with his 'servile humility', and yet the characters appear to be fused when Hermes translates from various languages for the tiresome audience, hinting at Harrison's polyglot persona (pp. 49, 48). Harrison might instead identify with the Old Man, but is clearly averse to his celebration of the destruction of Dresden by 'Bomber Harris'; as a non-smoker, he would also be unlikely to applaud his eulogy to 'weed'. Any correlation between the poet and miner-father is also undercut by the Dad's burning of the Boy's edition of *Prometheus Bound*. This replicates similar scenes in working-class fiction which depict a suspicion towards education. In Alan Sillitoe's *The Loneliness of the Long-Distance Runner*, an argument erupts between a wife and husband about reading: '"You booky bastard," she screamed, "nowt but books, books, books, you bleddy dead-'ead" – and threw the book on the heaped-up coals, working it further and further into their blazing middle with the poker' (London: W. H. Allen, 1959, p. 82). Harrison self-consciously refers to his younger self as a 'booky bastard' in the scene with the Boy: 'Book Ends' in the *Selected Poems* ends with 'books, books, books' that separate the grammar-school Boy from the working father; when the mother comes across his first collection, he notes in 'Bringing Up' that she would have flung it in the fire (due to the '"sordid lust"' therein) if it were not a library copy (pp. 126, 166). This scene in *Prometheus* also seals the connection between the destruction of cultural artefacts and Nazis: when the father throws the book into the fire, the Boy retorts that 'Burning books 's what Nazis do'; after receiving a slap, he calls his dad a 'Nazi get' (pp. 10, 11). 'Get' (or 'git') is a northern dialect word meaning 'donkey': in workbook 2, Harrison imagines a scene where the golden statue's hand snags on a washing line: a woman 'shrieks in Romanian', '"That's my washing, you great golden git"' (p. 257).
50. The last quotation is taken from Susan Sontag, 'Syberberg's Hitler', in

*Syberberg: A Filmmaker from Germany*, ed. Heather Stewart (London: British Film Institute pubs, 1992), p. 16. For a fuller discussion on the relationship between Harrison's poetry and conceptions of postmodernism and poststructuralism, see Sandie Byrne, *H, v. & O: The Poetry of Tony Harrison* (Manchester: Manchester University Press, 1998), pp. 92–7.

51. Colombat, p. 148.
52. Tony Harrison, 'The Tears and the Trumpets', *Arion*, 9: 2 (fall 2001), pp. 1–22, p. 13. The statue was erected during Mussolini's dictatorship, in 1930.
53. Zygmunt Bauman, *Modernity and the Holocaust* (Cambridge: Polity Press, 1989), p. xiii.
54. Nick Danziger, *Danziger's Britain* (London: HarperCollins, 1996), p. 325. The passage actually praises an example of free enterprise: Penrhys is contrasted with Tower Colliery in Hirwaun, where the miners used their redundancy money to re-open the mine. As stakeholders in their own company, 'They were all converts to free enterprise in possibly one of the strangest twists in industrial history' (p. 324); Danziger describes his visit to the pit as 'one of the most uplifting experiences of my journey through Britain' (p. 325). In contrast, in *Prometheus*, global free trade is written off as 'a crock of shit' (p. 75).
55. This may be the scene's main point, of course: that employers regard the workers as merely symbolic capital rather than as human brings.
56. Saul Friedlander, *Reflections of Nazism: An Essay on Kitsch and Death*, trans. Thomas Weyr (Bloomington and Indianapolis: Indiana University Press, 1993 [1982]), p. 21.
57. Aeschylus, p. 20 (see Note 42). Workbook 1 reveals that the fire sign was originally conceived as a 'nuclear symbol' for the play in Ferrybridge (p. 68); the 'flame logo' is first mentioned in workbook 2 (p. 309). Hermes's allegorical identity as a Nazi is indicated with his caduceus, which contains the same 'flame logo' sign. Workbook 4 lists ten proposed versions of the caduceus in the film, including a 'riot stick' and a 'lecturer's pointer' (p. 797).
58. Walter Greenwood, *Love on the Dole* (Harmondsworth: Penguin, 1969 [1933]), p. 13.
59. There are other similarities between *Brassed Off* and *Prometheus*: as well as the closing pits and frame of the miners handing in their tokens, there are comparable scenes of domestic strife. One of these ends with a mother leaving home with her children: they place their hands on the back window of the van in the same way as the women/Daughters of Oceanus do on the 'Oceanus' bus in Harrison's film.
60. Tony Harrison, *Selected Poems*, p. 247.
61. Io beats her wedding ring against the side of the cattle-truck; Hermes retrieves it later from the cattle-burning place. This partly represents Harrison's mother's ring in the earlier poem 'Timer', which survives the cremation service, and is returned to the poet. Harrison's continued interest in this poem – which won the National Poetry Competition in 1980 – is indicated with his reading of 'Timer' during *The South Bank Show* episode in 1999.
62. Quoted in Young, p. 32 (see Note 33).
63. Peter Lennon, 'Is This Any Way to Make a Movie?', *The Guardian*, 5 November 1998, p. 10.

64. Harrison discusses Pasolini in the introduction to the screenplay. An 'emergent [cinematic] "prosody"' is detected in films where, as Pasolini explains, 'we are aware of the camera and its movement' (p. xxvii). The self-conscious POV shot of the camera is defined as '"free indirect subjective"'.
65. Quoted in Woodward (see Note 13).
66. Tony Harrison, *Selected Poems*, p. 18.
67. Hilda Schiff, *Holocaust Poetry*, p. 157.
68. Quoted in Frieda W. Aaron, *Bearing the Unbearable: Yiddish and Polish Poetry in the Ghettos and Concentration Camps* (New York: State University of New York Press, 1990), pp. 153, 150.
69. Rebellions occurred in numerous places, such as Warsaw, Cracow, Czestochowa, Bendzin, Bialystok, Auschwitz, Sobibor and Treblinka.
70. Quoted in MacKinnon (see Note 13).
71. Bia may be displaying aspects of female masculinity: in some commentaries on myth Bia is referred to as a boy, but in others she is the daughter of the Titan Pallas.
72. In Hughes's 'A Woman Unconscious', European conflicts risk 'A melting of the mould in the mother' (Ted Hughes, *Collected Poems*, ed. Paul Keegan (London: Faber, 2003), p. 62). *Prometheus* explores the same paradox as Hughes's *Remains of Elmet*: the decline of working-class communities is lamented, at the same time as the author admits the environmental damage inflicted by industrialisation.
73. The gender politics are actually more complex in *Prometheus* than the binary between the 'female principle' and masculinity suggests. Woodward's article notes that Io's intervention is the most important episode in *Prometheus Bound*, since it connects, over the space of over three hundred lines, Zeus's mistreatment of Io with his persecution of Prometheus. In contrast, Io is virtually silent throughout *Prometheus*: she speaks twelve words throughout the film, one of which links her with Holocaust victims: whilst dreaming of Nazi persecution, she repeats the word '*Nein*' (p. 59). A counterargument might point out that she delivers twelve more words than the main protagonist, Prometheus. This would occlude the objectification of Io as a 'mad cow' throughout the film: in the very first frame, she appears wide-eyed, worried, and rather clueless. This links with Carol Chillington Rutter's description of Io in Theodoros Terzopoulos's 1995 performance of *Prometheus Bound* at Delphi in 'Harrison, Herakles, and Wailing Women "Labourers" at Delphi' (*New Theatre Quarterly*, 13: 50 [May 1997], pp. 133–43). Throughout the production, Io, 'bare-breasted in the background, tossed her head in endless cow-like convulsions' (p. 134). Rutter's 'uneasiness about Harrison's gender politics' is registered in the tension between the programme notes for the performance of *Labourers of Herakles* at the same festival of Ancient Greek Drama in 1995. The notes 'ask questions about male violence', whereas in the theatre Harrison marginalises 'women' by rendering them in parody as the Chorus of 'female' cement mixers (p. 139). Rutter notices that the statue of Herakles was castrated after the performance: rather than commenting on phallocentric power relations, and the destructive rage of Herakles during the play, the excision was actually carried out by the male actors, who 'signed it and gave it to their playwright as a souvenir' (p. 142). This fascination with fake penises continues in

*Prometheus*, which features several close-ups of Goldenballs's genitalia. One of these occurs in the scene in which Io kisses the statue's knee and foot, and makes it clear that this is a sequence of displaced sexual behaviour: the connection between Io and Prometheus in Aeschylus's play is rewritten as an erotic encounter. The binary between the male characters and the 'female principle' is thus subverted as she fawns on his dirty foot, and, as the screen-play illustrates (but not the film), *'wipes the feet clean with her hair'* (p. 73). (Since the statue consists partly of her recycled husband, perhaps her amorous attentions are directed towards him rather than the mythical figure.) In workbook 4, the first draft of this scene has Io maybe 'cleaning the feet cock etc.' and licking the neo-Nazi graffiti 'off the gold'; she then 'Licks with tongue, up to genitals', and 'Sucks the statue off' (p. 821).

# Chapter 4

# Ted Hughes, Peephole Metaphysics and the Poetics of Extremity

Ted Hughes is more commonly known as a eulogiser of sheep, pigs and Sylvia Plath than as a post-Holocaust poet. Of all the authors discussed in this book, Hughes seems to have taken Theodor Adorno's warning about 'barbaric' art most seriously, but references to the Holocaust do surface in his poetry. A relatively early poem, 'T. V. On', mentions the 'Jew-burning music' on the television, and describes sheepish characters on screen as 'those Jews who had not heard/ Where it was they had arrived/ On such a sunny day,/ Protesting as politely as/ A dignity requires'.[1] 'Karma', from *Wodwo*, refers to 'world-quaking tears . . . at Buchenwald': the typescript held at Emory University is entitled 'Ashes', and comprises a more specifically post-Holocaust poem (p. 167). It begins 'Auschwitz – a word hawked and spat out – Auschwitz!'; another draft of 'Karma' starts: 'Auschwitz, Auschwitz, Auschwitz'.[2] As Terry Gifford argues, Hughes's work engages with 'the aftermath of the Second World War, the Holocaust, the . . . horrible things that human beings could do to each other, and that were also happening . . . in the predatory, natural world'.[3] However, as opposed to the other post-Holocaust poets discussed in this book, Hughes declares in his prose statements that Britain remained relatively unaffected by the events of World War II, and that World War I had a much more profound effect on settlements that (allegedly) lost their entire male population in one day of trench conflict. Hughes's apparent lack of interest in the Holocaust is belied by the poems that do engage with the camps, such as 'Lines about Elias'. János Pilinszky – a Hungarian poet whom Hughes met after the inauguration of the *Modern Poetry in Translation* journal in 1966, and its attendant readings – appears to have influenced Hughes's poem. Pilinszky's lively correspondence with Hughes is held at Emory University in Atlanta: the opening of the Hughes archive has made the tracking of his comments about twentieth-century conflict much easier; references are made to unpublished letters and manuscripts throughout this chapter. Pilinszky's verse panegyrises the concepts of 'Being', and the 'poetry of extremity': his reliance on abstractions is perhaps partly attributable to his ambiguous status as a Holocaust poet, since he was enlisted by the retreating German army; his guilt betrays itself most memorably in the poem 'The French Prisoner', which describes a temporary escapee munching on a raw turnip. The Hungarian poet's concerns manifest themselves in Hughes's post-Holocaust poetry, such as when he suspends the conflict between the Nazi guards and inmates in 'Lines about Elias' with a concept of Being that is meant to transcend the blighted notion of humanity. This chapter argues that Hughes produces more successful post-Holocaust poems when he deploys what A. Alvarez has termed the poetics of indirection, as in 'Your Paris', 'Pike' and the Crow sequence.[4] Although 'Your Paris' criticises Alvarez's and Pilinszky's concept of the poetics of extremity, the poem does not comprise a self-conscious text in terms of its stylistic engagement with the events of the German occupation: awkward poetics arise more clearly in Hughes's work in the form of his critique of atrocity in the series of Crow poems; Paul Bentley refers to the 'awkward' and 'mangled' language of these texts.[5] In a letter to Gerald Hughes (27 October 1969) held at Emory, Hughes himself argues that the poems are 'actually very ugly . . . it's Crow-talk – plain and ugly'.[6] However, unlike the aesthetics of awkwardness in Geoffrey Hill's *The Triumph of Love*, the Crow sequence does not self-consciously discuss the possibility of aesthetic culpability within the texture of the poems themselves. The poems form 'barbaric' depictions of war's barbarism, but not critiques of the critique of war.[7]

## Hughes and ontology

The poems discussed in this chapter share an ontological need, which manifests itself as an encounter with a transcendent notion of Being ('Lines about Elias', 'Pike'), or post-Holocaust *Existenz* ('Your Paris', 'Crow's Account of the Battle'). This persistent desire pervades both Hughes's writing, and ensuing critical responses. It has manifested itself in various forms: Seamus Heaney senses a Hopkinesque penetration of the 'inner life', and the subsequent 'simple being-thereness' depicted in Hughes's work; Leonard Scijay detects a 'mystical consciousness of the oneness of Creation'; Craig Robinson has written of Hughes's discovery of 'an energy found at its purest in nature'; Keith Sagar eulogises the inner being of the poet.[8] Although different, these descriptions share an appreciation of Hughesian 'Being' (or '*Existenz*'): Scijay has located it more specifically in Eastern metaphysics, Zen, and the Japanese concept of *satori* (the 'totalistic unity with the infinite').[9] Critics have mostly agreed that Hughes does not adhere to an existentialist rewriting of *Existenz*, despite his predilection, as Alvarez notes, for black pullovers.[10] Critics have not always responded generously to confrontations with Being in Hughes's verse, in which the narrator may confront a fish or a harebell, and perceive a force at work beyond human understanding, but perhaps just glimpsed in the Tennysonian notion of wisdom as opposed to knowledge.[11] Just as reason lies beyond morality for Hegel, perhaps Being proliferates beyond ethics: Eric Homberger finds a version of the Nazi concept of *Rausch* in the poet's 'fascistic exaltation of violence for its own sake'.[12] Critics more sympathetic to Hughes have attempted to locate his sense of *Existenz* elsewhere. Dwight Eddins recognises *der Wille* in the 'inspiritedness' and 'universal force-field' confronted in the poetry, at the same time as recognising an anti-logical logos at work: the irony is that the 'wild, irrational instinctuality' of Schopenhauer's philosophy is ordered by the totalised concept of *der Wille* itself.[13] In contrast, Joanny Moulin uncovers the moments in which the narrators experience the imprint of the Lacanian 'real' in empirical reality.[14] All these different critical perspectives have provided valuable insights into Hughes's writing: it cannot be denied that the vigour of his work arises partly from his engagement with metaphysics of presence. Perhaps what could be added to this body of criticism is a critique of ontology itself.[15] The possibility remains that a requirement persists in Hughes's most sophisticated poetry to locate a form of Being that has been invented in order to find it. In *Negative Dialectics*, Adorno describes such an ontological need as a manifestation of 'peephole metaphysics'.[16]

*Guckkastenmetaphysik* (literally, 'peep-show' metaphysics) can be defined as philosophical thought in which the subject 'looks through' surface reality and discovers totalised Being.[17] *Negative Dialektik* is one of the most sustained critiques of ontology in twentieth-century philosophy; its main target in the second section ('Being and Existence') is the work of Hegel. The latter's exposition of *Existenz* is uncovered as an individual's search for transcendence: this occludes the absolute 'first' of Being, which is assumed to exist only because of the subject's acute ontological need. Reflective philosophy is concerned that the particular is increasingly at the mercy of overarching concepts such as *Existenz*; a connection is hinted at between the totality of fascism and the prevalence of Being. There is certainly a troubling, but not fascistic, concept of the self at work in much of Hughes's writing. Joyous immolations of the subject at the end of 'The Thought-Fox', 'Pike' and 'Milesian Encounter on the Sligachan' (to name but three poems) are potentially worrying in the light of Adorno's defence of the particular. An eco-critic might retort that the subject is immersed in the eco-system rather than sacrificed to other, more dangerous totalities. However, any sense of self must be qualified by the fact that it is a historical category; the augmented capitulation of the individual to ideology in the post-Enlightenment era would, therefore, be unsettling for any reflective philosopher studying the dissolution of the subject in Hughes's work. As Susan Gubar argues, post-Holocaust lyrics display 'the ironic friction between the lyric's traditional investment in voicing subjectivity and a history that assaulted not only the innumerable sovereign subjects but indeed the very idea of sovereign selfhood'.[18]

Any process in which the individual 'looks through' reality to a transcendent totality – as the narrators do in the poems listed above – is described by Adorno with the poetic image of the crenel: '*Wie durch die Scharten eines Turms blickt es auf einem schwarzen Himmel, an dem der Stern der Idee oder des Seins aufgehe*' (p. 143). E. B. Ashton translates this as follows: 'As through the crenels of a parapet, the subject gazes upon a black sky in which the star of the idea, or of Being, is said to rise' (pp. 139–40). '*Scharten*' literally means 'notches', but 'crenels' is more accurate in the context of the castle imagery. Instead of shooting arrows through the gaps, the idealist philosopher tries to prove *Existenz* by staring out from the parapet as if penetrating the veneer of rationality. Adorno's poetic analogy links with the phrase *Guckkastenmetaphysik* itself: the crenels become the peepholes through which the subject stares in awe. However, Ashton's phrase 'peephole metaphysics' loses the connotation in the original German of 'cheap entertainment'. 'Peep-show metaphysics', on the other hand, would retain Adorno's fear that Being evinces a 'cheap' aesthetic; that *Existenz* is a potentially mass-cultural phenomenon we can all revel in, as we naively attempt to affirm our existence through an outside force. 'Peep-show metaphysics' would also retain the meaning of 'looking through', since a peepshow is 'a small exhibition of pictures viewed through a magnifying lens inserted in a small orifice'.[19] George Bernard Shaw encountered this diminutive orifice in 1861 – resulting in one of the first instances of the word in English, according to the *OED* – when he 'did a cheap trip to Folkestone . . . [and] spent sevenpence on dropping pennies into silly automatic machines and peep-shows of rowdy girls having a jolly time'. Silly, yes, one might add, and yet the titillation is still spread across several pennies. Like philosophical evocations of Being, the peep-show is repeated precisely because it is such an accessible pursuit. Adorno's élitist concerns are expressed in relation to literature more forcibly when he asserts that Being, by the mid-twentieth century, is commensurate with poetic clichés, '*wie das Rauschen von Blättern in Wind schlechter Gedichte*' ('like the rustle of leaves in the wind of bad poems').[20]

Most of Hughes's poems are clearly not examples of bad wind, but awkward poetics do not occur in his *oeuvre* in the form of a critique of his concept of Being. Neither are the texts instances of 'cheap' aesthetics, since some of his most successful pieces engage in *Guckkastenmetaphysik*, such as the moment in which the narrator's blood prickles when he anticipates an encounter with a salmon in 'Milesian Encounter on the Sligachan', or when he enters the piling silence of the river in 'Stealing Trout on a May Morning'. 'Peep-show metaphysics' is thus a misleading translation in that it elides Adorno's admission that the ontological need can be partly condoned as a refulgent idea. Hence the celebratory – as well as accusatory – image of the philosopher waiting on the parapet for the 'star' of ontology to rise. Perhaps 'peephole metaphysics' is a more accurate phrase in the light of this positivity. An older word (the first English citation in the *OED* is 1681), 'peephole' is more apt in the context of the castle imagery. 'Show' also suggests something tangible can be adduced from the crenels' view, whereas 'hole' retains the possibility that there is nothing to be seen ('*hinaussehen*' literally means 'looking out', not 'peeping'). 'Peephole' focuses critical attention on the subject rather than the object; the (rather helpful) *OED* definition of the word is of 'A small *hole* through which *one* can peep' (my italics). As Adorno states after the 'crenel' passage, there may be a philosophical hole, but 'There is no peeping out' (p. 140); *Existenz* is a concept, not an empirical phenomenon.

Peeping is certainly an activity that runs through some of Hughes's more canonical pieces; for example, the moment in 'Pike' in which the narrator stares into the pond, and imagines the fish rising slowly towards him. The metaphysics of the gigantic pike enhance the epiphanic moment at the closure of the text. At this point, the divergence of *Negative Dialectics* and Hughes's *oeuvre* must be stressed: his poetry may be critiqued in terms of its conceptuality of Being, but this does not necessarily mean that it is diminished aesthetically in the process. Only occasionally, as in the poem 'Lines about Elias', does an assurance about *Existenz* result in a potentially reprehensible aesthetic, as I shall demonstrate later in this chapter. For the most part, a belief in Being instigates passionate poetics. Hughes's iterative confrontation with the 'star' of Being has lead to an abundant production of poems, as well as a distinctive style that is easily parodied, as in Wendy Cope's parody of *Crow*, 'God and the Jolly Bored Bog-Mouse'.[21] This abundance might appear to grate against Adorno's plea for stylistic wariness with his notion of artistic barbarism. Yet to confront the 'peephole' possibility in several poems that the poet might be confronting not Being, but a conceptual aporia, is a creative risk that Hughes was repeatedly willing to take.

## World War I, the Movement and the poetics of extremity

My focus for the rest of this chapter will be on the ways in which Hughes's 'peephole metaphysics' link with his vocation as a post-Holocaust poet; it is at this point that the letters held in the Emory Archives in Atlanta become particularly pertinent. His response to World War I as a moment of ontological 'extremity' is encapsulated in poems such as 'Six Young Men', 'Mayday on Holderness', 'Wilfred Owen's Photographs', 'Ghost Crabs', 'The Green Wolf', 'Scapegoats and Rabies', 'Out', 'Leaf Mould', 'Tiger-Psalm', 'Dust as We Are', 'The Last of the 1st/5th Lancashire Fusiliers', 'The Haunting', and has been well documented in the interviews and criticism.[22] A lesser-known fact can be added from the Emory collections: in a letter to Mr Fallon (9 January 1994), Hughes recounts that his first ambitious poetic project was to write a long poem about Gallipoli; the possibility that it might be read as an insult to the survivors – who famously included his father – stopped him from pursuing the topic.[23]

In contrast to this material available on Hughes and World War I, his status as a post-Holocaust writer has rarely been remarked. World War I is clearly his preferred area of concern, yet Holocaust synecdoches persist in his work: in addition to 'T. V. On', 'Karma', 'Ashes' and 'Lines about Elias', for example, 'The Locket' from *Capriccio* mentions the gas ovens 'Locked with a swastika' (p. 784), a pile of corpses opens *Gaudete*, and *Birthday Letters* refers to 'The stink of fear' of those hiding from Nazis during the occupation of France (p. 1,066).[24] In a letter to Nick Gammage (15 March 1991), Hughes explains that his particular interest in World War I arises from his generation's encounter with the event as a trauma recounted by fathers, whereas its experience of Britain after World War II registered no impact: 'As we became aware of the effects of the war in Eastern Europe, the holocaust, the Nuclear terror etc, they became just more news'.[25] Hughes contrasts the public 'news' of the Holocaust with his private, early days spent in 'a kind of Mental Hospital of the survivors' of World War I, in which 'the old understanding that war was fought by regular, professional armies had just been blown away like a wisp'. Instead of regarding many of the stories of the generation before 1936 (the date established in the letter) as equally mediated experiences, Hughes believes that, as a secondary witness of the 1914–18 conflict, he later created 'peepholes' through to the mythology or 'inner world' of his childhood. This important letter certainly accounts for the prevalence of World War I in his work: in another missive to Gammage (29 November 1989), Hughes reveals that it lies behind the relative absence of humans in the poem 'Wind'.[26] Nearly all of his father's friends who played football before the Great War were killed in action: on one occasion Hughes watched a soccer match through the window of the Heptonstall house and experienced an epiphanic moment in which he sensed a 'time-warp', and subsequently his father's boyhood; the result in writing was originally 'Wind', although he returned to the event in the later poem 'Football at Slack'.

Despite the example of these two texts, the Gammage letters risk over-shadowing Hughes's poems that include references to Holocaust icons, such as 'A Motorbike', where – as in Harrison's *Prometheus* – they inform working-class experience: the morning bus is reminiscent of a 'labour truck', the boss 'as bad as the S.S.', and the uniformity of ration-book Britain 'as bad as electrified barbed wire' (p. 547). 'A Motorbike' illustrates the Holocaust's increasing currency as a discursive figure for aspects of post-war Britain: Hughes comments in a letter to Derwent May (10 April 1992) – about the teaching of English in universities – that students negotiate literature and criticism as if the syllabus were a con-centration camp.[27] In a letter to Brenda and Charles Tomlinson (4 January 1989), Hughes depicts an antithetical succession relevant to both world wars in relation to family mythology: Wilfred Owen repre-sents his father, and Keith Douglas his brother Gerald.[28] This compari-son is supported by an earlier missive to Gerald, in which he mentions having sent some of Douglas's poems to him previously, and encourages his brother's writing by commenting that he has a similar talent to Douglas (10 May 1964). In a letter to Keith Sagar (4 April 1990), Hughes describes a similar epiphanic experience to that of the Heptonstall foot-ball match, this time in relation to the Holocaust rather than World War I. Hughes remembers peeping into a holly tree in Conisborough that a tawny owl was minded to frequent, and thinking: 'today is 4/4/44 and I shall never forget this moment. Now I orient all holocaust experiences all World War II events, by that fixed moment'.[29] This post-Holocaust ontology can be explicated in relation to the poetics of extremity outlined in the work of Alvarez and Pilinszky.

During an interview with Ekbert Faas, Hughes comments that Movement writers were deeply affected by the 'colossal negative revela-tion' of the 'death camps and atomic bombs', but produced poetic equiv-alents of the 'nice cigarette and a nice view of the park'.[30] Hughes, in his own words, 'came a bit later'; it was the early groundswell of post-Movement writing in Britain in the late 1950s – as well as Alvarez's reading of American poets (particularly Robert Lowell and John Berryman) – that inspired the seminal anthology *The New Poetry*, in which eighteen of Hughes's poems featured.[31] In a letter held in the archives of The Brotherton Library in Leeds, Philip Larkin asserts that he was attempting to make poetry 'clean' in 'At Grass'; in other words, free it from rhetorical excesses so apparent in 'The Horses', the Hughes poem that Alvarez compares with Larkin's in his introduction to *The New Poetry*.[32] In contrast, Alvarez argues that the 'extreme' poetics of Hughes's verse might be indicative of a new kind of post-war poetry.[33] Metaphysics of Being in these 'new depth' poetics are set against the 'gentility' of Movement writing, and its subsequent 'flatness of tone' (pp. 24–5). The poetry of extremity is that which, according to Alvarez, can face the advent of the death camps, psychoanalysis, and public savagery with the same panache as contemporaneous horror films. Despite only the vague edict that the poets of a 'new seriousness' should use the full range of their intelligence in order to achieve this, the polemical tract influenced many post-war poets, including, as Alvarez recounts in his autobiography, *Where Did It All Go Right?*, Sylvia Plath (p. 205).

Alvarez's comments on 'extreme' post-Holocaust poetics have not been without their detractors. John Lucas detects a tendentious form of ontology, in which artists are asked to 'take risks' in order to attempt to make their insignificant private insecurities comparable with public atrocities such as the Holocaust.[34] In a letter to C. B. Cox held in the archives of the John Rylands library in Manchester, Olwyn Hughes encloses an article by Margaret Newlin which attacks these 'extreme poetics' as an artistic invitation to insanity, violence, self-destruction, mania, depression, paranoia, hallucinations, psychosis, and drugs.[35] To be fair to Alvarez, he does not incite such proclivities in the introduction itself: 'peepholes' through to twentieth-century suffering should be tempered, Alvarez argues, with poetics of indirection (pp. 27–9). The self-consciousness of awkward poetics registers itself in his contention that pretending that private and public pain are commensurate will result in 'cheap' aesthetics: he calls instead for 'new depth' writing which will mix the formal grace of T. S. Eliot and Larkin with the savagery confronted in D. H. Lawrence and Hughes's work. Rather than engage with the possibility of aesthetic culpability, however, 'indirect' poetics are an attempt to solve the issue. Newlin, in relation to Plath, terms indirection the 'oblique' poetics of 'deflection'; Newlin and Lucas's criticisms of Alvarez can be more readily applied to less guarded statements in *The Savage God* and *Beyond All This Fiddle*, as in the comparison between Keats and Plath ('The very source of her creative energy was . . . her self-destructiveness').[36] In the latter collection of essays, the title piece suggests that peephole metaphysics might be the ontology of the bored: post-Holocaust writers confront ever more disturbing psychological phenomena in a self-effacing process of 'psychic Darwinism' (p. 17). However, the poetics of indirection outlined in *The New Poetry* do provide an insight into the modes of Being explored by Hughes in his post-Holocaust writing; especially in relation to the early collections *The Hawk in the Rain*, *Lupercal* and *Wodwo*, and his last one, *Birthday Letters*. These poetics chime with Adorno's charitable exposition of autonomous, and committed, art, such as that to be found in the poetry of Paul Celan, and, as I argue in Chapter two, Geoffrey Hill.[37] Instead of attempting to describe specific atrocities directly it is potentially less insulting – as Hughes recognised in relation to his abandoned Gallipoli piece – for the writer to engage with traumatic historical events at a tangent. This indirection – in a similar way to awkward poetics – might invite the counter-charge of insidious artistic profit gained whilst pretending to write about something else, but this technique has certainly proved fruitful for Hughes. 'Peephole metaphysics' produce much more successful poems when the texts invite the context of atrocity only indirectly, as in 'T. V. On', 'Karma', 'A Motorbike', 'Pike', 'Wodwo' and 'Your Paris'; these poems can be contrasted with the ontological muddle encountered in 'Lines about Elias'.[38]

## Extinction and creativity in 'Lines about Elias'

An increasing interest in 'new depth' poetics is evident in Hughes's work from the mid-1960s onwards, most obviously in his championing of various Eastern European poets such as Vasko Popa. Hughes was attracted to the writing of one Eastern European writer in particular, for no clear reason apart from the close friendship registered in the letters at Emory.[39] János Pilinszky was a Hungarian poet, but not, in fact, a victim of Nazism in a strict sense, given that he was enlisted with the retreating German army. In the 1975 introduction to his collection of Pilinszky's poetry – translated with János Csokits – ambiguous phrases obscure this fact, such as 'conscripted for military service' (with whom is not stated), and 'scooped up by the retreating German army' (as a prisoner or conscript?).[40] Nevertheless, Pilinszky's poems appear to have sharpened Hughes's conception of the poetry of extremity, since he argues in *The Desert of Love* that the tendency towards silence in the Hungarian's work is counterbalanced by 'the ecstasy of affliction', a 'passivity of transfiguration', which, 'when all the powers of the soul are focused on what is final . . . is indistinguishable from joy'; 'the moment closest to extinction turns out to be *the* creative moment' (p. 12). Pilinszky's fusion of near-death experiences and creativity – a conflation registered so controversially in Alvarez's introduction to *The New Poetry* – led to the lamentable Hughes poem 'Lines about Elias'. Aligning death with artistic ecstasy in the specific context of the Holocaust is problematic enough in the case of those (unlike Pilinszky) who suffered as camp inmates; for a post-Holocaust writer such as Hughes to assert that the moment before the gas chambers allows 'us' to appreciate an ontological 'truth' is insensitive, and yet this is exactly what occurs in 'Lines about Elias'. Moulin, in *Ted Hughes: New Selected Poems*, has gone a step further in his criticism and wonders 'whether such literature should not be damned' (p. 160). The following analysis investigates whether there are grounds in the text for Moulin's outraged critical response.

'Lines about Elias' describes an incident in an unnamed camp in which the inmates' orchestra played for the prison guards. There are no awkward poetics here in the form of a critique of *Existenz*: 'peephole metaphysics' are evident in that the music allows the narrator to 'see through' the inmates' pain, and appreciate a higher plain of Being in which victims, and non-victims, blend in ontological harmony. The second stanza highlights the suffering of Elias, since it opens with a description of the 'scabies on his belly the sores and/ Inflammations', but then the fourth stanza attempts to separate aesthetics from pain: the musical notes 'made them for those moments unaware/ Of their starvation' (pp. 742–3). Moulin rails against this shift towards transcendence by asserting Primo Levi's supposed hatred of music, but the Italian writer is not averse to celebrating moments of aesthetic pleasure within Auschwitz, as in the Ulysses chapter where he struggles to remember lines from Dante in *If This Is A Man*. Similarly, in 'The Literature of the Holocaust' from *Beyond All This Fiddle* (p. 22), Alvarez refers to Josef Bor's *Terezin Requiem*, in which the phenomenon of Verdi in Theresienstadt inspires both the book and the celebratory subtitle, 'A Narrative of the Human Spirit'. Music is the emphatic, single-line spondee of 'strange food' for the inmates in Hughes's poem (p. 743); in Levi's book, poetry momentarily attempts to fulfil this compensatory role. However, Levi does not place Dante above the need for the next piece of bread, as the post-Holocaust poet appears to do here. The character named Steinlauf in Levi's text provides a similar alternative to ontological extremity when he contends that washing allows the prisoner to escape the value system of the camp, 'a great machine to reduce us to beasts': 'to survive we must force ourselves to save at least the skeleton, the scaffolding, the form of civilization'.[41] Levi retorts by informing the reader that Steinlauf is an 'ex-sergeant of the Austro-Hungarian army', and partial to a moral discourse which is 'mid-European'; from 'the other side of the Alps' to Italy. '[W]ould it not be better,' Levi asks, 'to acknowledge one's lack of a system' in the disorientating space of the camp? Music and washing are only temporary escapes from the 'great machine' of Auschwitz, rather than instances that might lead to the overarching metaphysics located in the closure of Hughes's poem.

The nub of Moulin's critique is located in the last two verses, in which the guards are reborn as they bathe themselves in music; the poem concludes that they need this salvation more than the inmates. By turning Nazis into victims, Hughes risks obscenity. Perhaps the incriminating lines are ironic, yet the pious tone suggests no such complication. An ontological muddle is located in the anti-humanist verve which is simultaneously humanist; in this sense, my evaluation of the text is different from Moulin's, who argues that it reaches a nihilistic conclusion. Humanism, the poem implies, has lead to the advent of the camps (how is not explained); the prisoners and guards therefore need to merge in transcendent Being, 'Escaping their humanity' into a space outside 'the time corridor' (pp. 743, 742). Yet the gleaning of aesthetic purchase through the metaphysics of *Existenz* also forms an archetypal moment of humanist salvation. Anti-humanist critics in Holocaust studies such as Lawrence Langer and Theodor Adorno have been at pains to dismiss such epiphanies as hopelessly idealist, as I illustrated in my chapter on Harrison's *Prometheus*. In 'Lines about Elias', peephole metaphysics result in a capitulation of a victim/non-victim binary to a transcendence which elides any consideration of the self, replacing it with the spell of the whole. *Existenz* here 'eliminates all heterogeneous being', as Adorno warns in *Negative Dialectics* (p. 26).

Maybe Hughes can be excused of such indelicate poetry if he is not referring directly to the Holocaust: the identity of Elias remains obscure in the text; the capitalisation of the 'Camp' indicates that it might be referring outwards to all ontological discrepancies between victims and non-victims.[42] This hardly helps Hughes's case, since the Holocaust iconography is explicit: it recalls instances in several camps – including Terezín – where orchestras or individual inmates played for their captors. This particular synecdoche for the Holocaust indicates that the experience of music in the camps cannot be detached from the context of the inmates' suffering, whatever Hughes's poem may suggest. This inextricability was illustrated in the furore over the planned concert in Mauthausen in May 2000, in which Simon Rattle proposed to conduct the Vienna Philharmonic Orchestra: the journalist Stephen Moss asks in *The Guardian* why, when many artists and musicians in Austria had spoken out against Jörg Haider's Freedom Party, had the Vienna Philharmonic remained silent?[43] The orchestra maintained its historical privilege to remain apolitical, but a potentially obscene irony was not lost on the European press: musicians who refused to denounce a political party with a leader who praised Hitler's employment policies were due to play in a former concentration camp. Despite this, Rattle insisted that the concert should go ahead precisely because of the inextricability of aesthetics and history: he contended that a chord of B flat is political because 'music is intimately bound up with all the events of its planet'. Whereas the pan-European organiser Leon Zelman, a former inmate of Mauthausen, regarded the concert as a 'hymn of the new Europe', the Vienna journalist Marta Halpert saw it as evidence of the Holocaust industry, and 'event culture' in general, 'like the Three Tenors in the Baths at Caracalla'.[44]

'Lines about Elias' was written for a special edition of *P. N. Review* that celebrated the work of Thom Gunn: it appears to be a text written in haste, as the long, sparsely edited sentences and (sometimes) plain silly metaphors suggest.[45] Hughes has occasionally flirted with the label of a science fiction poet – as in 'Ghost Crabs', which was reprinted in Edward Lucie-Smith's sci-fi anthology *Holding Your Eight Hands* – but his predilection for spatial metaphysics results here in the offensive image of the camp inmates as 'baboons', 'under the effects/ Of a poisonous dust from space' (p. 742).[46] Any link between such effects and the playing of crude instruments is left uncertain; there may even be a distasteful connection between the 'dust' and the Zyklon-B particles that some of the musicians will encounter in the 'next few/ Frightful [frightful?!] possibly fatal days'. 'Frightful' appears in a letter to Nick Gammage about World War II (15 March 1991), describing the 'frightful time' that 'certain groups' suffered during the conflict: although the adjective means 'dreadful' or 'extreme', it cannot shake a sense of British understatement symptomatic of the officer class that Hughes displays his reservations about at the end of the missive.[47] Such careless metaphors ('baboons') and litotes can be contrasted with D. J. Enright's poem 'Apocalypse' from *The New Poetry* (p. 91), which attacks the German tourist board's celebration of an orchestra playing in the rubble of post-war Germany with the ironic retort, 'One Bach outweighs ten Belsens'.[48] If, following Pilinszky, 'the moment closest to extinction turns out to be *the* creative moment', it is also noticeable that the declaration suspends aesthetic judgements. It is ironic that the creative moment for the post-Holocaust writer in this instance produces one of the most insensitive poems that Hughes has ever written. This is certainly an occasion in which peephole metaphysics lead to the 'wind' of a bad poem.

## Paris and post-Holocaust *Existenz*

Perhaps it is unfair to begin a discussion of Ted Hughes's post-Holocaust poetry with such a controversial text. 'Your Paris' proves to be a much more successful post-Holocaust poem: it favours Alvarez's poetics of indirection, but also critiques 'new depth' poetics as the musings of a young, post-war poet unaware of his wife's suffering. Instead of attempting to speak directly for victims of the Holocaust – as in 'Lines about Elias' – it fulfils Alvarez's requirements for the poetics of extremity by interspersing references throughout the poem to the camps, World War II, and Verdun. Ostensibly, it depicts the visit (or visits) of Hughes and Plath to Paris in 1956.[49] Post-Holocaust poetry is here the preserve of the 'post-war utility survivor' (p. 1,066) – as Hughes terms Paris – who interprets the city through the drab viewfinder of a Yorkshireman used to rationing, and the 'utility' clothes worn during the war by much of the British populace. Peephole metaphysics arise in the comparison of Plath's suffering with the post-Holocaust *Existenz* recounted by the Hughes figure at the beginning of the poem. The narrator appears to be able to 'see through' to the psychological distress of the muse, at the same time as he admits his readings of her 'gushy burblings' were 'hopelessly wrong' (p. 1,067). Fate lies behind the surface action: *Birthday Letters* as a whole seems to implore Plath, or the reader, to answer the ultimate question from 'Setebos', 'Which play/ Were we in?', as if peepholes through to such elusive stories might assuage the pain of Plath's demise (p. 1,129).

In 'Your Paris', these worries are initially asides to the clash between American and European conceptions of the post-war capital. The irony of the name of the hotel at the beginning of the poem ('Hôtel des Deux Continents') indicates that there is no true ontology of Paris (p. 1,064).[50] A double narrative persists in which the poet describes incidents in the past, and records how he interprets them at the point of composition, as well as when the events of the war were still fresh in his mind. This distinction is sometimes blurred in the recounting of historical events: in relation to Holocaust literature, Sue Vice has termed this technique 'backshadowing'.[51] The process is immediately evident in that Hughes only *thought* Plath's Paris was 'American': this links with the patronising, 'bobby-soxer' version of Plath at the beginning of the text. Hughes appears conscious of this stereotyping in retrospect: 'You Hated Spain' from *Birthday Letters* refers similarly to Plath as – so he then thought – a naïve, over-exuberant, 'bobby-sox American' (p. 1,068). Hughes self-consciously criticises what he regarded as the typical American response to the city, uninterested in recent atrocities: Plath reads it in terms of a pre-war aesthetic which encompasses Impressionist paintings, and US writers living in Paris in the 1920s; in particular, 'Hemingway/ Fitzgerald, Henry Miller, Gertrude Stein' (p. 1,066). Hughes argues that his younger self perpetrated not a British, but European, reading of the post-war Île de la Cité. This initiated a 'new depth' sensibility: for him, Paris in 1956 was 'only just not German'; he cannot help but 'read' the bullet holes in the Quai, and ponders café chairs with 'SS mannequins' providing *tableaux vivants* ('visual entertainment') 'So recently the coffee was still bitter/ As acorns, and the waiters' eyes/ Clogged with dregs of betrayal, reprisal, hatred' (p. 1,066). Peephole metaphysics arise here in the form of the uncanny. There is something beyond the surface text of Paris that informs his reading: the post-Holocaust poet senses 'an eerie familiar feeling' as he contemplates the carnage of the Occupation; he becomes a 'ghostwatcher', in which history repeats itself as trauma in the faces of those 'closed by the Camps', or the '*Collaborateurs*'. Hughes 'had rehearsed' the 'old nightmare' repeatedly 'Most of [his] life'. These lines can be explicated in relation to his comments on 'A Masque for Three Voices': one of his 'earliest recurrent dreams, long before 1939, was clouds of German parachutists descending on the Calder Valley in West Yorkshire, and my constant fantasy was how this or that part of the valley could be defended . . . who would be traitors' (p. 1,219). These nightmares about infiltration inform – at this juncture in 'Your Paris' – the young Hughes's ontology of Paris. Whereas the Holocaust links with the previous atrocity of Verdun for Hughes – a former teacher of twentieth-century history – such connections for the Plath character are 'anecdotal aesthetic' touches, like the 'proleptic' ('anticipated') marker for the German bullet in Picasso's portrait of Apollinaire.

A narrative switch then occurs forty-six lines into the poem, in which 'new depth' poetics are uncovered, during the process of backshadowing, as a potential sham. Plath calls Hughes 'Aristide Bruant', and wants to draw *les toits* ('the roofs'): Bruant was the patron of Henri de Toulouse-Lautrec, and a *conferencier* (a singer, comedian and master of ceremonies); Plath may be referring to the famous poster of Bruant advertising his new club, with the caption '*Ambassadeurs . . . aristide Bruant dans sans caberet*'. Hughes appears to be the 'master of ceremonies' in 'Your Paris', presenting Plath as he chooses, and following her American reactions to the city, as he saw them, like the protective dog-figure in the text. Backshadowing subverts this presentation in the form of the metaphysics of Fate: in retrospect, Hughes thinks that her enthusiasm concealed an 'underground, your hide-out,/ That chamber' where she waits for her 'torturer' to remember 'his amusement'; the uncanny nature of the poem may also arise from the simultaneous appreciation of her future death in every detail of *Birthday Letters* (p. 1,067). If read in the light of this collection as a whole, and the biographical details it invites, these lines appear to refer to the suppression of her first mental breakdown, her electric-shock treatment, and the Freudian father figure who will encourage her to replace Hughes with his devilry. *Birthday Letters* tempts the critic into an unguarded evaluation of the collection as a true version of events, but despite the seductive device of the narrative switch in 'Your Paris', this remains an aestheticisation of the Plath figure; the 'peepholes' through to Fate and an Oedipal narrative clearly attempt (validly or not) to delimit the culpability of the narrator in her ultimate demise. Nevertheless, the poem remains disarmingly castigatory in its depiction of the deluded Hughes figure: Plath's inner 'chamber' critiques the earlier image of the post-Holocaust poet more concerned with the presence of Resistance members or hiding Jews in 'The stink of fear still hanging in the [Parisian] wardrobes'. These 'new depth' poetics are dismissed as 'plain paving, albeit/ Pecked by the odd, stray, historic bullet' compared to Plath's suffering (p. 1,067). This image undercuts the inseparability of aesthetics and history that Alvarez champions in *The New Poetry*: in retrospect, Hughes suspects the melodramatic, 'psychic Darwinism' of a young writer in the earlier images of the post-war city. Even a 'stricken, sunny exposure of pavement' is evidence of atrocity for the younger Hughes; this dialectic mirrors Adorno's potentially histrionic warning in *Minima Moralia* that 'Even the blossoming tree lies the moment its bloom is seen without the shadow of terror'.[52] The double narrative of the poem then gives way to Hughes's concluding critique of 'new depth' poetics: the primacy of his 'utility' imagination occluded the particularity of Plath's hidden distress.

Any clash between American, and European, versions of Paris is complicated at the end of the poem with an allusion to the various versions of the visit in the journals, letters, biographies and criticism; this phenomenon opens out in 'Your Paris' into a wider criticism of the reification of the relationship between Hughes and Plath. *Birthday Letters* can be read as a rewriting of the potential Hughes figures encountered in *Ariel*, but this poem reads more like a response to Plath critics in particular, the errant canines in 'The Dogs are Eating your Mother' who bit 'the face off her [Heptonstall] gravestone' (p. 1,169). This reading is supported by the Emory letters, in which Thom Gunn encourages Hughes to print material about Plath in a short book as a retort to certain anti-Hughes critics (14 April 1991); it is possible that these prose jottings metamorphosed eventually into the manuscript of *Birthday Letters*.[53] My argument arises from the final image in 'Your Paris' of the yawning Hughes, who watches Plath calm herself by drawing 'Roofs, a traffic bollard, a bottle, me' (p. 1,067). The last word emphasises Plath's transformation of Hughes into an aesthetic object. At this point, the comparison of the poet with roofs and a traffic bollard suggests mundaneness, and yet backshadowing occurs here in that it parallels the similar process to take place later, as Hughes saw it, in *Ariel*: in a letter to Janet Malcolm he criticises Plath for her 'incessant pushing of her immediate life (our life) into some limelit performance' (11 April 1994).[54] Behind the camp poetics of her dramatic monologues, he suspects personal melodrama; the irony is that in writing *Birthday Letters* there is a similar risk of 'limelit performance', this time from Hughes's perspective. The ending of 'Your Paris' anticipates this relativity of representation: Plath turns Hughes into aesthetic fodder by drawing the picture, and then writing *Ariel*; critics and biographers reify the relationship by perpetrating a critical industry; Hughes paradoxically perpetuates this by trying to draw the record straight in *Birthday Letters*. The representation of Plath in Paris is inevitably affected – as the poem admits – by Hughes's perspective: at other moments in *Birthday Letters*, Hughes innocuously corrects the details of *Ariel* poems: for example, the farmer's mug is blue in 'The Rabbit Catcher' (p. 1,138) rather than the 'dull' mug and 'white china' in Plath's original text.[55] Perhaps Hughes retained a journal where such details were there to be trawled through years later: in a letter to Aurelia Plath (12 January 1975) he mentions a written account of 1962.[56]

Even if a journal covering the Paris trip were available, Hughes's Paris would not be 'your' (Plath's) version of the city. Her sojourn is only mentioned briefly in her journals and letters; appendix ten of Kukil's edition of the journal (see Note 50) contains sketches of bottles, a fruit bowl (headed 'Café Franco-Oriental June 26 – Paris'), shoes and a café, fragments of verse ('Miss Drake Proceeds to Supper', 'Until bird-racketing dawn . . .'), and an anecdote about an old woman looking in a mirror (pp. 571–5). 'Your Paris' cannot help but rewrite Plath's positive version of the honeymoon in *Letters Home*: 'after meandering about Paris, sitting, writing and reading in the Tuileries, have produced a good poem apiece, which is a necessity to our personal self-esteem'.[57] Hughes subverts this cosy image of a blossoming literary relationship with the biographical details inserted into the last half of the poem. He 'backshadows' Plath's perceived suffering by arguing that 'her Paris' was tainted by 'a desk in a *pension*/ Where your letters/ Waited for him unopened' (p. 1,067). This refers to a well-known incident he may have read about in the journals: Plath visited the South of France on 1 January 1956 with Richard Sassoon; in March–April of the same year she visited Paris, hoping Sassoon would be there; she finds instead 'he had left no address, no messages, and my letters begging him to return in time were lying there blue and unread'.[58] In a journal entry of January 1958, Plath refers to her first visit as 'that terrible April in Paris'. This 'kept' secret may have sealed the retrospective spoiling of the honeymoon, and what Hughes refers to in a letter to Lucas Myers as his 'detestation of the French' (September 1961). Just as Plath satirises the fusion of history and spectacle with the camp poetics of 'Lady Lazarus', Hughes – as in 'T. V. On' – rails against the reification of the historical: 'Europe really has become an over-trodden over-photographed over-tipped over-cura-tored museum, and my mind faints slightly with sheer boredom when I think of it.' In the case of Hughes and Plath, this process continues in the personal sphere. Ironically, in 'Your Paris', Hughes anticipates the 'over-curatored' literary relationship that will be his first marriage. The poem berates the aesthetic 'doze' of the post-Holocaust *Existenz* he indulged in before the Plath industry began.

## Indirection and peepholes in 'Pike'

The self-conscious depiction, and subversion, of the poetics of extremity in 'Your Paris' compare favourably with the unreflective panegyric about Being in 'Lines about Elias', but the poem is inevitably responsive to the project of *Birthday Letters* as a whole. This, however, is partly its strength as a post-Holocaust poem. When Hughes tries to engage with the suffering of the camp inmates in 'Lines about Elias' – ignoring his earlier edict about Gallipoli – the narrative is tainted by his transcendent concept of Being. In contrast, 'Pike', like 'Your Paris', forms an example of a post-Holocaust poem that avoids controversy through indirection. These 'reflected' poetics operate beyond the self-consciousness of awkward aesthetics, and, in the case of 'Pike', authorial intention. Post-Holocaust poetics can only be detected in 'Pike', according to Hughes, if the reader chooses to ignore his intended system of symbols. Hughes remains open to the latter possibility in a letter to Janet Malcolm about 'Pike' (30 April 1990): 'People who tell me what a poem means to them are being interesting. Those who tell me what it <u>means</u>, on the other hand, are maybe being no more than bossy.'[59] He goes on to state that 'Pike' and 'Hawk Roosting' began as a series of poems in which the crea-tures were like angels 'hanging in the radiant glory around God's throne, composed of terrible Holy power'; whereas Hitler was 'truly "violent" – a man amok, simply mad, completely outside of any law, natural or human', animals kill because they adhere to their 'Law' of survival.[60] In a letter to Derwent May (10 April 1992), he expands on his initial plans for 'Pike': in the original draft, the fish represents Michael the Archangel, an angel of the water, the advocate of Israel, the personal chaperon of the Shekinah, and the female aspect of God.[61] As one Hughes critic retorted when I recounted these details from the letters, 'It's only a fucking fish.' Hughes himself may have endorsed such a response: in 'Milesian Encounter on the Sligachan', the melodramatic build-up to an encounter

with the erotic goddess is subverted with the bathos that she is actually
'Only a little salmon' (p. 655); in the letter to May, Hughes derides his
own reading of 'Pike' as 'Balderdash of course', and authorial propaganda, at the same time as going on to defend (with irony) its efficacy.
An interpretation of the pike as Michael relies on details outside the text;
in this sense authorial intention is being 'interesting' by telling the letter-
reader what it 'means' to the writer. If a mystified reader tried to tell
Hughes that his poem was about a small pie, the author's account would
clearly be superior, but reader-responses that utilise the actual details of
the text must be given credence.[62] A post-Holocaust reading of the poem
might similarly be alien to its primary meaning, but what, then, comprises the latter? After all, linkages between the violent pike and humans
are directly encouraged by the comparison of the iron in 'this eye' (the
poet's) to that of the dead fish (p. 85).

Also, within the first two stanzas, a potentially fascistic aesthetic
arises, but in a much more complex manner to that of 'Lines about Elias'.
The dominant 'grace' of the pike in its world of small fish appears to be
proportional to its aesthetic value. Hughes notes in both letters that it is
still, not violent, but this is not strictly true.[63] Hughes utilises adverbs
prolifically: 'properly', 'slightly', 'probably' (twice), 'presumably',
'hideously', 'aimlessly' and 'miraculously' appear in 'Eclipse' alone (pp.
347–50).[64] The main adverbs ('quietly', 'silently') in 'Pike' do indeed
denote passivity. However, in lines four and five respectively of 'Pike', the
fish are dancing and moving (albeit slowly): the poet is right in that they
do not indulge in the act of killing, but the stanzas make it clear that they
are celebrating their potential to do so with ease. 'A hundred feet long in
their world', the pike appear aware of their own superiority in the hierarchy of fish; this majesty increases their aesthetic value as they dance
among the flies on the surface of the pond (p. 85). Such a connection
between violence and aesthetics can be similarly adduced from the Nazi
icon of the Aryan soldier. As Hughes points out in the letter to Malcolm,
though, the fish kills for survival, not ideological reasons: it is 'subdued
to its instrument' in '*their* world' (my italics); in other words, ready to
kill when necessary, even though, at present, it is still, with its gills
'kneading quietly'. Nevertheless, for a post-Holocaust reader, the depiction of potential violence invites a comparison between the fish and
fascism, even if simplistic anthropomorphism is rejected by Hughes. Such
a reader-response to 'Pike' would not be telling the author what the poem
means – to use Hughes's phrases from the Malcolm letter – but what it
'means to them', without reducing the text to an authorial engagement
with 'motorcyclists with machine guns on the handlebars'.[65]

My argument above has assumed that the humans can be interpreted as being like violent fish; the allegory can also work the other way round. Given that pike cannot exist as autonomous objects beyond the artifice of language in terms of the poem, the phrases used to describe their voraciousness might necessarily carry the baggage of human violence. After all, the name of the fish, etymologically, is connected to a long wooden shaft with a pointed steel, or iron, head, an infantry weapon superseded by the bayonet, as well as the name for a peaked hill, from the Old English '*pic*' (a 'point' or 'prick').[66] Hence, when their underwater 'grandeur' demands a metaphor, threatening submarines are compared to the pike's 'horror' (pp. 84, 85). Potential violence is linked to rational estimations: the underwater craft, 'A hundred feet long', represents the gigantic size of the fish in relation to minnows (p. 85). In Hughes's work, reason and rationality are considered to be endemic in atrocity: for example, in the 'mishmash of . . . physics' which leads to the corpses in 'Crow's Account of the Battle' (p. 222). The juxtaposition of two subject positions in the first half of the poem might thus be a comment on aggression in both the pike and human worlds, as opposed to the more productive and irrational metaphysics of the second half. Numbers dominate until stanza eight: the fish is 'three inches long', 'A hundred feet long'; three of them are 'three inches, four,/ And four and a half'; suddenly 'there were two. Finally one'; others are 'six pounds each, over two feet long' (p. 85). As well as inscribing the sensibility of fishermen, this exactitude pits metaphysics of Being against the rationality of science, with a brief homage to Wordsworth. The second half of the poem begins in stanza eight, in which the dead fish shift to the narrator, who fishes a pond 'fifty yards across'. It recalls Wordsworth's 'The Thorn' in which the bush is located 'Not five yards from the mountain-path'; 'to the left, three yards beyond' there is a 'muddy pond'; the poet 'has measured it from side to side', and ''Tis three foot long, and two feet wide'.[67] Such bizarre measurements call attention to the fact that science can say nothing of much use to the poet about ponds; their echo in 'Pike' similarly means that the writer cannot complete his poem until he shifts from the descriptive nature of the first half of the text. Hughes's ensuing binary between reason and rationality on one hand, and the irrational and unconscious on the other, can certainly be critiqued as an instance of peephole metaphysics, and yet the closure of the text is composed of an ontological need that produces lyrical intensity, as opposed to the conceptual muddle of 'Lines about Elias'. This ending allows the poem as a whole to escape the status of a 'barefaced swindle' – as Adorno terms both *Existenz* and the concept of a 'world spirit' – and eschew the charge of the text being symptomatic of the 'wind' of the philosopher's 'bad poems'.

'Pike' is a description of a pike, at the same time as it is not a description of a pike. Poetics of extremity arise in the epiphanic moment at the end of the text:

The still splashes on the dark pond,

Owls hushing the floating woods
Frail on my ear against the dream
Darkness beneath night's darkness had freed,
That rose slowly towards me, watching (pp. 85–6)

A process of 'looking through' is afoot here as one eye watches for 'what eye might move': bathetically, in that the narrator stares into the pond searching for his prey; more poetically, in an encounter with the metaphysics of presence beyond the corporeal fish. '[D]ream' refers most obviously to the pike rising slowly to the surface. It is unsettling enough that it is 'watching' the fisherman; however, it is not only a fish, but a moment equivalent to that in which the 'star' of Being rises above the crenel of Adorno's castle. Ontological ennui is reflected in the similarity between Beckett's 'I can't go on, I'll go on' from *The Unnamable*, and Hughes's 'I dared not cast/ But silently cast' in the stanza above, but this gives way to an uncanny *Existenz* not dissimilar to that encountered in 'Your Paris'.[68] Attention is drawn away from the pike throughout the last three stanzas (the word is last used ten lines from the end). This is compounded by the lexical ambiguity: the oxymoron of 'still splashes' might be composed of an adjective and noun, an adverb and verb, or a noun and verb; the woods may be 'floating' in a surreal sense, or as they sway in the wind, making the sound of disturbed water, or when they are reflected in the pond; 'Darkness' may refer to the pike, or the water beneath the surface; 'night's darkness' may be the pitch-black scenario, or indicative of the fact that this is an imagined experience. The pike becomes a 'dream' (p. 85): 'Being' might be said to be 'rising' here in the sense of a threatening unconscious. This distancing of fish during the closure of the poem is supported by Hughes's comments in *Poetry in the Making*: rather than simply recounting an actual incident, 'bits of the . . . poem began to arrive' when he 'felt like doing some pike fishing, but in circumstances where there was no chance of it'.[69]

Peephole metaphysics are inextricably linked here to the process of writing itself: fishing the depths of ponds and lakes is connected to creativity throughout *Poetry in the Making*. In this sense, the ending of 'Pike' is equivalent to the closure of 'The Thought-Fox': both poems describe a creature, but the texts cannot be completed until the process of writing is commented upon self-referentially. In a letter to Gerald Hughes, a more intriguing interpretation of this phenomenon is offered by the connection between a dream about pike and Hughes's imminent marriage to Plath (24 February 1957). One of Hughes's last interviews describes this moment in 1956, but the letter to Gerald outlines it in much more detail: after not fishing for seven years, he recounts dreaming about 'the grandfather pike at Crookhill'; it was twenty feet long, 'and still most of it was in the pond. The next day I sold my first poem and got married.'[70] Rather than the nasty fish being equivalent to Plath, or the poetics of extremity symptomatic of his fear of marriage, the 'dream' pike represents 'luck'. In fishing dreams, Hughes explains, his arch-enemies are eels. This luckiness is both private and public: the chance encounter with Plath at St Botolph's merges with the ability to 'fish' a poem out of his mysterious mind. Hence, like 'Your Paris', 'Pike', first published in 1959, can be interpreted as a self-referential poem about the cusp of Hughes's literary career. Unlike 'Your Paris', which refers to distinct biographical details, it also forms a kind of allegorical epithalamium.[71]

## 'Ce n'est pas une phrase rèthorique': Crow and anti-rhetoric

In contrast with the indirection of 'Pike', the allegories of *Crow* mix responses to personal trauma with more self-conscious post-Holocaust poetics. The Emory letters highlight persistent connections between the collection and the deaths of Plath, Assia, Shura and Hughes's mother. In a letter to Lucas Myers (29 September 1984), he refers to the events of 1963 and 1969 as 'giant steel doors' that sapped his creativity: this is supported by a missive to Gerald Hughes (1971), where he states that he stopped writing *Crow* in 1969 just as he had reached 'the real starting place'.[72] Michael Parker insists that the fragments of the Crow poems be read biographically because Plath's 'death became Hughes's Auschwitz, the apocalyptic experience that to a major extent determined his poetic development' (p. 44) (see Note 24). Hughes himself is tempted by this rhetoric when he writes to Janet Malcolm (2 March 1994) about the 'torture and gas chamber of what [some] people were making of [Nick's] mother, me and everything about us'. In a letter to Lucas Myers (1961), Hughes also refers to the previous year as 'a sort of death-march, except for Frieda'.[73] Conflations of private bereavement with public atrocity are suspect, and yet Parker convinces with his reading of the late 1960s poems as engaging with such concerns at a tangent. As he demonstrates, Hughes's co-editorship of *Modern Poetry in Translation* with Daniel Weissbort (1966–71), and events such as the 1969 Poetry International conference (which included Pilinszky and Popa), increasingly influenced Hughes's poetics at the same time as his personal life was in turmoil. In 'Crow's Account of the Battle', for example, the trauma of Plath's death might be referred to indirectly in its apocalyptic narrative, as well as, more directly, his father's near-death at Gallipoli in the reference to the bullet hitting 'pocket-books' of the soldiers.[74] However, such biographical details are asides to the poem's overall depiction of warfare and survival: Moulin reads the text as an exposition of World War I, and the 'cataclysmic symptom[s] of the error of Western Civilisation' (p. 76). This 'error' could be the endorsement of the rational over the Lacanian 'real': in the manuscript version of the poem held at Emory, the study of language is paired with the (problematic) binary between reason and imagination, since 'the etymology of the word' joins 'Universal Laws' (not, of course, including Being), 'calculus' and 'Theorems' as the scourge of the West (p. 222); a 'good' watch becomes, more exactly, a 'proved' watch (p. 223). Due to the abstract nature of these 'cataclysmic' symptoms, it must be stressed that 'Crow's Account of the Battle' does not appertain to any specific historical period. Nevertheless, it forms an example of a self-conscious post-Holocaust poem by gesturing towards twentieth-century atrocity as a whole in the form of allegory. The poem is different from the texts I have discussed so far in this chapter in that, at this point in Hughes's career, peephole metaphysics are avoided in order to give priority to Crow's version of events. There is no 'looking through' from the perspective of the soldier on the battlefield: Fate, a transcendent humanism, and Being lurking at the bottom of a pond; all these expositions of *Existenz* I have outlined so far give way to a nihilistic depiction of warfare, in which recruits are humiliated by their own folly.

Moulin argues that the 'listing' technique in 'Crow's Account of the Battle' parodies that of the Bible (p. 70). Humanity's desperate worship of, paradoxically, both rationality and religion in the poem chimes with this reading. It is also, I would add, symptomatic of the increasing influence of Holocaust poetics on Hughes's work, particularly those of Pilinszky. In *The Desert of Love* collection, for example, the Hungarian poet's version of the poetics of extremity draws on this technique: in 'Fish in the Net', humanity's blighted ontological state is one in which 'Our hearts convulse . . . our writhings maim . . . Our cries conflict' (p. 17). In the manuscript at Emory, this repetition augments as the poem is amended: 'or potting' becomes 'too like potting'; the listing of 'likes' also originally included 'too like losing a milk tooth'.[75] This technique encourages the short lines of 'Crow's Account of the Battle' ('Too like dropping in a chair/ Exhausted with rage') (p. 223): the minimalism of many of the Eastern European poets had clearly influenced Hughes's writing by the late 1960s. Pilinszky praises Hughes's translations of his work in a letter to Hughes because '*Ce n'est pas une phrase rèthorique*' (18 April 1975). This anti-rhetorical style of writing allowed Hughes to eschew the melodramatic excesses of early poems such as 'The Horses', and produce the 'barbaric' aesthetics of *Crow*; poetics of extremity are paradoxically typified by a 'flatness of tone'. David Moody dismisses the collection as 'verbal sensationalism', yet a wariness of rhetoric persists, akin to that of awkward poetics.[76] Hughes appears to have been practising such anti-rhetorical strategies for some time: in one of the Emory notebooks (1961–6), a manuscript poem entitled 'The Haunting' bears remarkable stylistic similarities to 'Crow's Account of the Battle'. Instead of the matter-of-fact 'brains in hands' or 'legs in a treetop' (p. 222), 'The Haunting' contains details of 'The blown-off right hand swinging to the stride/ Of the stump-scorched + blown-off legs'; it also forms an early version of the 'listing' technique, with the repetition of phrases beginning with 'From' and 'Of' ('From their eyeless, earless hearts/ From their brainless hearts . . . Of their automatic rifles . . . Of their boots').[77] As opposed to the *Crow* collection, though, the manuscript poem appears to be much more obviously about World War I recruits: the lines of blind veterans recorded in much contemporaneous newsreel is referred to in the 'Marching in their boots blindfold + riddled,/ Rotten heads on their singing shoulders'. Historical specificity in the notebook gives way to the abstractions of *Crow*.

Peephole metaphysics lead to an exuberant lyricism in 'Pike'; by the time of the first published version of 'Crow's Account of the Battle' in 1967 ('A Battle'), the 'new depth' poetics give way to a more measured acceptance of personal trauma and 'public' history.[78] Bentley and Faas refer to the 'awkward, mangled' and 'super-ugly' language of *Crow* as symptomatic of Hughes's development of his own version of post-Holocaust aesthetics.[79] In this poem, battles are not only battles, just as fish are not just fish in 'Pike': Crow's account forms an allegory of post-Holocaust existence. Hughes could be accused of conflating victims and non-victims of atrocity in his struggle to represent post-Holocaust ontology, and yet this criticism could be defused by the details of the poem, which focus on the ease in which suffering co-exists with desensitisation during actual warfare. The list of 'likes' arises from the contention that shooting someone through the midriff is 'too like striking a match' (p. 223); the pretentious 'too like a twitching of nothingness' has been crossed out in the Emory manuscript, presumably to avoid the vacuous sensationalism that Moody detects in *Crow* as a whole. In an Emory letter (13 November 1989), Hughes castigates some modern poets as 'roaming around in the cast-offs of dead soldiers': 'Crow's Account of the Battle' cannot avoid this process of secondary witnessing in its attempt to focus on the insensitivity of the victors as they dispose of humans as if they were snooker balls.[80] Indirection is achieved through the lack of referents: Crow's testimony creates a distancing effect by making the atrocities appear like fairy-stories; the manuscript begins with 'Once upon a time' rather than the final version's 'There was this terrific battle' (p. 222); the title of the second version of the text highlights its subversion of children's tales ('Fifth Bedtime Story').[81] This may be critiqued as manna to neo-Nazi versions of the Holocaust as a fantastic narrative, but such criticism would plainly be blinkered to Hughes's attempt to record the ontology of the present as radically altered by twentieth-century atrocity.

Ironically, in terms of Adorno's critique of aesthetic 'wind' in *Negative Dialectics*, the poem ends with stasis, where 'Not a leaf flinched' (p. 223): 'Crow's Account of the Battle' succeeds in producing a poetics of extremity unburdened with the 'cheap' aesthetics of 'bad poems', either in the form of peep-show metaphysics, or a demeaning portrayal of victims. An inability to 'look through' to the compensatory 'star' of a transcendent Being in *Crow* as a whole – in the context of post-Holocaust *Existenz* – partly results in the bleak tone of the collection, and also a stymie – in terms of stylistic development – that would lead to the dead-end minimalism of *Prometheus on his Crag*, and the necessary release of the delicate lyrics at the closure of *Gaudete*. A reinvigorated interest in a transcendent concept of Being can also be located in the return to a more naturalistic poetry in the Moortown collections, and Elmet poems. Such creative developments were at the expense of the pursuit of a more radical engagement with post-Holocaust aesthetics, but the nihilism of *Crow* would have been difficult to iterate throughout the 1970s and 1980s. Hence the 'new depth' poetics of 'Pike', 'Wodwo' and 'Crow's Account of the Battle' disperse into the environmental concerns of these later collections, only to return (with an added critique) in 'Your Paris'. Peepholes through to the refulgent 'star' of Being in the early poems avoid the post-Holocaust ontology of *Crow*, but they do not negate Adorno's warning in *Negative Dialectics* that there is no 'looking through'. The metaphysics of Fate in 'Your Paris', the transcendent humanism in 'Lines about Elias', and the sublime fish in 'Pike'; all these instances of 'peeping' might deflect the reader of Hughes's work from the more unpleasant prospect that Being is a peep-show where the viewer's gaze is reflected back onto the initial, ontological need.

## Notes

1. Ted Hughes, *Collected Poems*, ed. Paul Keegan (London: Faber, 2003), pp. 192–4, p. 192. All further references to Hughes' poems appertain to this collection, unless otherwise stated.
2. I am grateful to Neil Roberts for bringing to my attention these variations in the typescript and manuscripts of 'Karma'. Roberts notes that the typescript is dated '61': there may be a connection between suggestions of inarticulacy surrounding the word 'Auschwitz', and the German language, in 'Karma' and Plath's poem 'Daddy', which was written in 1962.
3. Terry Gifford's comments come from BBC2's *Ted and Sylvia: Love and Loss* (2004).
4. Given that my analyses are spread across several collections and anthologies of Hughes's work, my readings of the poems will make reference to the critical contexts surrounding the poems' original publication, such as the furore surrounding the representation of Plath in *Birthday Letters*, and discussions about the relationship between aesthetics and violence in relation to 'Pike' and the early poems.
5. Paul Bentley, *The Poetry of Ted Hughes* (London: Longman, 1998), p. 54.
6. Letters to Gerald Hughes 1952–91 (Box 1), Ted Hughes archives, Emory University.
7. This does not mean that Hughes is beyond self-critique in his poetry as a whole. 'Egg-head' engages in (partly) playful self-parody: the daring poet who contemplates 'hurtling endlessness' is actually 'Peeping through his fingers at the world's ends' (p. 33). The egg-head is accused of 'Braggart-browed complacency in most calm/ Collusion with his own/ Dewdrop frailty' (p. 34).
8. Seamus Heaney, 'Hughes and England', in *The Achievement of Ted Hughes*, ed. Keith Sagar (Manchester: Manchester University Press, 1983), pp. 14–21, p. 21; Leonard Scijay, 'Ted Hughes and Ecology: A Biocentric Vision', in *The Challenge of Ted Hughes*, ed. Keith Sagar (London: Macmillan, 1994), pp. 160–81, p. 173; Craig Robinson, 'The Good Shepherd: *Moortown Elegies*' (*The Achievement of Ted Hughes*, pp. 257–84, p. 261); Keith Sagar, *The Laughter of Foxes: A Study of Ted Hughes* (Liverpool: Liverpool University Press, 2000).
9. Leonard Scijay, 'Oriental Mythology in *Wodwo*' (*The Achievement of Ted Hughes*, pp. 126–53), p. 133.
10. A. Alvarez, 'Ted Hughes', in *The Epic Poise: A Celebration of Ted Hughes*, ed. Nick Gammage (London: Faber, 1999), pp. 207–11, pp. 207–8. Alexander Davis argues that 'Wings' and 'Mr Sartre Considers Current Affairs' are attacks on existentialist 'freedom' in 'Romanticism, Existentialism, Patriarchy: Hughes and the Visionary Imagination' (*The Challenge of Ted Hughes*, pp. 70–90, p. 75). Hughes's concept of human nature 'is that of an essence', which, as opposed to existentialism, precedes existence (p. 76). See also Michael Parker's anti-existentialist interpretation of 'Existential Song' in 'Hughes and the Poets of Eastern Europe' (*The Achievement of Ted Hughes*, pp. 37–51, p. 46).
11. In Tennyson's *In Memoriam* (NewYork and London: Norton, 1973), the validity of, and Victorian obsession with, scientific knowledge is countered

by wisdom, in which the metaphysics of the 'heart' are expressed, such as in the concept of the soul. See parts 112 and 113 (pp. 74–5).

12. Eric Homberger, *The Art of the Real* (London and Toronto: Dent, 1977), p. 213.

13. Dwight Eddins, 'Ted Hughes and Schopenhauer: The Poetry of the Will', *Twentieth Century Literature* (Spring 1999), pp. 94–109, pp. 97, 98.

14. Joanny Moulin, *Ted Hughes: New Selected Poems* (Paris: Didier, 1999).

15. James Booth discusses how Hughes 'converts metaphor into metaphysics' in 'Competing Pulses: Secular and Sacred in Hughes, Larkin and Plath', *Critical Survey*, 12: 3 (2000), pp. 3–26, p. 9.

16. Theodor Adorno, *Negative Dialectics*, trans. E. B. Ashton (London: Routledge, 1990 [1996]), p. 138.

17. Theodor Adorno, *Gesammelte Schriften, 6: Negative Dialektik, Jargon der Eigentlichkeit* (Frankfurt: Suhrkamp, 1973), p. 143.

18. Susan Gubar, *Poetry after Auschwitz: Remembering What One Never Knew* (Bloomington: Indiana University Press, 2003), p. 12.

19. *OED*, 2nd edn.

20. *Gesammelte Schriften*, 6, p. 83; *Negative Dialectics*, p. 76.

21. Wendy Cope, *Making Cocoa for Kingsley Amis* (London: Faber, 1986), p. 55.

22. See *The Achievement of Ted Hughes*, p. 10. 'The Haunting' is held in the notebooks at Emory. It finally forms the first part of 'Scapegoat and Rabies' ('I. A Haunting'), published in the American edition of *Wodwo*, and reprinted in the *New Selected Poems 1957–1994* (London: Faber, 1995), pp. 65–6. See *Collected Poems* (p. 1,253).

23. Ted Hughes Correspondence (Box 64). Unless otherwise stated, all citations in brackets appertaining to letters refer to those held in the Emory Archives. In this letter, Hughes writes that 'I learned early that for a non-combatant to say anything, about that campaign, that could honourably exist in the same world as those who survived it – would need divine help. So I never completed what I began.'

24. Exceptions include Michael Parker, 'Hughes and the Poets of Eastern Europe', *The Achievement of Ted Hughes*, pp. 37–51, which I discuss later in this essay in relation to 'Crow's Account of the Battle'.

25. Series 1: Correspondence (Ted Hughes) (Box 61). These comments mirror those that Hughes made in a radio interview quoted in Keith Sagar's essay 'Hughes and his Landscape' from *The Achievement of Ted Hughes* (pp. 2–13): 'It was right there from the beginning, so it was going on in us for eight years before the Second World War came along . . . The First World War was our sort of fairy-story world – certainly was mine' (p. 10). Some of these ideas are also repeated in Hughes's comments on 'A Masque for Three Voices' (*Collected Poems*, pp. 1,219–20): World War I is, for him, 'virtually the Creation Story' (p. 1,219).

26. Box 61 (F14).

27. Box 61 (F17). In a letter to C. B. Cox held in the Critical Quarterly Archive, Philip Larkin makes a similar comment about school children (13 December 1974). They must be allowed to leave school at fourteen, he contends, since teachers must be allowed to focus on those who are capable of learning, as opposed to 'concentration-camp child minding'.

28. Box 64.
29. Box 64.
30. Ekbert Faas, *Ted Hughes: The Unaccommodated Universe* (Santa Barbara: Black Sparrow Press, 1980), p. 201. There is surely a specific reference here to Philip Larkin's beloved Pearson Park in Hull.
31. A. Alvarez, *The New Poetry* (Harmondsworth: Penguin, 1966 [1962]).
32. Letter to Mrs McGrigor Phillips (20 February 1956), Special Collections, The Brotherton Library, University of Leeds.
33. A. Alvarez, *Where Did It All Go Right?* (London: Richard Cohen, 1999). *The New Poetry* was published in spring 1962 (p. 213).
34. John Lucas, *Modern English Poetry: From Hardy to Hughes* (London: B. T. Batsford Ltd, 1986). 'Poetry should take risks, Alvarez proclaimed. (He also, very stupidly, suggested that poets themselves should take risks: "poetry is a murderous art", he announced)' (p. 193).
35. Olwyn Hughes, letter to C. B. Cox (6 November 1971); Margaret Newlin, 'The Suicide Bandwagon', *Critical Quarterly* 14: 4 (winter 1972), pp. 367–78, p. 367. Despite the influence of Olwyn Hughes, Cox published the article because of its critical integrity: it forms an early example of the (then sparse) voices that critiqued Alvarez's poetics of extremity.
36. Newlin, p. 370; A. Alvarez, *The Savage God: A Study of Suicide* (Harmondsworth: Penguin, 1974 [1971]); *Beyond All This Fiddle* (London: Penguin, 1968). 'Keats wrote so much about death that death became inevitable, and this was the same for Plath' (*Beyond All This Fiddle*, p. 57). Sagar follows this logic when he writes that Plath might have saved her life if she had written less confessional-style poetry (*The Laughter of Foxes*, p. 57).
37. Theodor Adorno, 'Commitment', in *Aesthetics and Politics*, ed. R. Livingstone, P. Anderson and F. Mulhern, trans. F. MacDonagh (London: New Left Books, 1977), pp. 177–95. I discuss this in *Tony Harrison and the Holocaust* (Liverpool: Liverpool University Press, 2001). Although he does not mention Adorno, Alvarez argues by proxy against the philosopher's concept of committed autonomous art in 'The Literature of the Holocaust' from *Beyond All This Fiddle*. Whereas Adorno praises Beckett's politics of indirection, Alvarez criticises the abstractions in the playwright's autonomous art, and requests that post-Holocaust literature should comprise 'detached' but direct engagements with the event (p. 33). This stance, in relation to first-hand witnesses of the Holocaust, is different from the conception of indirection for 'non-victim' writers in *The New Poetry*.
38. *Crow* might seem a more obvious place to begin a discussion of Hughes's post-Holocaust poetics, but I have left a discussion of the collection until the end of the essay precisely because it has been written about in these terms before. 'Lines about Elias' is a much more recent text, which has not, as yet, received much critical attention.
39. Many of these letters are under restricted access, but Box 6 (F7), 'Series 1.1 János Pilinszky 2/72–11/78' does contain twelve items. The archives at Emory also contain critical essays about, and by, Pilinszky, including the poet's essay 'The Fate of the Creative Imagination in our Time' (translated by Steven Polgar and Tomas Keri) (Subseries 2.7), as well as Hughes's notes on his translations of the Hungarian poet's work. In one letter from Box 6

(18 April 1975), Pilinszky praises Hughes's '*traduction* [translation] *de mes poèmes*', and his '*générosité . . . artistique*'; another missive (5 August 1976) eulogises Hughes's preface to his poems as the best analysis of his 'poor' poetry ('*le premier analyse valable . . . ma "pauvre" poésie*'). Hughes picks up on the latter phrase in 'Notes on Translating János Pilinszky' when he refers to the 'linguistic poverty' of the original verse, and the 'unadorned language of the dispossessed'. The Hungarian poet then mentions that he is writing again ('*de nouveau*') from '*une clinique psychiatrique*' (6 October 1976). Suffering from '*Depression*', the missive reminds him of his previous visit to the Hughes household, '"*les beaux jours" chez vous, chez Nicol* [*sic*]'. (Hughes clearly corrected Pilinszky's spelling [or translation] of 'Nick/Nicky' in his reply, since the next letter refers to '*Nicky*'; Pilinszky adds, '*[est-ce correcte comme ça]?*') This letter (8 December 1976) mentions that he is ill again ('*je suis un peu malade encore*'), but that Hughes's reply was a real joy to read ('*Ta lettre était une vrais joie pour moi*'). Pilinszky announces that he would like to produce a selection of Hughes's poems in Hungarian ('*une livre [Poèmes choisis] en Hongrois de Toi*'), and asks whether he would prefer him to translate the Crow sequence in its entirety ('*la traduction intégrale de Crow*'). This developed into a plan for a selection of Hughes's, Tomas Tromströmer's and Pilinszky's work in a single volume (13 January 1978). Pilinszky was clearly struggling with this project, since he adds that 1977 was quite a bad year for him ('*L'année passé était assez grave pour moi*'). Pilinszky reveals (21 November 1978) that he is working slowly ('*lentement*'), but that he still hopes to finish his '*grand projet*', which is to interpret the depth and infinitely rich texture of Hughes's poetry ('*la profondeur, et la richesse infiniment . . . de ta poésie*'). Pilinszky committed suicide before he finished this project.

40. János Pilinszky, *The Desert of Love* (London: Anvil, 1989 [1976]), p. 9.
41. Primo Levi, *If This Is A Man/The Truce*, trans. Stuart Woolf (London: Abacus, 1987 [1958]), p. 47.
42. Elias may be a reference to a character known personally to Hughes. I have discovered other characters of the same name in Holocaust literature and criticism, but none is definitive. Elias Lindzin in *If This Is A Man* (pp. 101–4) does not fit the description (unless the 'baboon' image is specific), since he is a 'madman, incomprehensible and para-human . . . an atavism, different from our modern world, and better adapted to the primordial conditions of camp life' (p. 103). Norbert Elias was a German Jew and former Professor Emeritus at the University of Frankfurt, who wrote about Mozart in the tradition of court music, in which musicians were regarded as labourers who produced aesthetic pleasure for a more refined audience (*Mozart: Portrait of a Genius*, trans. Edmund Jephcott (Oxford: Polity, 1994)). The theme of this book fits the action of the poem, and would provide a more political reading of the relationship between the inmates and guards than Hughes provides, but it was published in Britain in translation five years after 'Lines about Elias' first appeared in *P. N. Review*. Perhaps Elias is most likely to refer to a name given to Christ at Calvary, as in St Mark (v.34–7), when Christ cries out 'Eloi Eloi' on the Cross, and the crowd below say 'Behold, he called Elias'. Someone then fills a sponge full of vinegar and gives it to Jesus to drink, saying '"Let us see whether Elias will come to take

him down.''' At this point, Jesus cries with a loud voice and 'gave up the ghost'. Thus, 'about Elias' might mean 'after the death of Christ'; this is potentially worrying, if the deaths of the inmates are regarded as a sacrifice. Plath and Harrison make similar comparisons between Christ and Holocaust victims in, respectively, 'Mary's Song' and *Prometheus*; I discuss both these texts earlier in this book. Another possible reference is Richard Glazar's account of '"little Edek playing his accordion and the young singer singing *Eli Eli*"' (quoted in Gubar, p. 186).

43. *The Guardian*, 10 March 2000. (www.guardian.co.uk)
44. *The Guardian*, 28 April 2000. (www.guardian.co.uk)
45. *P.N. Review* 16: ii (1989), p. 44.
46. 'Ghost Crabs', in *Holding Your Eight Hands: An Anthology of Science Fiction Verse*, ed. Edward Lucie-Smith (Rapp & Whiting, 1970), pp. 42–3.
47. Box 61 (F16). Hughes is discussing his ambivalent attitude towards Wilfred Owen. Whilst he 'swallowed Owen as deeply as anybody well could', he notes that he did have a 'reservation' about him as an officer: Hughes's father refused promotion, and remained an infantryman, telling 'strange stories about some officers'. (One of my own relatives, Charles Rowland, served as an infantryman, and was convinced that he had to refuse promotion in order to have a better chance of surviving the conflict.) Hughes also notes that Owen did not join the conflict until late 1916, and that he 'held it against him'. He adds that this is clearly a 'foolish reservation', which he disowns, but still knows that 'it's there'.
48. Gubar notes that Dannie Abse's 'No More Mozart', Peter Porter's 'May 1945' and Barry Ivker's 'Art and Politics' 'link music to genocide' (p. 276).
49. The poem possibly conflates two of the Hughes's visits to Paris in 1956, since they only definitely stayed in the Hôtel des deux Continents (mentioned in 'Your Paris') on the shorter, second visit, even though the temporality of 'Your Paris' appears to present us with one, longer visit.
50. Plath describes the hotel in a journal of 26 August 1956 (*The Journal of Sylvia Plath: 1950–1962*, ed. Karen V. Kukil (London: Faber, 2000), pp. 578–9).
51. Sue Vice, *Holocaust Fiction* (London: Routledge, 2000).
52. Theodor Adorno, *Minima Moralia*, trans. E. F. N. Jephcott (London: Verso, 1978 [1951]), p. 25.
53. Box 6 (F7) 'Series 1.1 Thom Gunn 5/68–8/92'. Moulin, in *Ted Hughes: New Selected Poems*, refers to a letter in which Hughes claims the collection is not poetry, since the poems are simply pieces of writing that connected him with the ghost of Plath for as long as possible (p. 142). Another reading of the awkward style of the texts is provided by the Emory letters: if Hughes transferred prose accounts (many of which, he says, were stolen over the years) into elegies, the result might necessarily be a tad prosaic.
54. Box 62.1 (Ted Hughes Correspondence).
55. Sylvia Plath, *Collected Poems* (London: Faber, 1981), pp. 193–4, p. 194.
56. Box 64. In another letter (22 April 1992), Hughes writes that it 'looks as though I've lost a huge amount of rough drafts of my life with S. P. – probably walked. A lot of my things have walked, over the years' (Box 64).
57. Sylvia Plath, *Letters Home* (London: Faber, 1976), p. 259.
58. *The Journals of Sylvia Plath*, p. 553.

59. Box 61 (F15), 'Ted Hughes Correspondence to Others'. Hughes elaborates on these points in *Winter Pollen* (London: Faber, 1994), pp. 261–7. The Emory files contain an archive of photographs about Hughes: one of them, entitled 'Seamus Heaney and Unidentified', depicts a sign for 'Ted Hughes Motor Cycles'. A hand-written banner has been added: 'Bike three inches long/ Perfect bike in all p. . .'.

60. Hughes's interpretation of Hitler grates against recent studies of Nazism in relation to the wider anti-Semitism prevalent in Germany and other European countries during the 1930s and 1940s, such as Daniel Jonah Goldhagen's *Hitler's Willing Executioners: Ordinary Germans and the Holocaust* (London: Abacus, 1997 [1996]). In this sense, Hitler was a symptom of wider ideologies rather than a figure operating outside any human law.

61. Box 61 (F17).

62. This point is an important one in the context of Hughes studies as a whole. The Hughes conference in Lyon (2000) demonstrated a possible rift between 'authorial' readings of Hughes (typified by Sagar's and Ann Skea's) and 'theoretical' interpretations of the texts (as with the papers influenced by Lacanian theory). This led to a discussion between participants and other Hughes critics on this issue in Klaus Kasser's informative website (www.uni-leipzig.de/~angl/hughes).

63. This dominance has lead to some strange activity. In 1999, Darren Blake was bitten on the foot by a pike whilst water-skiing on Llangorse lake, near Brecon, Powys ('Water Skier Bitten by Giant Pike', *The Guardian*, 1 September 1999). (www.guardian.co.uk)

64. 'Accurately', 'blackly', 'blindly', 'bodily', 'brilliantly', 'carefully', 'casually', 'closely', 'completely', 'concentratedly', 'confidently', 'deliberately', 'delicately', 'doggily', 'endlessly', 'evidently', 'expertly', 'extraordinarily', 'faintly', 'finally', 'foolishly', 'freshly', 'frowningly', 'furiously', 'gently', 'ghostly', 'gracelessly', 'grandly', 'gravely', 'grotesquely', 'guiltily', 'happily', 'hardly', 'heavily', 'helplessly', 'hopefully', 'hopelessly', 'horribly', 'immensely', 'instantly', 'kindly', 'leisurely', 'lightly', 'limply', 'loosely', 'lucidly', 'mercilessly', 'miserably', 'mockingly', 'momentarily', 'monotonously', 'nearly', 'nightly', 'numbly', 'oddly', 'other-wordly', 'painfully', 'quickly', 'quietly', 'religiously', 'savagely', 'scarcely', 'shiningly', 'silently', 'simply', 'simultaneously', 'sleekly', 'slowly', 'softly', 'sparely', 'staringly', 'startlingly', 'stately', 'steadily', 'stiffly', 'stupidly', 'suddenly', 'summarily', 'suspiciously', 'tentatively', 'thoroughly', 'thrillingly', 'tinily', 'tribally', 'truly', 'unearthly', 'unfathomably', 'ungainly', 'unpredictably', 'utterly', 'valiantly', 'violently', 'visibly', 'warily', 'whitely', 'widely', 'weirdly', and 'wishfully', appear elsewhere in the *New Selected Poems*.

65. Faas, p. 201 (see Note 30). Hughes famously used this phrase in relation to an 'over-reading', as he regarded it, of 'Hawk Roosting' and 'The Jaguar' ('Where I conjured up a jaguar, they [critics] smelt a stormtrooper').

66. *OED*, 2nd edn.

67. *The Oxford Authors: William Wordsworth* (Oxford and New York: Oxford University Press), p. 60.

68. Samuel Beckett, *The Beckett Trilogy* (London: Picador, 1976 [1959]), p. 382.

69. Ted Hughes, *Poetry in the Making* (London: Faber, 1967), p. 21.
70. 'Poet, Pike and a Pitiful Grouse', *The Guardian* (8 January 1999). 'As it came up, its head filled the lake. I brought it out and its girth filled the entire lake. And I was backing up, dragging the thing out.' In the letter to Gerald, he is joined in his exertions by Gerald and 'Johnny'. (www.guardian.co.uk)
71. A typescript of 'Pike' is held in the 1958 folder at Emory. In contrast to 'Pike' and 'Your Paris', 'Wodow' manages to eschew almost completely any connection between biographical details and the depicted creature. Blake Morrison appears close to reading the wodwo's angst as symptomatic of Hughes's state of mind after Plath's suicide (*The Epic Poise*, p. 28) (see Note 10), but the poem was first published long before this incident in the *New Statesman* (15 September 1961). In a similar moment to the pun in Larkin's 'The Whitsun Weddings', in which porters are larking with the mails, the poet only enters the text as an author figure in the anticipated misreading of 'huge' as Hughes (p. 183). There may, however, be an allusion to the author's reputation as a nature poet in the 'interesting' inspection of the frog: perhaps this indicates that the poem is meant to mark a new beginning, and anticipate the less naturalistic, and more mythopoeic, verse of Hughes in the late 1960s and early 1970s. Hence Morrison is correct in his assertion that 'Wodwo' is about poetic identity; however, his contention that the text is primarily about survival is more revealing. As with 'Pike', 'Wodwo' can be read as an allegorical poem, but instead of confronting peephole metaphysics at the closure of the piece, the whole text can be interpreted as a refutation of ontology: the creature wants to know who he/she/it is; there is no concept of Being available to provide an easy answer. Clearly, the poem is not a 'direct' representation of the Holocaust, as in 'Lines about Elias': here, the poetics of indirection can be seen to be at work if placed in the wider context of the wodwo's confusion. It would be tempting to argue that this arises from Hughes's increasing familiarity with post-Holocaust poetics in terms of European 'survivor' figures such as Pilinszky, but such supposition might be anachronistic given the 1961 publication date. Nevertheless, the wodwo's suffering, like the pike's violence, invites an anthropomorphic comparison with the difficulties of 'surviving' a century of atrocity. In *Poetry in the Making*, Hughes comments that the poem depicts the bewilderment of a creature 'just discovering that it is alive in the world': as many critics have noted, the 'half-man half-animal spirit of the forests' is gleaned from *Sir Gawain and the Green Knight*, a version of the medieval poet's forest troll 'who lived in rocks' (W. R. J. Barron, *Sir Gawain and the Green Knight* (Manchester: Manchester University Press, 1998), p. 68). This may be what it 'means' to the author, but the stream-of-consciousness narrative of 'Wodwo' results in open signification; the ensuing deferral of meaning opens up the possibility of a post-Holocaust reading of the text. Written only weeks before Alvarez began to pen the introduction to *The New Poetry*, it uncannily anticipates his rallying cry for a poetics of extremity. 'Bewilderment' is certainly at the heart of the poem: essence, in this case, does not precede existence for the wodwo, who attempts, and fails, to find traces of his/her/its identity throughout the piece.
72. Lucas Myers Correspondence, Ted Hughes archives, Emory University. Hughes adds in the Myers letter that he wonders 'if things might have gone

differently without the events of 63 and 69'. The Emory letter also provides various mythic frameworks for interpreting *Crow*: in a letter to Gerald Hughes (27 October 1969), Crow is created by God's nightmare: he then eats God, and liberates His mother in the form of 'God's mother's daughter i. e. the daughter not of God but of the Creation, the mother of all the gods, and her he marries'. Keith Sagar has always maintained that the poems are part of a much larger series of myths; he applies such mythic narratives to the poems in the excellent chapter on *Crow* in *The Art of Ted Hughes* (London and Cambridge: Cambridge University Press, 1978 [1975], pp. 101–45). He also provides a condensed narrative of Crow's epic journey in *The Laughter of Foxes* (pp. 170–80). Crows in their ornithological form appear to have preoccupied Hughes in the late 1960s: in a letter to Gerald (27 April 1967) he refers to them returning to the elm in his home; he adds that if he catches one like he did last year, he will tame it.

73. The letter is dated 'winter/spring 1961'.
74. Parker refers to this incident (p. 39).
75. Box 69.
76. David Moody, 'Telling It Like It's Not', *Yearbook of English Studies*, 17 (1987).
77. Box 65 'Series 2: Writings by Ted Hughes'.
78. 'A Battle' appeared in *Outposts* 74 (autumn 1967), pp. 6–8.
79. Bentley, p. 54 (see Note 5); Faas, p. 209.
80. Box 61 (F14). The letter is addressed to 'Tony'.
81. 'Fifth Bedtime Story' was printed in *New American Review* 8 (January 1970), pp. 40–3.

# Conclusion

Awkward poetics in post-war British poetry form a retort to Ted Hughes's claim in an Emory letter that the 'news' of the Holocaust has registered no impact in Britain.[1] This book has argued that the aesthetics of awkwardness comprise an urgent response to the current stage of post-Holocaust literature: the Holocaust is 'dying', according to Susan Gubar, so British writers must strive – alongside other European, and American, authors – to 'keep it alive as dying', and confront 'a past as it passes out of personal recollection'.[2] Poets' confrontations with the traumatic past can encompass self-conscious recognitions of their non-participation in atrocity, registering their mediated reception of the event. Awkward poetics in this sense provide a self-reflexive counterpoint to the rise of memory-envy and the fake memoir, as Holocaust synecdoches become so widely circulated that they risk exploitation. One of the ways in which post-Holocaust poets can resist the latter process is to counter the unreflective regurgitation of Holocaust icons. Sylvia Plath's camp poetics in particular call attention to the inextricability of icons and media spectacle; the secondary witness's duty is to try and unravel this 'hardening' relationship.[3] Such an ethical response to history counters previous suspicions that post-Holocaust poetry commits an 'appropriative act of arrogance' rather than an 'empathetic identification' with those that suffered during the Holocaust.[4] '[E]mpathetic identification' can take the form of an engagement with Holocaust poetry and poetics; for the British poets discussed in this book, the abstract lyricism of Paul Celan, János Pilinszky's concept of 'Being' and the final poems of Miklós Radnóti prove particularly influential. Intertextual references to Holocaust poets do not result in a relativity of suffering: instead of aestheticising a self unaffected by the 'news', post-Holocaust poets display, overall, a moral intelligence attuned to the interpretative responsibility bound up with the reception of eye-witness accounts. Such sensitivity is not equivalent to artistic piety, but evidence of reflective writing conscious of the limitations of post-Holocaust literature; for example, in relation to the possibility of aesthetic larceny. Awkward poetics respond to Theodor Adorno's edict about potentially exploitative art in the wake of the Holocaust by registering the philosopher's concerns in the texture of the artworks themselves.

Adorno's exposition of 'barbaric' poetry latently anticipates artistic ruptures: rigorous self-critique (Geoffrey Hill), internal subversions (Tony Harrison), 'ugly' semantics (Ted Hughes) and outrageous criticism of the imagined reader (Plath) illustrate the response of awkward poetics to the philosopher's plea that poetry should never be the same after the advent of Auschwitz. The campy rhetoric of many of the poems Plath wrote in October 1962 calls attention to the dramatic monologue's resistance to traditional notions of poetry based on exemplary renditions of the epiphanic, lyrical moment. Awkward poetics similarly indicate that that classification is belied by the genre's aesthetic itinerancy, and its specific ability to metamorphose in the wake of an event that seemed to endanger the notion of aesthetics entirely. Poetry should no longer be regarded as the equivalent of the 'well-groomed memorial'.[5] As one critic commented to me in relation to Hill's poem *Comus* – where a passage of lyrical intensity is interrupted with (for most readers) unintelligible Icelandic – awkward poetics are like sipping ambrosia, and finding a thistle. Rather than regurgitate an unreflective version of pre-Holocaust poetics which celebrates mellifluous writing, post-Holocaust poets embrace the regular irregularities of awkward poetics in order to emphasise the pitfalls of writing about an event plainly so resistant to artistic representation. The irascible narrator in Hill's *The Triumph of Love* openly discourses on the possibility of aesthetic culpability in the text itself; self-critique is registered elsewhere in the juxtaposition, and undercutting, of various voices in Harrison's *Prometheus*, and the criticism of 'limelit' performances in Plath's 'Lady Lazarus'.[6] Hughes is the only poet discussed in this book who attempts to 'solve', rather than ruminate on, the problem of potentially exploitative poetry: the Crow poems comprise 'barbaric' depictions of war's barbarism, but they do not self-consciously critique their critiques of atrocity. This study has been attentive to the different versions of awkward poetics evident in each poet's work, and also their rejection, as well as endorsement, of self-conscious, and self-critical, writing: Hughes boldly attempts to transcend the notion of humanity, and turn Nazis, rashly, into victims in 'Lines about Elias'; Harrison's (and Nick Danziger's) concept of 'industrial genocide' risks conflating unemployment with mass murder.

Hughes is also the exception in terms of the poets' investigation of the negotiations between poetry, history, and subjectivity. All the authors discussed are para-Marxists in that they worry, as in *The Triumph of*

*Love*, about the effects of the fascistic mob '*A se stesso*' ('To the self'): post-Holocaust poets invest in a genre traditionally associated with sub-jective ruminations partly because the Nazis attacked so precisely the concept of the freedom of the self-determining subject.[7] The archaeology of various civilians affected by atrocity in Hill's long poem emphasises the potential victimhood of twentieth-, and twenty-first-, century sub-jects, since wars are no longer fought by professional armies clashing by night on obscure plains.[8] In contrast with the other poets' concerns about the dissolution of the subject, however, Hughes's poetry delineates the joyous immolation of the self in poems such as 'Milesian Encounter on the Sligachan'. In a sense, Hughes depicts what the other poets' fear (but in relation to ecology rather than fascistic ideologies). The lamented triumph of ideological will is evident in Lady Lazarus's impotent railing against Herr Doktor, the Old Man's futile defiance towards Führer Zeus in *Prometheus*, and the murders committed by Jacques Callot's soldiers in *The Triumph of Love*. Awkward poetics may be regarded as evidence of an artistic rupture sensitive to recent history, but – to echo Seamus Heaney – they cannot stop any tanks.[9]

Heaney's critique of poetry's efficacy should not overshadow post-war British poets' contribution to the process of postmemory in keeping the Holocaust 'alive as dying'. How long, though, does (or maybe should) postmemory last? If for many mid-Victorians the Crimean War com-prised the trauma of recent history, these particular memories of memory are now limited to street names rather than literary representation. The advent of genocide might be expected to initiate a more capacious instal-ment of postmemory, but it is impossible to forecast the vicissitudes of post-war culture. The impossibility of an exact temporality of postmem-ory is registered in the Hughes letter (to Janet Malcolm, quoted above) on this unpredictable process:

> It's dawned on me gradually . . . that the First World War is remote history. They know about the trenches as they know about the squares at Waterloo or the archers at Agincourt – as curious fact about other people's excitements and woes. Rather as they know about that wipe-out on the Kuwait Basra road last month. They know about it, but it doesn't mean much to them.

The 'news' of the Holocaust that Hughes refers to in the same letter may also dissipate into 'curious' facts for 'them', the (elusive) general public. His reference to the Gulf War registers a contemporary dissatisfaction with the (inevitable) intertwining of technology and history, which has a tendency, for Hughes, to make recent events appear as obscure as med-iaeval warfare. Gubar has expressed her concern that the proliferation of mass media is inseparable from postmemory: 'as decades intervene with their stupefying disasters in tow, it may be impossible to keep the Shoah from declining into just one among numerous horror shows at the cultural multiplex' (p. 26). For Geoffrey Hartman, the pressing burden is 'how to be a witness to the witness', or – in the light of Gubar's comment – a discerning secondary witness to contemporary, sensationalist narratives in films and novels, as well as contemporaneous testimonies. Awkward poetics, symptomatic of the reinvigorated art of poetry, comprise one of the ways in which to counter unreflective art at the multiplex. The modern poets discussed in this book are representative of a generation of secondary witnesses born in the 1930s who were shocked, as children, by the 'news' of the Holocaust in the form of newsreels, testimonies and photographs; this resulted later in their reflections on the event in poetry. Whether the next generation of British poets will assimilate their legacy of awkward poetics remains a moot point, since most of contemporary, mainstream poetry in Britain today is responding to Adorno's 'lacerating cry' about barbaric art with 'blank-faced' indifference.[10]

## Notes

1. Letter to Nick Gammage (15 March 1991). Correspondence (Ted Hughes) Series 1 (Box 61). In an interview with Ekbert Faas, Hughes contradicts this statement in arguing that the 'colossal negative revelation' of the 'death camps' deeply affected the Movement poets (*Ted Hughes: The Unaccommodated Universe* (Santa Barbara: Black Sparrow Press, 1980), p. 201).
2. Susan Gubar, *Poetry after Auschwitz: Remembering What One Never Knew* (Bloomington: Indiana University Press, 2003), pp. 1, 7, 9.
3. James E. Young discusses this 'hardening' process in *At Memory's Edge: After-Images of the Holocaust in Contemporary Art and Architecture* (New Haven and London: Yale University Press, 2000). (See my discussion of Plath's poetry and the spectacle of Holocaust icons in Chapter one.)
4. Gubar, p. 53.
5. James E. Young, *The Texture of Memory* (Yale: Yale University Press, 1993), p. 70.
6. This refers to Hughes's comment in a letter to Janet Malcolm (11 April 1994) that he was not enamoured with Plath's 'incessant pushing of her immediate life (our life) into some limelit performance.' Box 62.1 (Ted Hughes Correspondence).
7. Geoffrey Hill, *The Triumph of Love* (London and New York: Penguin, 1999 [1998]), p. 21. Gubar discusses the connection between history's threat to 'sovereign subjects' and the lyric (p. 12).
8. I am echoing Matthew Arnold's 'Dover Beach': 'And we are here as on a darkling plain/ Swept with confused alarms of struggle and flight,/ Where ignorant armies clash by night' (*Arnold: Poems*, selected by Kenneth Allott (Harmondsworth and New York: Penguin, 1985 [1954]), p. 182).

  9.  Quoted in Gubar, p. 9.
 10.  William Logan, 'The Triumph of Geoffrey Hill', *Parnassus*, 24: 2 (May 2000), pp. 201–20, p. 208.

# Bibliography

## Primary Texts

Celan, Paul [1988] (1996), *Selected Poems*, London: Penguin.

Gunn, Thom, Letters to Ted Hughes, Box 6 (F7) Series 1.1, 'Thom Gunn 5/68–8/92', Ted Hughes Archives, Emory University (unpub.).

Harrison, Tony (1998), *Prometheus*, London: Faber.

Harrison, Tony (2001), 'The Tears and the Trumpets', *Arion*, 9: 2 (fall), pp. 1–22.

Heyen, William (1984), *Ericka: Poems of the Holocaust*, New York: Vanguard Press.

Hill, Geoffrey (1959), *For the Unfallen*, London: André Deutsch Ltd.

Hill, Geoffrey (1968), *King Log*, London: André Deutsch Ltd.

Hill, Geoffrey (1971), *Mercian Hymns*, London: André Deutsch Ltd.

Hill, Geoffrey (1978), *Tenebrae*, London: André Deutsch Ltd.

Hill, Geoffrey (1991), *The Enemy's Country: Words, Contexture, and other Circumstances of Language*, Oxford: Clarendon Press.

Hill, Geoffrey [1998] (1999), *The Triumph of Love*, London and New York: Penguin.

Hill, Geoffrey (1999), 'Tacit Pledges', in A. W. Holden and J. R. Birch (eds), *Housman: A Reassessment*, London: Palgrave, pp. 53–75.

Hill, Geoffrey (2000), 'The Art of Poetry LXXX', *Paris Review*, 154 (spring), pp. 270–99.

Hill, Geoffrey (2002), 'Gold out of Loss', *PBS Bulletin*, 194 (autumn), p. 5.

Hughes, Olwyn, Letter to C. B. Cox, 6 November 1971, Brian Cox and Critical Quarterly Archives, John Rylands Library, University of Manchester (unpub.).

Hughes, Ted, Letters to Gerald Hughes 1952–91 (Box 1), Ted Hughes Archives, Emory University (unpub.).

Hughes, Ted, Ted Hughes Correspondence (Box 64) (also Box 61 Series 1: Correspondence [Ted Hughes]), Ted Hughes Archives, Emory University (unpub.).

Hughes, Ted, Box 65 Series 2: 'Writings by Ted Hughes', Ted Hughes Archives, Emory University (unpub.).

Hughes, Ted (1995), *New Selected Poems 1957–1994*, London: Faber.

Hughes, Ted (2003), *Collected Poems*, ed. P. Keegan, London: Faber.

Larkin, Philip, Letters to C. B. Cox, Brian Cox and Critical Quarterly Archive, John Rylands Library, University of Manchester (unpub.).

Larkin, Philip, Letter to Mrs McGrigor Phillips, 20 February 1956, Special Collections, The Brotherton Library, University of Leeds (unpub.).

Larkin, Philip (1988), *Collected Poems*, London: Faber.

Lawson, Peter (ed.) (2001), *Jewish Poetry in Britain Since 1945: An Anthology*, Nottingham: Five Leaves Pubs.

Levi, Primo [1958] (1987), *If This Is A Man/The Truce*, trans. S. Woolf, London: Abacus.

Levi, Primo (1986), *The Drowned and the Saved*, trans. R. Rosenthal, London: Abacus.

Levi, Primo (2000), *The Periodic Table*, trans. R. Rosenthal, London: Penguin.

Myers, Lucas, Letters to Ted Hughes, Lucas Myers Correspondence, Ted Hughes Archives, Emory University (unpub.).

Peake, Mervyn (1949), *Drawings by Mervyn Peake*, London: The Grey Walls Press.

Peake, Mervyn (1967), *A Reverie of Bone and Other Poems*, London: Bertram Rota.

Pilinszky, János, Letters to Ted Hughes, Box 6 (F7), Series 1.1 'János Pilinszky 2/72–11/78', Ted Hughes Archives, Emory University (unpub.).

Pilinszky, János, 'The Fate of the Creative Imagination in our Time', trans. S. Polgar and T. Keri, Subseries 2.7, Ted Hughes Achives, Emory University.

Pilinszky, János [1976] (1989), *The Desert of Love*, trans. J. Csokits and T. Hughes, London: Anvil.

Plath, Sylvia (1981), *Collected Poems*, London: Faber.

Plath, Sylvia (2000), *The Journals of Sylvia Plath 1950–1962*, ed. K. V. Kukil, London: Faber.

Radnóti, Miklós (2000), *Camp Notebook*, trans. F. Jones, Todmorden: Arc.

Replansky, Naomi (1994), *The Dangerous World: New and Selected Poems, 1934–1994*, Chicago: Another Chicago Press.

Resnais, Alain (dir.) (1955), *(Nuit et Brouillard) Night and Fog*.

Różewicz, Tadeusz (1982), *Conversations with the Prince and Other Poems*, trans. A. Czerniawski, London: Anvil.

Schiff, Hilda (ed.) (1995), *Holocaust Poetry*, London: Harper Collins.

Sebald, W. G. [2001] (2002), *Austerlitz*, trans. A. Bell, London: Penguin.

Silkin, Jon (1971), *Amana Grass*, London: Chatto & Windus.

## Secondary Texts

Aaron, Frieda W. (1990), *Bearing the Unbearable: Yiddish and Polish Poetry in the Ghettos and Concentration Camps*, New York: State University of New York Press.

Adorno, Theodor (1967), 'Cultural Criticism and Society', in *Prisms*, trans. S. and S. Weber, London: Neville Spearman, pp. 17–35.

Adorno, Theodor [1966] (1990), *Negative Dialectics*, trans. E. B. Ashton, London: Routledge.

Adorno, Theodor [1957] (1974), 'Rede über Lyrik und Gesellschaft', in *Gesammelte Schriften II: Noten Zur Literatur*, Frankfurt: Suhrkamp, pp. 49–68.

Adorno, Theodor [1962] (1977), 'Commitment', trans. F. MacDonagh, in R. Livingstone, P. Anderson and F. Mulhern (eds), *Aesthetics and Politics*, London: New Left Books, pp. 177–95.

Adorno, Theodor [1951] (1978), *Minima Moralia*, trans. E. F. N. Jephcott, London: Verso.

Adorno, Theodor [1957] (1991), 'On Lyric Poetry and Society', in *Notes to Literature*, trans. S. W. Nicholsen, New York: Columbia University Press.

Adorno, Theodor (1991), 'On Epic Naiveté', in *Notes to Literature*, vol. 1, trans. S. W. Nicholsen, New York and Chichester: Columbia University Press, pp. 24–9.

Adorno, Theodor [1967] (1992), 'On the Classicism of Goethe's *Iphigenie*', in *Notes to Literature*, vol. 2, trans. S. W. Nicholsen, New York and Chichester: Columbia University Press, pp. 153–70.

Alexander, Michael (1991), 'Tony Harrison in Conversation with Michael Alexander', *Verse*, 8: 2, pp. 84–93.

Alvarez, A. (1968), *Beyond All This Fiddle*, London: Penguin.

Alvarez, A. (1971), *The Savage God: A Study of Suicide*, London: Weidenfeld & Nicolson.

Apel, Dora (2002), *Memory Effects: The Holocaust and the Art of Secondary Witnessing*, New Brunswick, NJ and London: Rutgers University Press.

Arendt, Hannah [1963] (1964), *Eichmann in Jerusalem: A Report on the Banality of Evil*, London: Penguin.

Astley, Neil (ed.) (1991), *Critical Anthologies. 1. Tony Harrison*, Newcastle: Bloodaxe.

Avisar, Ilan (1988), *Screening the Holocaust: Cinema's Images of the Unimaginable*, Bloomington: Indiana University Press.

Bauman, Zygmunt (1989), *Modernity and the Holocaust*, Cambridge: Polity Press.

Bedient, Calvin (1979), 'Sylvia Plath, Romantic . . .', in G. Lane (ed.), *Sylvia Plath: New Views on the Poetry*, Baltimore: Johns Hopkins University Press, pp. 3–18.

Bentley, Paul (1998), *The Poetry of Ted Hughes*, London: Longman.

Caws, Mary Ann (1977), *The Surrealist Voice of Robert Desnos*, Amherst: University of Massachusetts Press.

Cayrol, Jean (1963), Interview with Raymond Bellour, *Les Lettres françaises*, 967: 28 (February), pp. 17–18.

Cheyette, Brian (2000), 'Between Repulsion and Attraction: George Steiner's Post-Holocaust Fiction', in A. Leak and G. Paizis (eds), *The Holocaust and the Text: Speaking the Unspeakable*, London: Macmillan, pp. 67–82.

Cluysenaar, Anne (1972), 'Post-Culture: Pre-Culture?', in M. Schmidt and G. Lindop (eds), *British Poetry since 1960: A Critical Survey*, Manchester: Carcanet, pp. 215–32.

Collins, Jeff (2000), *Heidegger and the Nazis*, Cambridge: Icon Books.

Colombat, André Pierre (1993), *The Holocaust in French Film*, Metuchan and London: Scarecrow Press.

Douglas, Lawrence (1998), 'The Shrunken Head of Buchenwald: Icons of Atrocity at Nuremberg', *Representation*, 63 (summer), pp. 39–64.

Eddins, Dwight (1999), 'Ted Hughes and Schopenhauer: The Poetry of the Will', *Twentieth Century Literature* (spring), pp. 94–109.

Edwards, Michael (2000), 'Quotidian Epic: Geoffrey Hill's *The Triumph of Love*', *The Yale Journal of Criticism*, 13: 1, pp. 167–76.

Ezrahi, Sidra DeKoven (1991), '"The Grave in the Air": Unbound Metaphors in Post-Holocaust Poetry', in S. Friedlander (ed.), *Probing the Limits of Representation: Nazism and the "Final Solution"*, Cambridge, MA and London: Harvard University Press, pp. 259–76.

Faas, Ekbert (1980), *Ted Hughes: The Unaccommodated Universe*, Santa Barbara: Black Sparrow Press.

Felstiner, John (1995), *Paul Celan: Poet, Survivor, Jew*, New Haven: Yale University Press.

Ferrier, Carole (1976), 'The Beekeeper's Apprentice', in G. Lane (ed.), *Sylvia Plath: New Views on the Poetry*, Baltimore: Johns Hopkins University Press, pp. 208–11.

Flanzbaum, Hilene (1999), *The Americanization of the Holocaust*, Baltimore and London: John Hopkins University Press.

Ford, Mark (1999), 'Missing the Vital Spark', *London Review of Books*, 13 May, pp. 25–6.

Friedlander, Saul (1993), *Reflections of Nazism: An Essay on Kitsch and Death*, trans. T. Weyr, Bloomington and Indianapolis: Indiana University Press.

Gammage, Nick (ed.) (1999), *The Epic Poise: A Celebration of Ted Hughes*, London: Faber.

George, Emery (1986), *The Poetry of Miklós Radnóti: A Comparative Study*, New York: Karz-Cohl.

Gervais, David (1996), 'An "Exemplary Poet": Geoffrey Hill's Wordsworth', in W. Cookson and P. Dale (eds), *Agenda: A Tribute to Geoffrey Hill* (summer), pp. 88–103.

Gervais, David (2002), 'Geoffrey Hill: A New Direction?' (rev. of *Speech! Speech!*), *The Reader*, 11 (autumn/winter), pp. 77–88.

Goldhagen, Jonah [1996] (1997), *Hitler's Willing Executioners: Ordinary Germans and the Holocaust*, London: Abacus.

Greenhalf, Jim (1998), 'Making Poetry an Open Book', *Telegraph & Argus*, 18 December, p. 25.

Gubar, Susan (2001), 'Prosopopoeia and Holocaust Poetry in English: Sylvia Plath and her Contemporaries', *The Yale Journal of Criticism*, 14: 1, pp. 191–215.

Gubar, Susan (2003), *Poetry after Auschwitz: Remembering What One Never Knew*, Bloomington: Indiana University Press.

Haffenden, John (1981), *Viewpoints: Poets in Conversation*, London: Faber.

Hall, Edith (2002), 'Tony Harrison's *Prometheus*: A View from the Left', *Arion*, 10: 1 (spring/summer), pp. 129–40.

Hamilton, Ian (1999), 'Between Me and We' (rev. of *The Triumph of Love*), *Sunday Telegraph*, 21 February, p. 12.

Hammond, Wally (1999), '"Prometheus"', *Time Out* (14–21 April), p. 77.

Hardwick, Lorna (1999), 'Placing Prometheus', The Department of Classical Studies Open Colloquium, http://www.open.ac.uk/Arts/Colq99/hardwick.htm.

Harris, Jon (1992), 'An Elegy for Myself: British Poetry and the Holocaust', *English*, 41:171, pp. 213–33.

Hartman, Geoffrey (2002), *Scars of the Spirit: The Struggle against Inauthenticity*, New York and Basingstoke: Palgrave.

Haughton, Hugh (1985), '"How Fit a Title . . .": Title and Authority in the Work of Geoffrey Hill', in P. Robinson (ed.), *Geoffrey Hill: Essays on his Work*, Milton Keynes: Open University Press, pp. 128–48.

Hayman, Ronald (1991), *The Death and Life of Sylvia Plath*, London: Minerva.

Heaney, Seamus (1989), 'The Indefatigable Hoof-taps', in *The Government of the Tongue*, London: Faber, pp. 148–70.

Herbert, Zbigniew (1993), 'Why the Classics?' and 'A Poet of Exact Meaning: A Conversation with Marek Oramus', in D. Weissbort (ed.), *The Poetry of Survival: Post-war Poets of Central and Eastern Europe*, London: Penguin, pp. 330–5; 322–9.

Hirsch, Marianne (2003), 'Mourning and Postmemory', in N. Levi and M. Rothberg (eds), *The Holocaust: Theoretical Readings*, Edinburgh: Edinburgh University Press, pp. 416–22.

Howe, Irving (1977), 'The Plath Celebration: A Partial Dissent', in E. Butscher (ed.), *Sylvia Plath: The Woman and the Work*, New York: Dodd, Mead and Co., pp. 223–35.

Huk, Romana (1996), 'Poetry of the Committed Individual: Jon Silkin, Tony Harrison, Geoffrey Hill, and the Poets of Postwar Leeds', in J. Acheson and R. Huk (eds), *Contemporary British Poetry: Essays in Theory and Criticism*, New York: State University of New York Press, pp. 175–220.

Kaes, Anton (1992), 'Holocaust and the End of History: Postmodern Historiography in Cinema', in S. Friedlander (ed.), *Probing the Limits of Representation: Nazism and the "Final Solution"*, Cambridge, MA and London: Harvard University Press, pp. 206–22.

Kendall, Tim (1998), 'He Makes it Rhyme', (rev. of *Tony Harrison: Loiner*), *Times Literary Supplement*, 30 January, p. 13.

Kendall, Tim (2001), *Sylvia Plath: A Critical Study*, London: Faber.

Kirsch, Adam (1999), 'A Stick to Beat the Century With', *Times Literary Supplement*, 29 January, pp. 7–8.

Kushner, Tony (1994), *The Holocaust and the Liberal Imagination: A Social and Cultural History*, Oxford: Blackwell.

Kustow, Michael (1999), 'Burning Ambition: The Producer Michael Kustow Relives the Making of Tony Harrison's *Prometheus*', *The Observer*, 11 April, http://film.guardian.co.uk/Feature_Story/Observer/0,4120,41473,00.html.

Lang, Berel (2000), 'Holocaust Genres and the Turn to History', in A. Leak and G. Paizis (eds), *The Holocaust and the Text: Speaking the Unspeakable*, London: Macmillan, pp. 17–31.

Langer, Lawrence (1995), *Admitting the Holocaust*, Oxford: Oxford University Press.

Langer, Lawrence (2002), 'Recent Studies on Memory and Representation', *Holocaust and Genocide Studies*, 16: 1 (spring), pp. 77–93.

Laub, Dori (1984), 'Holocaust Themes: Their Expression in Poetry and in the Psychological Conflicts of Patients in Psychotherapy', in *The Nazi Concentration Camps: Structure and Aims; the Image of the Prisoners; the Jews in the Camps*, Jerusalem: Yad Vashem, pp. 573–87.

Lezard, Nicholas (1999), 'Fire in his Belly', *The Independent on Sunday*, 11 April, pp. 5–6.

Logan, William (2000), 'The Triumph of Geoffrey Hill', *Parnassus*, 24: 2 (May), pp. 201–20.

Lomas, Herbert (1999), 'Rhyming Film', *Thumbscrew*, 13 (spring/summer), pp. 52–5.

Longley, Edna (1999), 'All You Need Is Love' (rev. of *The Triumph of Love*), *Metre*, 6 (summer), pp. 70–4.

Lowell, Robert (1966), 'Foreword', in S. Plath, *Ariel*, New York: Harper & Row, pp.vii–ix.

Lyon, John (1999), '"Pardon?" Our Problem with Difficulty (and Geoffrey Hill)', *Thumbscrew*, 13 (spring/summer), pp. 11–19.

MacKinnon, Kenneth (1999), 'Film Adaptation and the Myth of Textual Fidelity', The Department of Classical Studies Open Colloquium 1999, http://www.open.ac.uk/Arts/Colq99/hardwick.htm.

Markey, Janice (1993), *A Journey into the Red Eye: The Poetry of Sylvia Plath – A Critique*, London: The Women's Press.

Mauriac, François (1981), 'Foreword', in Elie Wiesel, *Night*, trans. S. Rodway, London: Penguin, pp. 7–11.

Maxwell, Glyn (1999), Review of *Prometheus*, *Sight and Sound* (April), pp. 55–6.

McDonald, Peter (2001), '"*Violent Hefts*": Geoffrey Hill's *The Triumph of Love*', *Metre*, 10 (autumn), pp. 65–78.

Meiner, R. K. (1991), 'Mourning for Ourselves and for Poetry: The Lyric after Auschwitz', *The Centennial Review*, 35: 3 (fall), pp. 545–90.

Moulin, Joanny (1999), *Ted Hughes: New Selected Poems*, Paris: Didier.

Murdoch, Brian (1974), 'Transformations of the Holocaust: Auschwitz in Modern Lyric Poetry', *Comparative Literature Studies*, 11: 2 (June), pp. 123–50.

Myers, D. G. (1999), 'Responsible for Every Single Pain: Holocaust Literature and the Ethics of Interpretation', *Comparative Literature*, 51: 4 (fall), pp. 266–88.

Newlin, Margaret (1972), 'The Suicide Bandwagon', *Critical Quarterly*, 14: 4 (winter), pp. 367–78.

Orr, Peter (1966), *The Poet Speaks*, London: Routledge & Kegan Paul.

Padley, Steve (2000), 'Fruitility', *P. N. Review*, 27:1 (September/October), pp. 56–7.

Padley, Steve (2003), 'Poetry and Atrocity' (rev. of *Tony Harrison and the Holocaust*), *English*, 52: 204 (autumn), pp. 278–82.

Parmet, Harriet L. (2001), *The Terror of Our Days: Four American Poets Respond to the Holocaust*, Cranbury: Rosemont pubs.

Parmet, Harriet L. (2003), Review of *Tony Harrison and the Holocaust*, *Holocaust and Genocide Studies*, 17: 3 (winter), pp. 515–17.

Paulin, Tom (1992), 'A Visionary Nationalist: Geoffrey Hill', in *Minotaur: Poetry and the Nation State*, London: Faber, pp. 276–84.

Perloff, Marjorie (1979), 'Sylvia Plath's "Sivvy Poems": A Portrait of the Poet as Daughter', in G. Lane (ed.), *Sylvia Plath: New Views on the Poetry*, Baltimore: Johns Hopkins University Press, pp. 155–78.

Peterson, Joan (2000), '"Some Gold Across the Water": Paul Celan and Nelly Sachs', *Holocaust and Genocide Studies*, 14: 2 (fall), pp. 197–214.

Poole, Adrian (1999), 'Harrison and Marsyas', The Department of Classical Studies Open Colloquium 1999, http://www.open.ac.uk/Arts/Colq99/hardwick.htm.

Przyrembel, Alexandra (2001), 'Transfixed by an Image: Ilse Koch, the "Kommandeuse of Buchenwald"', trans. P. Selwyn, *German History*, 19: 3, pp. 369–99.

Pybus, Rodney (2002), 'What Fun . . . and Strange Beauty', *Stand*, 3 (4) and 4 (1): 712, pp. 30–6.

Rawlinson, Mark (1996), 'This Other War: British Culture and the Holocaust', *Cambridge Quarterly*, 25: 1, pp. 1–25.

Ricks, Christopher (1986), '"The Tongue's Atrocities"', in H. Bloom (ed.), *Modern Critical Views: Geoffrey Hill*, New York: Chelsea House Pubs, pp. 55–68.

Roberts, Neil (1999), *Narrative and Voice in Postwar Poetry*, Harlow: Longman.

Robinson, Peter (1999), 'Facing Up to the Unbearable: The Mythical Method in Tony Harrison's Film/Poems', The Department of Classical Studies Open Colloquium 1999, http://www.open.ac.uk/Arts/Colq99/hardwick.htm.

Rose, Gillian (1996), *Mourning Becomes the Law: Philosophy and Representation*, Cambridge: Cambridge University Press.

Rosenbaum, Alan (ed.) (1996), *Is the Holocaust Unique? Perspectives on Comparative Genocide*, Oxford and Boulder, CO: Westview Press.

Rosenfeld, Alvin H. (1979), 'The Holocaust as Entertainment', *Mainstream*, xxv: 8 (October), pp. 55–8.

Rothberg, Michael (2000), *Traumatic Realism: The Demands of Holocaust Representation*, Minneapolis and London: University of Minnesota Press.

Rowland, Antony (2001), *Tony Harrison and the Holocaust*, Liverpool: Liverpool University Press.

Rutter, Carol Chillington (1997), 'Harrison, Herakles, and Wailing Women "Labourers" at Delphi', *New Theatre Quarterly*, 13: 50 (May), pp. 133–43.

Sagar, Keith (ed.) (1983), *The Achievement of Ted Hughes*, Manchester: Manchester University Press.

Sagar, Keith (ed.) (1994), *The Challenge of Ted Hughes*, London: Macmillan.

Sagar, Keith (2000), *The Laughter of Foxes: A Study of Ted Hughes*, Liverpool: Liverpool University Press.

Schwarz, Daniel R. (1999), *Imagining the Holocaust*, London: Palgrave.

Sexton, David (2002), 'The Strongest Voice' (rev. of *The Orchards of Syon*), *Evening Standard*, 9 September, p. 45.

Shapiro, David (1979), 'Sylvia Plath: Drama and Melodrama', in G. Lane (ed.), *Sylvia Plath: New Views on the Poetry*, Baltimore: Johns Hopkins University Press, pp. 44–53.

Sicher, Efraim (2000), 'The Future of the Past: Countermemory and Postmemory in Contemporary American Post-Holocaust Narratives', *History and Memory: Studies in Representations of the Past*, 2, pp. 56–91.

Silkin, Jon (1958), 'Editorial', *Stand*, 4: 1, pp. 3–4.

Simon, Roger, Sharon Rosenberg and Claudia Eppert (eds) (2000), *Between Hope and Despair: Pedagogy and the Remembrance of Historical Trauma*, New York: Rowman and Littlefield.

Sinclair, Andrew (1989), *War Like a Wasp: The Lost Decade of the 'Forties*, London: Hamish Hamilton.

Sinclair, Andrew (ed.) (1989), *The War Decade: An Anthology of the 1940s*, London: Hamish Hamilton.

Sontag, Susan (1992), 'Syberberg's Hitler', in H. Stewart (ed.), *Syberberg: A Filmmaker from Germany*, London: British Film Institute pubs, pp. 13–25.

Spufford, Francis (1999), 'Geoffrey Hill goes into Injury Time' (rev. of *The Triumph of Love*), *Evening Standard*, 1 February, p. 50.

Steiner, George (1967), 'Dying is an Art' (rev. of *Ariel*), in *Language and Silence*, London: Faber, pp. 324–34.

Stevenson, Anne (1990), *Bitter Fame: A Life of Sylvia Plath*, London: Penguin.

Stone, Dan (ed.) (2001), *Theoretical Interpretations of the Holocaust*, Amsterdam: Rodopi.

Strangeways, Al (1996), '"The Boot in the Face": The Problem of the Holocaust in the Poetry of Sylvia Plath', *Contemporary Literature*, 37: 3, pp. 370–90.

Suleiman, Susan Rubin (2000), 'Problems of Memory and Factuality in Recent Holocaust Memoirs: Wilkomirski/Wiesel', *Poetics Today*, 21: 3 (fall), pp. 543–59.

Szirtes, George (2000), 'Introduction', in M. Radnóti, *Camp Notebook*, trans. F. Jones, Todmorden: Arc, pp. 13–16.

Thomson, Ian [2002] (2003), *Primo Levi*, London: Vintage.

Tonkin, Boyd (1999), 'Hard Lines from the Bitter Bard', *The Independent*, 6 February.

Vice, Sue (2000), *Holocaust Fiction*, London: Routledge.

Vice, Sue (2000), 'The Demidenko Affair and Contemporary Holocaust Fiction', in A. Leak and G. Paizis (eds), *The Holocaust and the Text: Speaking the Unspeakable*, London: Macmillan, pp. 125–41.

Vice, Sue (2003), 'Binjamin Wilkomirski's *Fragments* and Holocaust Envy: "Why Wasn't I There Too"?', in *Representing the Holocaust: In Honour of Bryan Burns*, London and Portland: Vallentine Mitchell, pp. 249–68.

Wainwright, Jeffrey (2000), 'Geoffrey Hill: *The Triumph of Love*', *P. N. Review*, 26: 5 (May/June), pp. 13–21.

Webb, Igor (1977), 'Speaking of the Holocaust: the Poetry of Geoffrey Hill', *The Denver Quarterly*, 12: 1 (spring), pp. 114–24.

Wood, James (1999), 'Too Many Alibis' (rev. of *Canaan* and *The Triumph of Love*), *London Review of Books* (1 July), pp. 24–6.

Woodward, Steve (1999), 'Voices in the Past and in the Present: Tony Harrison's Reworking of the Prometheus Myth', The Department of Classical Studies Open Colloquium 1999, http://www.open.ac.uk/Arts/Colq99/hardwick.htm.

Wroe, Nicholas (2000), 'Tony Harrison: Man of Mysteries', *The Guardian*, 1 April, pp. 6–7.

Young, Gloria (1993), 'The Poetry of the Holocaust', in S. S. Friedman (ed.), *Holocaust Literature: A Handbook of Critical, Historical, and Literary Writings*, Westport and London: Greenwood Press, pp. 547–74.

Young, James E. (1988), 'The Holocaust Confessions of Sylvia Plath', in *Writing and Rewriting the Holocaust*, Bloomington and Indianapolis: Indiana University Press, pp. 117–33.

Young, James E. (1993), *The Texture of Memory*, Yale: Yale University Press.

Young, James E. (2000), *At Memory's Edge: After-Images of the Holocaust in Contemporary Art and Architecture*, New Haven and London: Yale University Press.

Žižek, Slavoj (2000), 'Camp Comedy', *Sight and Sound*, 10: 4, pp. 26–9.

# Index